Fasten seatbelts –
Stories of British civil aviation

Roger James Newton

Table of Contents

To my wife Susan, who has provided constant support and encouragement for this project along with her clear recollections during her time when working at Rolls-Royce in Derby during the late 1960s and early 1970s.

About the Author

Roger James Newton was born in Stockport and attended Stockport Grammar School, followed by the University of Sheffield, where he graduated in Law in 1970. He then trained and practised as a Solicitor in the Greater Manchester area before choosing a career in Industry and Commerce. In early 1974, he joined Rolls-Royce (1971) Limited in Derby as a Commercial Legal Adviser and was later Deputy Company Secretary of the Engineering Group, Babcock International plc. At that time Lord King of Wartnaby was Chairman of both Babcock and of British Airways.

After holding later management roles in the Food Manufacturing sector, Roger retired from full-time work in 2008 and then established and ran a Legal and Trustee Services Consultancy for the following fifteen years. Roger met his wife, Susan, at Rolls-Royce in the 1970s and they have lived in Sonning, near Reading since 1986.

This is Roger's first book, which presents stories of British civil aviation from its inception in 1919. His interest and involvement in the subject now extends to a period of well over half a century, commencing from his times as a teenage plane spotter at Manchester Airport in the early 1960s.

Prologue

Civil aviation is a glamorous but also a high-risk and reward business for both aircraft and aero-engine manufacturers and for airlines. For aviation enthusiasts, civil airliners are seen as objects of grace and elegance, but they are also expensive to acquire and to maintain and they make money only when they are in the air, carrying viable passenger or freight loads. The British civil aviation sector has shown huge volatility over its lifetime and its past is sadly littered with many failures by both manufacturers and airlines. Quick fortunes have been made by some individuals and have been equally rapidly lost by others.

Britain was an early leader in the development of civil aviation and the Nation has since experienced many changes in this important sector of the Economy. The instruction to "Fasten seatbelts" is possibly the only aspect of British civil aviation remaining unchanged since the first official international passenger flight took off from London Hounslow on 25 August 1919 and arrived two and a half hours later at Le Bourget, Paris.

This book presents stories which trace the subsequent development of British civil aviation over the past more than one hundred years and progressing through to the present day. The stories are concise and non-technical, recording both times of high elation and sometimes moments of deep tragedy. This book is also intended to provide some insight into those strong personalities whose skill, entrepreneurship and drive created today's British civil aviation. Many of these individuals were later rewarded with knighthoods and peerages for their endeavours.

Air travel nowadays is very safe when compared with most other means of mass transport. The last British Airways fatality was over forty years ago, and none of the other leading British airlines, EasyJet, Jet2.com and Virgin Atlantic, together with predominantly United Kingdom-based Ryanair, now Europe's largest airline, have ever been involved in fatal accidents. In the most recent airlineratings.com report on airline safety, British Airways was placed a creditable seventeenth out of nearly four hundred airlines assessed with regard to operating incidents and the age of their aircraft. The assessment also included a range of other factors, such as reported incidents, governing body audits, safety initiatives and pilot training programmes.

Easyjet and Ryanair, with their comparatively young aircraft fleets, were rated highly in the budget airline category. Overall, there has recently been a slight increase in the average age of civil aircraft. The International Air Transport Association (IATA) states this increase is because of the high demand for air travel and the inability of the two remaining large civil aircraft manufacturers, Airbus and Boeing, to match the airlines' consequent huge demand for new aircraft.

The world has discovered that travel experiences can be life-changing, and air travel is now regarded as being a necessary part of modern everyday life. It is readily and widely available, and the sheer increase in the scale of worldwide civil aviation, particularly over the past sixty years, has been truly amazing. On a good day in the 1960s, Manchester Airport plane spotters would have seen twenty to thirty aircraft movements. In comparison, on 23 June 2024, a power failure at the Airport cancelled the one hundred and forty flights scheduled for the following six-hour period. This event revealed that more than twice the number of flights is now handled, each hour, at Manchester Airport than in a whole day in 1960!

Statistics from "Our World in Data" have reported that global air passenger numbers in 1960 were 106 million and that, by 1990, numbers had increased more than ten-fold to 1.17 billion. In 2024, passenger numbers were nearly 5.0 billion and, subject to the world economy continuing to expand, IATA is forecasting further growth in global passenger numbers in 2025 and in future years. That this growth is critically dependent upon secure digital technology was starkly illustrated on 19 July 2024 when the distribution of a defective cyber security update occasioned the disruption of flights across the world. Five per cent of the incredible number of 110,000 flights scheduled worldwide to take place on that single day needed to be cancelled.

This book comprises five parts as follows:

Part 1 - 1919-49 (The Formative Years) includes the formation of Rolls-Royce, following the 1904 "meeting of minds" of the unlikely pair, and then covers the creation of Imperial Airways. The development of the early British Aero Industry is described as Britain headed towards the Second World War. The Brabazon Committee's recommendations set the scene for British civil aviation in the post-war period. New State-owned airline corporations also emerged and re-established domestic and international air travel using a variety of Interim Types and imported American airliners. A number of post-war

6

entrepreneurs registered Independent airlines and The Berlin Airlift, in 1948, provided some with a vital lifeline.

The Formative Years closed with the prospect of new Brabazon Types, as recommended by the Committee's 1945 Report, mostly powered by that most fundamental change in the method of aircraft propulsion, the gas turbine engine. International air regulation was now in place and more capable aircraft opened the way for the massive expansion of air travel in the second half of the twentieth century and continuing into the twenty-first century.

Parts 2, 3 and **4** describe each of the three decades from 1950 to 1980, which were a Golden, if not entirely successful, Era for British aircraft manufacturers. The topics covered are:

The 1950s: Post-war British Aero Industry; Brabazon Types; The Comet disasters; new opportunities for Independent airlines; Freddie Laker, the early years; The English Channel and Passenger experiences. This decade also saw intrepid members of the baby-boomer generation embarking upon their first "package holidays" to exciting new European destinations.

The 1960s: British Aero Industry consolidation; State-owned airline corporations' woes; second generation British jets; varying fortunes for the leading Independent airlines (British Eagle International; British Midland, British United, Caledonian, Monarch and Skyways/Euravia/Britannia).

The 1970s; The introduction of wide-bodied passenger aircraft (including the fabulous Boeing 747 Jumbo – the "Queen of the Skies"); A Second Force Private Sector airline; The New British Airways; Rolls-Royce – disaster and recovery; Working at

Rolls-Royce; Airbus Industrie; Laker Airways & Skytrain and Concorde.

Part 5 - 1980 to the current day (The Modern Era). Most of the post-war British Independent airlines now say their last farewells to British civil aviation. Terrorism rears its ugly head and the production of complete British-built airliners ceases. In the early 1990s, Richard Branson, the Aviation Virgin, and his upstart Virgin Atlantic Airways won a dramatic battle (the "Dirty Tricks" affair) against Lord King and British Airways.

Low-cost air travel emerged during the Modern Era creating further huge passenger capacity demands. Third and fourth generation jets and aero engines came into service from the mid-1990s. The International Airlines Group (IAG) was created in 2010 through the merger of British Airways with the Spanish carrier Iberia. Open Skies and Markets are now the norm, in complete contrast to the highly regulated commercial environment and, at times, politically driven agendas of the past. The environmental aspects of civil aviation, which were not a significant consideration prior to the Modern Era, are now a major focus and have become a potentially existential issue for the Industry.

The primary objective for today's air travellers is, quite correctly, to reach their destinations as efficiently and safely as possible. However, hopefully, air travellers might still find sufficient time to read the stories in this book and to discover and enjoy the fascinating world of British civil aviation, as it has evolved since 1919. Civil aviation is an important part of our British heritage and it continues to be a significant contributor to the British Economy, providing a large number of highly skilled jobs and keeping the Nation at the forefront of modern technology.

The subject matter of this book predominantly concerns British civil aviation; however the reader will note some occasional references to military aircraft projects, where an important part of British aviation history is concerned or where there is an association with or a bearing upon civil aviation matters. An example is the 1950s "V Bomber" saga, which arises at a number of points.

Brief summaries of contemporary politics and economics, from time to time, are also included in order to provide background to events which influenced the development of British civil aviation at various times in its history.

Part 1 -
The Formative Years (1919 – 1949)

Key events

1919 – The first official international passenger flight took place on 25 August when a converted ex-First World War Bomber (an Airco DH.4A) powered by a single Rolls-Royce Eagle engine carried its pilot and a sole passenger, together with freight, from London to Paris. Rolls-Royce had produced its first cars in 1904 and its first aero-engine in 1914.

1924 – State-owned Imperial Airways was created in order to provide air services within the United Kingdom and Europe and to establish connections to the further reaches of the British Empire. Steady but slow progress is made during the early 1930s in developing the "Empire Routes".

1935 – The Hawker Engineering Company buys the businesses of John Davenport Siddeley and thereby creates the major future British aircraft manufacturer, Hawker Siddeley Limited.

1936 – The commencement of more extensive services on "Empire Routes" is facilitated by the introduction of Imperial Airways' fleet of Empire Flying Boats produced at Rochester, Kent by the aircraft manufacturer, Short Brothers Limited.

1939 – Prime Minister Neville Chamberlain announces that Britain is at war with Nazi Germany and civil aviation activities are largely suspended. The new British Overseas Airways Corporation (BOAC) assumes the operations of Imperial Airways and of privately-owned British Airways Limited.

1942 – Rolls-Royce's General Manager, Ernest Hives, and Dr Stanley Hooker meet representatives of the Rover Car Company at Clitheroe, Lancashire and acquire the designs and production facilities for the Whittle gas turbine engines.

1946 – British civil aviation is re-launched. BOAC and two other new State-owned airline corporations commence services with a number of "Interim Types" supplemented by American imports. The British Aero Industry progresses work on its responses to the Brabazon Report's specifications for a new generation of British civil aircraft.

1947 – The Chicago Convention sets the framework for the regulation of worldwide aviation, including the "Freedoms of the Air" and the creation of the International Civil Aviation Organisation (ICAO). The "End of Empire" commences with the hasty and brutal independence of India and with the creation of Pakistan. De-colonisation continues rapidly during the following two decades.

1948 – The USSR closed land routes to Berlin and The Berlin Airlift lasted for fifteen months, providing a financial lifeline for a number of Independent airlines. The British Monarchy quietly relinquished use of the title of "Empress of India", first bestowed upon Queen Victoria some seventy years previously.

The Beginnings

A small number of the over 6,000 bombers produced for war-time service by The Aircraft Manufacturing Co Ltd (Airco) were converted for civil operations and were designated the DH.4A. The aircraft which flew the service on 25 August 1919 was operated by the fledgling airline Aircraft Transport & Travel Limited (AT&T) and was piloted by Lieutenant EH "Bill" Lawford. It had left London Hounslow at 9.10 am, arriving at Le Bourget at 11.40 am with a sole passenger, journalist George Stevenson – Reese. Freight on board included mail and leather, together with the braces of grouse and the jars of Devonshire cream which had been ordered by a Paris restaurant!

An Airco DH. 4A one of which performed the world's first official international passenger flight on 25 August 1919

Airco was created before the First World War by pioneer aviation industrialist George Holt Thomas, and the initials "DH" identified the DH.4A as having been designed by Geoffrey de Havilland. The young engineer, born in July 1882, had joined Airco in 1914, having first developed his design skills in the motor industry. De Havilland also had interesting personal connections, being the cousin of the Hollywood superstars, later deadly rivals, Olivia de Havilland and Joan Fontaine.

Geoffrey de Havilland serving as a First World War officer in the Royal Flying Corps.

Frederick Handley Page in 1936, midway through an illustrious aviation career

The tall and imposing Frederick Handley Page was an aviation engineer with a flair for marketing. Handley Page was born in Cheltenham in November 1885 and, after being sacked by his electrical engineering employers for alleged unauthorised experimentation, he established the Handley Page Aircraft Company Limited in June 1909. Initial finances were so precarious that the founder had to support the struggling company through his earnings from journalism, patent royalties and from lecturing in aeronautics. The company specialised in larger aircraft and early development work for the Admiralty had led to the First World War production of its successful twin-engine 0/400 and 0/1500 bombers.

A Handley Page 1920s airliner derived from the company's First World War bombers.

The Air Navigation Act of 1919 permitted the commencement of civil aviation services from 1 May. From that day, the Handley Page Aircraft Company used its converted 0/400s to ferry newspapers within the United Kingdom. Frederick Handley Page then set up an airline subsidiary, Handley Page Transport Limited, which, earlier in the day of 25 August 1919, had upstaged that "official" first international passenger flight by flying one of its 0/400s from the Handley Page airfield at Cricklewood to Le Bourget.

The 0/400 had arrived at Le Bourget ninety minutes before the AT&T flight, with its seven passengers being seated on either side of the aisle in single, uncomfortable, low back and easily flammable wicker seats. The instruction to "Fasten seatbelts" would not have applied to this particular flight because there were no seatbelts to be fastened in the 0/400s. Although seatbelts were widely provided on most passenger aircraft during the Formative Years, it was not until a flying boat crash in 1935 that they were made compulsory for passengers.

At the conclusion of the First World War in 1918, large quantities of war-surplus aircraft had become available. There was, therefore, only a small likelihood of orders for new military aircraft in the post-war years. Demand for civil aircraft was also low. Without Government support and, in common with a number of other aircraft manufacturers, Airco rapidly became unprofitable. By 1920, Holt Thomas was effectively forced to sell the company to the Birmingham Small Arms Company Limited (BSA), which was primarily interested in acquiring Airco's factories for its diverse engineering operations.

Because BSA had carried out inadequate pre-purchase enquiries on Airco, it subsequently found the aviation activities to be unprofitable and soon announced their closure. However, de Havilland, with financial backing from Holt Thomas, purchased sufficient Airco assets to enable him to form the de Havilland Aircraft Company. The new company found initial work on ongoing Government contracts, and it was destined to become a major force in British aircraft manufacturing over the next forty years.

Holt Thomas also owned AT&T, and the airline was experiencing financial difficulties, similar to those of Airco, becoming insolvent in December 1920. In those bleak post-First World War years there were sufficient passengers wishing to explore the exciting new world of flying and who were able to pay the average return fare to Paris of around £20 - £30 (£1000-£1500 in today's money!). However, the trips across the Channel were barely profitable for the airlines, even with a full load.

AT&T's successor was Daimler Airway, which took up the challenge of establishing sustainable services by commencing operations from Croydon Airport to Paris, using six of the larger DH.34 aircraft. Instone Air Line was another early operator created by the shipping company S. Instone & Company in 1919. Its initial purpose was the speedy transit of the company's documents between London and Continental ports, thereby saving on port charges.

Under the leadership of Sir Samuel Instone and his brother and chief pilot, Captain Alfred Instone, the airline commenced a London to Paris service in April 1920, later also serving Cologne. This interest or, more correctly, this self-interest on the part of shipping companies in having an involvement in British civil aviation would feature for many years ahead.

The aviation community's prevailing conservative attitudes in the early 1920s were demonstrated by its ridicule of what was actually a farsighted January 1922 decision by Instone Air Line, to be the first airline to issue uniforms to pilots and staff. The airline also operated DH.34s, together with a civil version of the Vickers Vimy. This was the aircraft that had made the first non-stop crossing of the Atlantic Ocean on 14/15 June 1919. It was piloted by Captain John Alcock and navigated by Arthur Whitten Brown, both of whom were knighted by King George V during the following week.

Cabins on these early passenger services were unheated. The well-dressed occupants needed not only to be wealthy but also hardy and well-wrapped up, sometimes wearing flying helmets and coats loaned to them by the operators. The pilots, by choice, initially sat in open cockpits. It would be some years before enclosed Flight Decks were introduced. Some tickets included transport from London to the departing airport and then from the arriving airport to the final destination. This type of marketing ploy is, of course, still employed by some of today's travel companies.

An unlikely pair

An important meeting with significant future implications for British aviation had taken place many years earlier, on the 4 May 1904, at the newly-opened Midland Hotel in Manchester. Travelling that morning to Manchester and enjoying a leisurely breakfast in the dining car of the Midland Railways train from London was the Hon Charles Stewart Rolls. It had been arranged for Rolls to meet Mr Frederick Henry Royce, the owner of a Manchester-based electrical engineering business. The twenty-seven year old Charles Rolls, member of a wealthy Monmouthshire family, had been educated at Eton, followed by studying Engineering at Trinity College, Cambridge. In contrast, Royce had been born into relative poverty in Peterborough in 1863 and had left school at the age of fourteen for a railway apprenticeship. Through subsequent hard work, drive, and ability, Royce was able to establish his own successful business.

The Hon Charles Stewart Rolls, a very resolute and determined person, but regarded by some as being rather strange and idiosyncratic.

Sir Frederick Henry Royce

Royce's objective was to build the best car in the world. Rolls, amongst his many other interests, had a car business in Fulham and was the purveyor of automobiles to the gentry from his West End of London showroom. Most of these vehicles were foreign sourced and Rolls now wished to sell high-quality, British-manufactured vehicles to his customers.

Rolls and Royce were a most unlikely pair, but a famous "meeting of minds" proceeded to take place, with Rolls later commenting that:

"In Mr Royce, I found the man I had been looking for, for years." A partnership agreement was signed under which Rolls undertook to sell every car that Royce could produce. The partnership was converted to become Rolls-Royce Limited in 1906, which was then registered as a public company later that year.

Charles Rolls at the wheel of a Rolls-Royce Silver Ghost hosting, on behalf of the Royal Aero Club, the bowler-hatted Wright Brothers during their 1909 visit to England.

Charles Rolls was also interested in aviation and was a founder member of the Royal Aero Club. He then became one of the first British purchasers of a private aircraft in the form of a Wright Flyer manufactured by Short Brothers Limited, a company established by brothers Eustace, Horace and Oswald Short.

Short Brothers Limited purchased the British rights to the aircraft designs of the American brothers, Orville and Wilbur Wright, following their success in achieving the world's first controlled sustainable flight in December 1903. On 2 June 1910, Charles Rolls completed the first return flight across the English Channel, but sadly, on 12 July 1910, he was the first Briton to be killed in a powered aircraft accident. The tail of his Wright Flyer had failed with fatal consequences during a display at Bournemouth.

Rolls-Royce transferred its main operations to Derby in 1908, primarily because of reasonably priced electricity and the good availability of labour and land. However, Royce was suffering increasingly poor health, a situation not assisted by his inadequate eating and sleeping habits, often working in the factory through the night. Royce's principle was one of constant engineering improvement and he insisted on personally checking every drawing and calculation, often with consequent production delays. By 1912, the Board had concluded that Royce's behaviour was: "inconsistent with the efficient management of a public company and was prejudicial to the interests of the shareholders".

Quarndon House where Royce lived from 1908-11. The Author

As a result, Royce was removed from future involvement in day-to-day matters at the company. He then separated from his wife and he left his resplendent home at Quarndon House in the exclusive Derbyshire village of that name. Royce headed south accompanied by his nurse and housekeeper, Miss Ethel Aubin, subsequently settling at West Wittering on the West Sussex coast and wintering at his villa in the village of Le Canadel on the French Cote d'Azur.

For the next twenty years, during which he was appropriately supervised and well looked after by Miss Aubin, Royce continued his work on new projects and maintaining his strong belief that; "Whatever is rightly done, however humble, is noble". Enjoying beach walks with visiting Rolls-Royce development engineers, Royce would often sketch out his new design concepts in the sand.

Charles Rolls was quick to initiate the marketing of Rolls-Royce cars. Rolls-Royce initially supplied only engines and chassis and the various body styles were provided by independent firms of coachbuilders.

Royce enjoying later life at his home in West Wittering with the redoubtable Miss Aubin in close attendance.

So, after a relatively short period of time, neither of the Rolls-Royce founders had any direct involvement in the business. Also, there were no off-spring to continue an association with Rolls-Royce. However, the company was fortunate to have, as its Managing Director, the designer and marketing genius, Claude Johnson, who described himself as being the hyphen in Rolls-Royce. Johnson led the company successfully until his early death in 1926 and he established the basis for significant expansion in the years ahead.

Imperial Airways

In February 1923, the Hambling Committee was set up to review the payment of operating subsidies to the early airlines. It extended its remit and recommended the establishment of a single, financially secure airline operation. Such an airline would have the ability to undertake the expansion of air services as perceived necessary by the Government.

The Committee therefore proposed a merger of the previously mentioned most prominent airlines, including Daimler Airway, Handley Page Transport, Instone Air Line, and British Marine Air Navigation Co Limited. This latter airline was a venture in which flying boat manufacturer, Supermarine Aviation Works, was interested. It operated cross-Channel services to Cherbourg, Le Havre and the Channel Islands, using Supermarine-designed Sea Eagle flying boats.

Imperial Airways Limited was the name chosen for the combined airline, which was created on 31 March 1924. The merger negotiations were partially orchestrated by Holt Thomas. Instone Air Line initially held back, but the appointment of Sir Samuel as a director of the new airline company was probably a deciding factor in its eventual participation. Holt Thomas passed away in 1929, but would be remembered for his pioneering work in the early years of British civil aviation.

Imperial Airways proceeded to commence services, in April 1924, using aircraft inherited from its predecessor airlines, primarily the civil derivatives of the Handley Page bombers and the de Havilland DH.34s. A Government subsidy of £1m (£75m in today's money) was to be paid over ten years, with £137,000 (£13m today) paid during the first year. Land-based aircraft were operated from Croydon, with seaplane services from Southampton. Internal services within the United Kingdom were suspended initially in order to focus on growing services to the already-established European destinations.

There was strong political pressure for Imperial Airways to initiate air services more widely and, in particular, to connect with the further reaches of the British Empire, then the largest formal empire that the world had ever known and "upon which the sun never set". The British Empire comprised eleven million square miles, with four hundred million subjects. A further one million square miles and thirteen million more subjects had been added by the peace settlement at the conclusion of the First World War. Lord Curzon, the then Viceroy of India, commented at the time that:

"The British flag never flew over a more powerful or united Empire than now".

It seemed that those then in authority were assuming that Britain would continue to maintain its Empire indefinitely through the exercise of military, economic and diplomatic power. In reality, large numbers of Empire troops had died in the First World War and many of the survivors had returned to their countries with growing doubts about previous instinctive loyalties to the British Crown. The seeds of the decline of the Empire had been sown but, in the meantime, the pressing need was to plan and test long-distance air routes.

The British aviator Alan Cobham, born in May 1894, was an entrepreneur who undertook a number of route-proving flights in the 1920s. The services required to connect the Empire included routes to Africa and the Middle East and also to the "Jewel in the Crown" of India. The flights would then continue to Burma (now Myanmar), Singapore, Malaya (now Malaysia), Hong Kong, Australia, and finally, New Zealand. However, it would not be until the early 1930s that regular Imperial Airways' services to these Empire destinations would commence. The small number of passengers on those early services comprised mostly businessmen and colonial administrators, sometimes travelling with their families in order to take up Empire postings.

Early British Aero Industry

Imperial Airways required suitable long-haul aircraft for these challenging Empire Routes, but the Government prohibited the purchase of aircraft and aero-engines other than those produced by the British Aero Industry.

In addition to Handley Page and de Havilland, Armstrong Whitworth Aircraft Limited (AW) was then the only other sizeable British producer of land-based civil aircraft. By 1927, AW, originally established by the engineering giant, the Sir W G Armstrong Whitworth & Co Limited, had passed into the ownership of the shrewd John Siddeley, born in Manchester in August 1866. Siddeley, who would later become the 1st Baron Kenilworth, proceeded to expand AW in 1928 by purchasing AV Roe Limited (Avro) from Alliott Verdon-Roe, the Manchester-born aviation pioneer. Siddeley also owned Armstrong Siddeley Limited (AS) which produced both aero-engines and Armstrong Siddeley motor cars. Imperial Airways commenced long-haul services in the early 1930s, mostly using the AW Argosy airliner powered by three AS Jaguar engines.

The Armstrong Whitworth Argosy enabled Imperial Airways to commence services on Empire Routes from the early 1930s. British Airways Museum.

Interior of the Armstrong Whitworth Argosy. Note the non-reclining wicker seats without retaining belts! British Airways Museum.

In 1935, the H G Hawker Engineering Company purchased both AW and AS from John Siddeley for £1m (£88m today). The Hawker Company was formed in 1920 by Thomas Sopwith, the designer of the famous First World War Sopwith Camel fighter aircraft, and his Australian chief test pilot, Harry Hawker. Now extremely wealthy, Siddeley donated some of his fortune to charity, including gifting Kenilworth Castle to the Nation, before retiring to Jersey. Hawker Siddeley Limited, the new combined company, would feature significantly in the future of British civil aviation, retaining the separate identities of its aircraft manufacturing operations and associated aircraft until becoming part of British Aerospace in 1977.

Imperial Airways also operated the de Havilland DH.66 Hercules to carry out services during the 1930s. The Hercules was powered by three Bristol Jupiter engines. These engines were produced by the Bristol Aeroplane Company Limited, which had been founded in 1910, originally as the British and Colonial Aeroplane Company Limited. During the First World War, Bristol produced over five thousand Bristol Fighters and continued to specialise in military aircraft in the inter-war period. By the commencement of the Second World War, its works at Filton was the largest aircraft manufacturing unit in the world. It would play an important role in post-war British civil aircraft manufacturing.

Rolls-Royce's first aero-engine, the Eagle, which powered the DH.4A and other types of that era. Rolls-Royce Museum. The Author.

In 1914, the Government pressured Rolls-Royce to enter the aero-engine market and the company then produced the Eagle engine, which powered the aforementioned Vickers Vimy and which was the preferred engine choice for the Airco DH.4A. Aero-engines would later become Rolls-Royce's main activity.

In a similar manner, Bristol Engines had succumbed to Government "encouragement" in the form of a 1920 Air Ministry "suggestion" that it should acquire the bankrupt Cosmos Engineering Company Limited, led by the talented Roy Fedden (later Sir Roy). Whilst Rolls-Royce produced liquid-cooled, in-line piston engines, Feddon had taken an alternative approach with an air-cooled, radial engine, the Jupiter, which was correctly considered by the Ministry to have future potential. Over the following thirty years, Bristol Engines would expand its aero-engine business. Its highly successful range of air-cooled, radial piston aero-engines were named after figures from Greek mythology and they were widely used for both military and civil purposes.

Liquid-cooled, in-line and air-cooled radial piston engines each have their respective advantages and disadvantages. Liquid-cooled engines facilitate better streamlining and are more aesthetically pleasing. However, air-cooled radial engines were preferred for civil use, particularly by the increasingly dominant American civil aircraft manufacturers.

A 1930s de Havilland Dragon Rapide, operating a British European Airways flight from the mainline to the Isles of Scilly in 1959. Air Team Images

Returning to the evolution of the de Havilland Aircraft Company Limited, in addition to producing the DH.66, de Havilland had, through the 1930s, also developed small passenger aircraft for shorter routes. Its most successful design was the DH.89 Dragon Rapide, which first flew in 1934. The Rapide was a plywood box fuselage biplane capable of carrying eight to ten passengers with a range of around 550 miles, at a cruising speed of over one hundred and thirty miles per hour (mph). Over seven hundred Rapides were produced until 1946, with the aircraft continuing in airline service well into the 1960s.

Handley Page HP 42/45, the pre-Second World War flag-ship of Imperial Airways. Air Team Images

Some Rapides are still flying today, offering the Public an opportunity to experience this historic aircraft.

Frederick Handley Page was not to be ignored, and he ensured his company's continuing involvement in British civil aviation through his successful response to a 1928 Imperial Airways specification for an aircraft to be the flagship of its land-based fleet. The airline ordered eight of the resulting Handley Page HP 42/45, the world's largest biplane, powered by four Bristol Jupiter engines. This aircraft would provide the backbone of Imperial Airways' land fleet up to the Second World War.

A BOAC Short Solent S45 Empire Flying Boat in the pool of London in 1949. The advent of more capable land planes brought the Flying Boat era to an end in 1954. British Airways Museum.

Aircraft range limitations at the time determined that a combination of land aircraft and flying boats supported, in some cases, by connecting rail services were, on occasion, the only solution for long-haul routes. Accordingly, Short Brothers Limited developed a range of suitable flying boats from its then main base at Rochester, Kent. The elegant and graceful Empire Flying Boats, forty-two of which were built, were introduced into service by Imperial Airways on its Empire Routes in 1936. The Empire Flying Boats would take six days to reach Cape Town and a further ten days of flying, with nine overnight stops, to reach Sydney. The Empire Flying Boats were operated by an all-male crew, and Imperial Airways carried around 50,000 passengers to these long-haul destinations during the 1930s.

Vickers-Armstrongs Limited was created by the 1927 merger of Vickers Limited, a predominantly military aircraft manufacturer since 1911, with the previously-mentioned Sir W G Armstrong Whitworth & Company Limited. In 1928, the company had grown further by acquiring the financially struggling Supermarine business. During the pre-Second World War period Vickers-Armstrongs did not engage significantly in the production of civil aircraft, but the company was destined to play a major role in post-war British civil aviation.

Heading for War

It became clear, as the 1930s progressed, that further hostilities in Europe were threatened. The Nazi party had assumed power in Germany under the leadership of its fanatical Chancellor, Adolf Hitler, who had territorial expansion ambitions. The British Government, belatedly recognising that its armed forces and particularly the RAF were inadequately equipped for a new war in Europe, directed the Air Ministry to issue specifications for much-needed, more advanced military aircraft.

This unsettling situation significantly impacted the development of British civil aviation by changing the immediate priorities of British aircraft and aero-engine manufacturers away from civil projects in favour of the preparation of responses to these military specifications. If the companies were successful, then follow-up work on profitable Government contracts was virtually guaranteed.

AW was concentrating its efforts on a Government contract for the Whitley bomber, and civil aircraft projects were consequently delayed, such as the 1935 Imperial Airways' order for fifteen of the AW Ensign, powered by AS Tiger engines and seating forty passengers. The Ensign did not fly until early 1938 and then suffered technical and engine problems. The Handley Page Aircraft Company was similarly focussing its main efforts on the development of its Hampden bomber. The Hampden and the Whitley both later proved to be ineffectual and they were removed from service as soon as four-engine heavy bombers became available.

Reginald Joseph ("RJ") Mitchell, born in 1895 and a son of Staffordshire, had been precluded from serving in the forces during the First World War because of his essential occupation as an aeronautical engineer. In 1917, Mitchell joined the Southampton-based Supermarine Aviation Works and, four years later, he was appointed Chief Engineer. By 1927, he was Supermarine's Technical Director, serving under a ten-year contract! It was fortuitous that Supermarine had secured Mitchell's services in this manner because a key stipulation of the Vickers-Armstrongs take-over of the company, in the following year, was that he would transfer with the business!

RJ Mitchell, designer of the Spitfire. His life was cruelly cut short by cancer.

Since the mid-1920s, Mitchell had been engaged in an "unofficial" collaboration with Frederick Henry Royce on concepts for a new engine, the "R" engine. This engine was to be used to power Supermarine's S.6 and later its S.6B seaplanes, which were being designed by Mitchell to compete for the Schneider Trophy. The Schneider Trophy was first awarded by Jacques Schneider in 1913 to incentivise manufacturers to progress in seaplane development, which he considered was lagging behind that of land-based aircraft.

The RJ Mitchell designed Supermarine S.6B, winner of the Schneider Trophy.

Rolls-Royce Management had previously declined involvement in competing for the Trophy, and it was annoyed to discover Royce's collaboration with Mitchell and Supermarine. However, the Ministry overruled Rolls-Royce and limited production of a small number of "R" engines was authorised. The "R" engine powered Supermarine's S.6B which was victorious in the 1929 and 1931 Schneider Trophy competitions, thereby enabling Britain to retain the trophy permanently. It is still held at the Science Museum in South Kensington. Shortly after the 1931 race, the S.6B broke the world air speed record with a speed of 407.5 mph. In the late 1930s, Sir Malcolm Campbell's Bluebird, also powered by an "R" engine, increased water speed records to over 140 mph.

In 1934, Supermarine responded to an Air Ministry specification for a day and night fighter aircraft in the form of RJ Mitchell's Type 300. This aircraft incorporated much of the learning from the Schneider Trophy seaplanes. The Air Ministry rapidly accepted Supermarine's proposal and authorised the construction of a prototype aircraft named the "Spitfire". This name was chosen by Sir Robert McLean, the Managing Director of the Vickers aviation business. It is said after his feisty and energetic daughter, Annie Penrose, who was nicknamed "little spitfire".

Avro Lancaster and Vickers Supermarine Spitfire. Two classic Merlin-engined war planes which are now exhibits at the superb Imperial War Museum, Duxford. The Author

The Spitfire first flew in June 1936, powered by a developed version of the "R" engine, which was now poised to become the hugely successful Rolls-Royce Merlin. The Air Ministry promptly placed a £1.25m (£1bn today) order for three hundred and ten aircraft. The Spitfire remained in continuous development and production throughout the Second World War, with over 21,000 being built in many different versions. Nearly 170,000 Merlin engines were produced up to 1950, including 55,000 built by Packard under licence in the USA. Merlins powered other famous Second World War military aircraft, including the Avro Lancaster, of Dam Busters fame, the de Havilland Mosquito, the

Hawker Hurricane and the North American Mustang. Merlins were also installed as the power plants of some of the early, post Second World War interim airliners.

Mitchell and Royce left a great and long-lasting legacy for British aviation. Sadly, Mitchell died of cancer in 1937, at just forty-two years of age, unable to see his children grow up or to witness the huge later success of his creation. Mitchell's life story is sensitively portrayed by Leslie Howard in the 1942 film "The First of the Few".

A Rolls-Royce Merlin exhibited at the Rolls-Royce Museum.
The Author

Meanwhile, Royce, despite his earlier ill health, had apparently benefitted from the sea air and from his new lifestyle, strictly overseen by Miss Aubin. He had died four years earlier, in April 1933, at the good age of seventy for those times, still working feverishly on new engine concepts. Miss Aubin, clearly a most capable and efficient lady, had then proceeded to marry Royce's Solicitor!

During the autumn of 1938, Neville Chamberlain, the British Prime Minister, made a number of trips to Germany to meet with Adolf Hitler. On 30 September 1938, he landed at Heston airport near Hounslow, emerging from his aircraft an American-manufactured, metal-skinned, twin-engine Lockheed Electra. Chamberlain was brandishing a piece of paper, which had been signed at a conference in Munich with Hitler, Mussolini, the Italian fascist leader, and the French Prime Minister.

Chamberlain claimed that the signed document meant "peace in our time", but contrary events were happening in Europe. In less than twelve months, on 3 September 1939 and following Hitler's refusal to withdraw Nazi invading forces from Poland, Chamberlain would again be speaking to the British people with the shocking news that:

"This country is at war with Germany".

The Second World War

Upon the declaration of war, all civil air services to Europe were immediately suspended, and most civilian airports were taken over by the military. The Government created the National Air Communications Centre to assume responsibility for civil aircraft and administration. Operations were initially physically transferred to Bristol (Whitchurch) Airport and this transfer effectively signalled the end of Croydon's role as the principal airport for London.

The so-called "Phoney War" was initially to follow. The British Expeditionary Force (BEF), comprising large numbers of British troops and equipment, was sent to northern France. Most civil aviation operations then focussed on flights across the English Channel in order to supply the troops with food and ammunition. On 10 May 1940, the Phoney War ended with the Nazi blitzkrieg invasion of Holland, Belgium and Luxembourg.

The German Panzer tanks, with strong air support from the Luftwaffe, proved to be unstoppable, soon moving into France and threatening the total annihilation of the French army and the enforced complete surrender of the BEF. British and French troops retreated to the beaches around Dunkirk. Total disaster loomed, saved only by The Admiralty-organised Operation Dynamo. Between 26 May and 3 June 1940, a huge fleet of vessels of all types ferried over 300,000 British and French troops back from the Dunkirk beaches to safety in England, although most arms and equipment were lost. Hitler then commenced Nazi preparations, in northern France, for Operation Sea lion, the invasion of the United Kingdom.

However, it was first necessary to gain air superiority. Following his appointment in July 1936 as Head of Fighter Command, Air Chief Marshall Hugh "Stuffy" Dowding had ensured the replacement of the RAF's obsolete biplane fighters. In the ensuing Battle of Britain, commencing on 10 July 1940, the RAF's fourteen hundred pilots, supported by their ground crews, pitted their modern Rolls-Royce Merlin-powered Hawker

Hurricanes and Vickers-Supermarine Spitfires against much superior Luftwaffe aircraft numbers.

Infuriated by an RAF bomber attack on Berlin on 25 August 1940, which had caused minimal damage but which had forced Berliners to run for the bomb shelters, a vengeful Hitler then critically blundered. He ordered the Luftwaffe to divert its attacks to London rather than continuing to disrupt the south of England fighter airfields. This change enabled the RAF to re-group and also spared the remaining coastal Radio Direction Finding stations (an initiative which had been championed by Dowding), which were giving the RAF vital advance notice of Luftwaffe attacks. On 15 September 1940, the Battle of Britain reached its climax, with every available RAF fighter being deployed successfully to repulse two waves of massive Luftwaffe attacks. Two days later, Hitler postponed his invasion preparations.

The Battle of Britain had been won with Winston Churchill, the British Prime Minister since 10 May 1940, celebrating the victory with the immortal words;

"Never in the field of human conflict was so much owed by so many to so few".

Mitchell and Royce would have been proud of the Spitfire's vital role in the Battle, powered by its Rolls-Royce Merlin engine. However, Britain was now standing alone in Europe against the Nazis. In August 1941, Churchill sailed across the Atlantic for a secret rendezvous with President Franklin D Roosevelt in Placentia Bay, Newfoundland. The Atlantic Charter was signed, under which America agreed to provide wartime equipment and economic support to Britain. A key proviso was that the two Governments would:

"Respect the right of all peoples to choose the form of government under which they will live; and wish to see sovereign rights and self-government restored to those who have been forcibly deprived of them".

The USA was signalling that it had no intention of assisting a post-war perpetuation of the British Empire. Later, the USA formally entered into the Second World War following the Japanese attack on its Navy at Pearl Harbour, Hawaii, on Sunday, 7 December 1941.

The Mediterranean area was now closed to civil aviation, so flights to Empire destinations required to be re-routed around the West African coast, across the African mainland to Khartoum in Sudan and then up to Cairo in order to link with the routes to India and then on to Australia. The ignominious fall of the British colony, Singapore, to the Japanese in February 1942 was a further humiliation for Britain. Japanese forces had surged down the Malay Peninsula from Thailand using nothing more sophisticated than large fleets of bicycles. Empire flights were then ended for the duration of the war.

JuanTrippe the founder of Pan Am. An American aviation legend who pioneered global travel and who placed the first order for the Boeing 747 Jumbo.

A Hawker Hurricane at White Waltham. Wartime HQ of the Air Transport Auxiliary (ATA). The Author

Whilst travel across the North Atlantic in the 1920s and 1930s was very much the province of the magnificent ocean liners of the period, exploratory transatlantic flights had commenced in July 1937 in collaboration with the legendary Juan Trippe, the founder and President of Pan American Airways (Pan Am). The first scheduled Imperial Airways transatlantic service from Southampton was undertaken by a Short Empire Flying Boat in early August 1939. The aircraft had in-flight refuelled over Foynes in Southern Ireland and then, battling strong headwinds, had reached Botwood in Newfoundland over sixteen hours after leaving Southampton.

With the advent of the Second World War, Empire Flying Boat operations were relocated to Poole. To maximise cargo capacity, passenger seats were reduced to twenty-eight and the fleet received more powerful Bristol Pegasus radial engines. A skeleton wartime transatlantic air service was maintained by way of Trippe facilitating the supply to BOAC of three of the more capable Boeing 314A flying boats, which could accommodate sixty-eight day passengers or thirty-six sleepers.

The practical war-time support provided by the USA to the Allies included its "Lend-Lease programme". Under this arrangement, the Atlantic Return Ferry Service was established to ferry American-produced aircraft across the Atlantic to the United Kingdom. Their American, British and Canadian delivery crews were then shuttled back to North America in a small fleet of American-produced Consolidated Liberator bombers. The process was repeated many times over. Much valuable experience was gained during this period about future transatlantic air travel.

Commander Pauline Gower
at a Women's Engineering Society dinner in March 1940.

Separately, within the United Kingdom, the Air Transport Auxiliary (ATA) was formed in early 1939 at the instigation of Gerard d' Erlanger, a merchant banker who had been involved with a number of aviation projects during the 1930s. From its headquarters at White Waltham airfield near Maidenhead, Berkshire, the ATA organised the ferrying of new and repaired aircraft, to the front-line squadrons, from British factories and maintenance units and also from the transatlantic delivery points. Pilots were widely recruited, including a number of older senior ex-Imperial Airways pilots.

Thankfully attitudes were changing from those which had been demonstrated at a meeting of the International Commission for Air Navigation in April 1925, when it had excluded women "from crews of aircraft engaged on public transport activities"! One-eighth of the pilots recruited by the ATA were women, and they received equal pay in 1943. By the conclusion of the Second World War, the ATA had ferried to the front line over 300,000 aircraft of many different types. Commander Pauline Gower, an experienced aviator, was the organiser of the ATA's women's section, but sadly, she did not survive the war for long, dying at the age of just thirty-six, in March 1947, when giving birth to her twin sons.

The Brabazon Committee

By late 1942, the British Government was already considering the future of post-war British civil aviation. The Allies had agreed that the USA should be the main provider of wartime transport aircraft. Winston Churchill foresaw that post-war Britain would therefore most likely become largely dependent upon the USA for supply of new civil aircraft. Churchill considered that British aircraft manufacturers needed to be incentivised to design and produce a new post-war generation of airliners, particularly for long-haul routes. Otherwise, British manufacturers would be able to offer, for civil use, only conversions and derivatives of military types.

Churchill's views were probably influenced by his uncomfortable war-time flights in a noisy Avro York VIP transport. The York, a civil derivative of the Avro Lancaster bomber, was the best British manufacturers could then currently offer, but it compared unfavourably with emerging airliners from the leading American manufacturers, Boeing, Douglas and Lockheed. American civil aviation had developed significantly during the 1930s, particularly for long-haul routes, reflecting its large internal land mass. The USA was geographically different from Europe, without the difficulties of national borders. A strong American Economy was driving a growing demand for everyday air travel.

A Douglas DC-3, still serving in 1994 in New England with Providence Boston Airlines, nearly sixty years after the first flight of the type. The Author

Donald Willis Douglas founded the Douglas Aircraft Company in 1921 as a rival to its nearest competitor, the Boeing Airplane Company. In 1936, Douglas produced the twin-engine DC (Douglas Commercial) -3 and its military equivalent, the C-47 Skytrain, later known as the "Dakota" in British military service. The DC-3 was to be a highly successful aircraft with its cruising speed of around two hundred mph, carrying up to thirty-two passengers over a range of 1500 miles. By 1939, around 90% of all world passenger flights were being performed by DC-3s.

On 6 June 1944, over 800 C-47 Skytrains were involved in the D-Day landings to drive the Nazis from northern France, either towing troop-carrying gliders or delivering a force of over 13,000 American para-troopers into Normandy. Douglas produced large numbers of C-47s/DC-3s during the period 1936-43. It also developed the larger DC-4 and its military equivalent, the C-54 Skymaster. This was a four-engine tricycle undercarriage airliner, seating up to fifty passengers, and it first flew in February 1942, with nearly 1200 aircraft in various versions being produced over the following five years.

Separately, the American business magnet, the reclusive Howard Hughes and one of the most influential and richest people in the world had instigated the development of the Lockheed Constellation, a transcontinental airliner powered by four piston engines. The Constellation would feature the newly introduced concept of cabin pressurisation, a process in which conditioned air is pumped into and out of the aircraft's cabin, enabling the cabin to be kept at a pressure of between sea level and 8000 ft. In an unpressurised cabin, passengers required additional oxygen at higher altitudes because of reduced air density. The consequent risks of hypoxia would then lead to the loss of cognitive ability. All modern airliners today have pressurised cabins.

The Constellation first flew in January 1943 and, with the benefits of its pressurised cabin, it was able to reach a service ceiling of 24,000 ft. It could carry fifty passengers or more over a range of 3,500 miles at a cruising speed of 340 mph. Hughes, a major stockholder in Trans Continental and Western Airlines (TWA), had agreed personally to finance TWA's purchase of the Constellation. The Constellation's level of performance far exceeded the capabilities of any then-current or projected British civil aircraft. Further, Boeing was planning to enter the post-war civil aircraft market with its two decks and pressurised Stratocruiser. This large aircraft could carry up to one hundred passengers on its main deck, with a further fourteen travelling in the lower deck lounge.

To address Churchill's concerns about future British airliner manufacturing, the Government decided to establish the Brabazon Committee, its purpose being to:

"Investigate the future needs of the British Empire's civilian airliner market following the Second World War, recognising that the British Empire and the Commonwealth (Australia, Canada and New Zealand) as both a political and economic entity would have a vital need for aviation systems (principally aircraft) to facilitate its continued existence and self -reliance".

The Committee's terms of reference indicate how many within the British Establishment were still failing to recognise changing attitudes. The end of what remained of the "British Empire" was actually very close to hand. Canada had been a largely self-governing country since the mid-19th century and Australia and New Zealand, also South Africa had been granted "dominion" and self-governing status in the mid-1920s. The successor Commonwealth would be a much looser and more independent association.

Lord Brabazon. Despite its best endeavours his Committee ultimately failed to achieve a long term future for British civil aircraft manufacturing.

Further, there was an underlying assumption that the Government would control the production, distribution and pricing of aircraft through "command economy" style principles. The Government also envisaged retaining a direct involvement in civil aviation through its State-owned airline corporations. Market forces later demonstrated this approach to be unsustainable and that the Government's role in aviation should not extend beyond Defence and Regulation, together with precisely targeted support of development projects.

John Moore-Brabazon, a contemporary of Charles Rolls at Trinity College, Cambridge, was appointed Chairman of the Committee, which was to bear his name. A pioneer aviator,

Moore-Brabazon was the first person to qualify as a pilot in the United Kingdom, being awarded the Royal Aero Club Aviator's Certificate number 1, on 8 March 1910, the same day as Charles Rolls was awarded Certificate number 2.

Four months later, Moore-Brabazon's wife, shocked and concerned for her husband's safety following the death of Rolls in the July 1910 accident, had persuaded him to relinquish his Certificate. The First World War then intervened and Moore-Brabazon served as a pilot in the Royal Flying Corps, winning the Military Cross. He was later a Conservative MP, becoming Minister of Aircraft Production in 1941. He was ennobled as Baron Brabazon of Tara in April 1942.

The Brabazon Committee commenced its formidable task in early 1943, with Flight magazine at the time describing what little then remained of the operational fleet of British transport aircraft and current offerings by the British aircraft manufacturers as comprising:

"Conversions, makeshifts, and cast-offs, totally inadequate to represent the Empire in serving the air routes of the world in the peace to come".

Moore-Brabazon was very well aware of the rapid civil aviation developments in America. At a luncheon on 25 August 1944, held to celebrate the twenty-fifth anniversary of the previously-mentioned first official international passenger flight, he "jovially" suggested to the then Secretary of State for Air that he should visit America because:

"You are being manoeuvred off the earth".

The war in Europe ended in early May 1945, following Hitler's suicide at the end of the previous month and the recognition by the German High Command that the military situation was hopeless for Germany. The war in Asia was brought to an end with the Japanese surrender on the deck of the battleship USS Missouri on 14 August 1945. This surrender followed the dropping of an atomic bomb over the city of Hiroshima and the detonation of a plutonium implosion bomb over Nagasaki.

With the Second World War now being over in its entirety, the Brabazon Committee issued its final report in December 1945. The Report called for the construction of seven new aircraft types, and the British aircraft manufacturing industry immediately took up the challenge of presenting appropriate responses. The re-launch of British civil aviation took place on 1 January 1946.

State-owned airline corporations

Whilst Churchill had been a great war-time leader, the Labour Party's promise to the British Public of "food, work and homes" in peace time meant that the Conservative Party duly lost the general election, held on 5 July 1945. A Labour Government was elected, led by Clement Attlee, and included within its Manifesto was the proposed nationalisation of public utilities and major industries. For civil aviation purposes, the ensuing Civil Aviation Act 1946 would enable the Government to:

"Secure the development of air transport services by corporations operating under public control".

In August 1939, the British Overseas Airways Corporation (BOAC) Act had received Royal Assent. It provided that the newly-created BOAC would be the sole recipient of subsidies for overseas air services, but the corporation would not be granted a monopoly over commercial flying. BOAC had taken over operations from Imperial Airways, effective 1 April 1940. Commander Pauline Gower had achieved another first for women by being appointed to the BOAC Board in 1943. After just fifteen years of operations, Imperial Airways had now become another part of British civil aviation history and the use of the word "Imperial" was quietly dropped.

The American-produced Lockheed Electras, which had transported Chamberlain on his various pre-Second World War trips to meet with Hitler, were operated by British Airways Limited, an Independent airline originally known as Allied British Airways Ltd. The airline had been formed in 1935, with the involvement of Gerard d' Erlanger, through the merger of Hillman Airways, an operation started in 1931 by the gregarious Essex coach entrepreneur Edward Henry Hillman, with two other small independents, Spartan Airlines and United Airlines. British Airways Limited had been able to purchase its Electras because it was not subject to the Government restrictions on foreign-produced aircraft. Its operations and assets were now also acquired by BOAC. British Airways Limited then became a dormant entity until its re-activation on 1 April 1974, with the creation of the British Airways that we know today.

Sir Alan Cobham (left) with Air Vice-Marshall Don Bennett both important British aviation figures. British Airways Museum.

In addition to BOAC, there would be two new State-owned airline corporations, one of which would be British South American Airways (BSAA). BSAA had already been established in early 1944, initially as British Latin American Airways. The founders were five major shipping lines with the intention of complementing their shipping services to South America. BSAA was taken into state ownership in 1946. Its first Chief Executive was the RAF's former youngest Air Vice-Marshall, Donald

Clifford Tyndall Bennett. Don Bennett, regarded as being one of the most brilliant technical airmen of his generation, was the wartime leader of RAF's Pathfinder Force. A number of ex-Pathfinder pilots were recruited by BSAA.

The second new airline corporation was British European Airways (BEA), an airline which had commenced operations in February 1946, initially as a division of BOAC. BEA took over routes from RAF Transport Command, together with some of its DC-3 Dakotas and became State-owned on 1 August 1946. It then increased its fleet to comprise a total of twenty-one Dakotas, based at Northolt Airport in north London.

The pre-war British Airways' Lockheed aircraft had not resumed service, but BEA inherited the forty-five de Havilland Dragon Rapides of the ten small independent airlines, which had been controlled during the war by a Government organisation known as the Associated Airways Joint Committee. The Rapides were put to work alongside BEA's Dakotas in order to provide domestic and some initially limited European services.

Peter Masefield in wartime, at the controls of a USAAF B17 bomber. He was later CEO of BEA and Managing Director of Bristol Aircraft.

Gerard d' Erlanger was appointed as BEA's first Chairman, and he promptly recruited Peter Masefield from the Civil Aviation Ministry to be his assistant. Masefield was another Cambridge engineer who had entered journalism pre-war after failing the RAF's eyesight test. However, he managed to fly with the USAAF as a gunner and occasional co-pilot in its Boeing B17 Flying Fortresses. He had then worked for Lord Beaverbrook, the war-time Minister of Aircraft Production, and was later appointed Secretary to the Brabazon Committee.

Former Marshall of the Royal Air Force and First World War aviation hero William Sholto Douglas, now Lord Douglas of

Kirtleside, replaced d' Erlanger as BEA Chairman in early 1949. Lord Douglas was the fourth person in the UK to obtain a commercial pilot's licence, and he was a Captain with Handley Page Transport in the 1920s. BEA promptly promoted the thirty-five year old Masefield to the position of Chief Executive.

Handley Page Halton a Halifax bomber conversion. BOAC's fleet was later acquired by Freddie Laker's Aviation Traders Limited. Some were converted for use in The Berlin Airlift. British Airways Museum.

The three new State-owned airline corporations were now operational. However, as predicted by Churchill those three years previously, they were attempting to re-launch scheduled services with the motley group of aircraft, which had previously been so disparagingly described by Flight magazine. The remaining AW Ensigns, operated briefly pre-war by Imperial Airways, had been written off and had been replaced by twenty-one Avro Lancastrians, transferred from the RAF. BOAC had also acquired a fleet of Handley Page Haltons. The Lancastrians and the Haltons were the predicted very basic civil conversions of the military Lancaster and Halifax bombers, respectively. BSAA also operated a small fleet of Lancastrians.

Avro Lancastrian, a Lancaster bomber conversion. The aircraft on which Richard Branson's mother worked as an Air Stewardess in the late 1940s. Air Team Images

Interim Types

In addition to producing its specifications for the new Brabazon Types, the Committee also had the foresight to acknowledge the need for a number of "Interim Types" to enable the operation of an adequate and competitive network of scheduled air services pending the arrival of the Brabazon Types. These Interim Types were forecast to be required for service for at least the initial five years of the post-war period. The Interim Types comprised:

The **Avro York -** The previously mentioned York was a high-wing aircraft powered by four Rolls-Royce Merlins. It served on BOAC's African routes from 1944 until the introduction of the pressurised Canadair Argonaut in 1949. Two hundred and fifty-eight Yorks were produced between 1943 and 1948 and the aircraft continued in service with the Independent sector until its last commercial flight in 1964.

A Hunting Clan Avro York at Manchester in August 1955. The noisy and unpressurised York was no match for the emerging new American types. Creative Commons Attribution RuthAS

The **Avro Tudor -** was an aircraft proposed by the Ministry of Supply for use by BOAC on both the North Atlantic and on some Commonwealth routes. BSAA, charged with the task of developing services from the UK to South America and including the West Indies and Central America, also had a keen interest in the four Rolls-Royce Merlin-powered, pressurised Tudor. The Tudor first flew in June 1945 but it suffered from aerodynamic problems and was rejected by BOAC in April 1947 as being unsuitable. Confidence was further seriously undermined a few months later when the prototype crashed on take-off from the Avro facility at Woodford, near Stockport, due to an assembly error. All on board were killed, including Roy Chadwick, Avro's chief designer. Chadwick had been responsible for the war-winning Lancaster bomber, of which over 7000 had been produced, and he had died during an ill-fated "hands-on" effort to sort out out the Tudor's problems.

The Avro Tudor. The interim type, which served only a short period with British South American Airways, after a series of unexplained aircraft losses. Air Team Images

The Ministry of Supply nevertheless continued its support of the Tudor project, and BSAA, seeking to replace its Avro Lancastrians, commenced services with six Tudor 1Vs in late 1947. On 30 January 1948, BSAA Tudor, Star Tiger, with a crew of six and with twenty-five passengers aboard, bound for Bermuda from the Azores, last reported its position as being 380 miles north east of the island. Nothing further was heard from the aircraft. The Tudor fleet was immediately grounded, and passenger services were not resumed until August 1948.

Don Bennett strongly objected to the grounding and was promptly dismissed by BSAA after having unwisely used the media to state his case. On 17 January 1949, BSAA Tudor, Star Ariel, carrying a crew of seven and thirteen passengers, was also lost over the Atlantic Ocean, this time on a flight from Bermuda to Jamaica. The Tudors were again grounded, and, separately, the Ministry of Aviation announced that, with effect from 1 January 1950, BSAA would cease to exist and would become the South American Division of BOAC.

After leaving BSAA, Bennett had formed Airflight, a charter and cargo airline based at Langley Airfield in Berkshire, maintaining his faith in the Tudor and operating two aircraft during The Berlin Airlift. Bennett personally flew all of the night time services.

On 12 March 1950, Airflight Tudor, Star Girl, was returning seventy-eight Welsh Rugby Union supporters from Dublin to Llandow Aerodrome in South Wales. They had watched the game against Ireland in the Five Nations Championship. Eyewitnesses observing its landing approach saw that the Tudor was at an abnormally low altitude. Corrective actions were attempted by the pilot, but the Tudor stalled and plummeted to the ground. All but three of the passengers on board were killed, together with all of the five crew members.

The terrible Llandow crash is still remembered in Wales and its seventy-fifth anniversary was marked, on 15 March 2025, by a one minute silence at the Six Nations game between England and Wales. The crash was, at the time, the worst recorded disaster in civil aviation history. A Court of Enquiry determined the cause as being overloading, which had moved the centre of gravity aft.

The Tudor would never play its intended significant role in the re-establishment of British civil aviation, but it still had a limited future use, as we shall see later.

The **Handley Page Hermes** – The Hermes was an Interim Type proposed by the Handley Page Aircraft Company, where Frederick Handley Page, knighted in 1942 for services to the war effort, was still very much in charge. The Hermes, powered by four Bristol Hercules engines, was intended for use primarily on BOAC's routes to Africa. BOAC placed an order for twenty-five aircraft in early 1945. The Hermes was specified to carry up to eighty passengers over a range of around 3000 miles at a cruising speed of 266 mph. Sir Frederick succeeded in negotiating a parallel RAF order for one hundred and fifty of the similar Hastings transport aircraft. The combined orders secured a viable production run for Handley Page in those difficult early post-war years.

An ex-BOAC Handley Page Hermes at Blackbushe in September 1954. Airwork operated the type mostly on trooping contracts.

Development issues delayed Hermes' service entry with BOAC until August 1950. Subsequent reliability and performance problems, some attributable to an excessively heavy wing derived from the Halifax bomber, resulted in its early withdrawal in favour of the Canadair Argonaut. By 1954, the Hermes fleet was out of service and was standing forlornly at BOAC's Heathrow maintenance base, looking for a new home.

Sales of redundant Hermes aircraft to Independent airlines were delayed by Union officials representing BOAC maintenance staff. The Unions were demanding assurances that the aircraft "would not be engaged on flights which could be undertaken by BOAC" and they also required that BOAC's facilities be used to carry out Hermes' engine overhauls. The disputes were eventually resolved, and the Hermes fleet progressively passed into the hands of the Independents, serving reasonably successfully until the aircraft's final flight in December 1964.

The **Canadair (DC-4M) Argonaut** – The Argonaut was a pressurised Douglas DC-4 powered by four Rolls-Royce Merlins and fitted with various components from its more advanced Douglas DC-6 successor. BOAC, anticipating possible problems with the Tudor and the Hermes, had secured Government permission for a fall-back solution in the form of an order for twenty-two Argonauts from Canadair (formerly Canadian Vickers Limited). The Argonauts were delivered an unprecedented eight months ahead of schedule during March-November 1949 and proved to be a very cost-effective purchase.

An ex- BOAC Canadair Argonaut at Manchester in June 1965. Two years later, this particular aircraft was the subject of the Stockport air crash. Air Team Images.

Members of the Public attending today's flying displays will have heard the very distinctive and stirring sound of the four Merlins powering the Lancaster of the Battle of Britain Memorial Flight. The external sound of the Argonaut was very similar, but passenger comfort was affected by high internal noise levels, which could only be partly addressed by modifications to the exhaust systems.

Notwithstanding these passenger comfort issues, Argonauts were used to transport Royalty. On 1 February 1952, BOAC Argonaut Atalanta carried Princess Elizabeth and her husband, the Duke of Edinburgh, to Kenya in order to commence a Commonwealth Tour. The Tour had to be cancelled, and five days later, the same aircraft returned to Heathrow. On board was Her Majesty, Queen Elizabeth the Second, the Princess having acceded to the throne following the death of her father, King George VI.

Argonauts were extensively used on routes to South America, Africa and the Middle East and they continued in BOAC service until 1960, flying on with some of the Independents until 1967. They also serviced the Far East, covering the trip to Hong Kong in three days, compared with five days for the Empire Flying Boat service. A further two days were taken off the Flying Boat schedule for the onward journey to Tokyo.

It was these improvements which ended BOAC's Empire Flying Boat services in 1954. The remaining United Kingdom flying boat operator, Aquila Airways, made gallant efforts to expand holiday flights but, with no available successor for its ageing Short Solent aircraft, all Aquila operations ceased in

September 1958. So ended the glamorous era of the flying boat in British civil aviation.

After being superseded by Viscounts, ex-BEA' Vikings then successfully served with many Independent airlines. Air Team Images

The **Vickers- Armstrongs Viking** – The Viking was selected by BEA as being a suitable Interim Type to service its European routes. It was a development of the Wellington bomber powered by two Bristol Hercules engines. The Viking first flew in June 1945, and it was the first twin-engine airliner able to comply with a recent ICAO requirement for such airliners to be able to take off with one engine stopped. Vickers-Armstrongs produced one hundred and sixty-one Vikings, up to 1948. Over four hundred of the military Varsity and Valetta versions were also produced, again making this combined order viable for the manufacturer. As BEA progressively phased out the type, from the early 1950s, in favour of its turboprop Viscounts, the Viking was to become a mainstay of the newly-emerging British Independent airlines.

The Bristol freighter, an aircraft which facilitated cross-Channel car ferry services, operating here on behalf of Freddie Laker's Air Charter in the mid-1950s. Air Team Images

The **Bristol Freighter** – This aircraft was not strictly an Interim Type, but it was an important participant in early post-war British civil aviation. A high-winged, twin Bristol Hercules engined, monoplane, the aircraft had a Flight Deck elevated above the load space which was accessed by large hinged nose doors. It flew in December 1945 as a stop-gap project to fill capacity after the failure of Bristol's Brabazon and during the development of the later Britannia airliner. The aircraft also had special future potential for service as a car ferry.

American Types were also recognised by the Government as being necessary to enable BOAC to be internationally competitive. Accordingly, it approved the purchase of American-produced Lockheed Constellations and Boeing Stratocruisers. On 14 June 1946, the first BOAC Constellation arrived at Heathrow from New York, having completed the 3,520-mile Atlantic crossing in the then-record time of eleven hours and twenty-four minutes. The previous month, a Pan Am Constellation was the first international flight to land at the newly-opened Heathrow airport. Later problems and delivery delays with the Brabazon Types would require BOAC to operate a fleet of around forty Constellations and Stratocruisers much longer than anticipated and into the late 1950s.

Lockheed 749A Constellations, in preparation at Heathrow, in the early 1950s, for service during the remainder of the decade with BOAC. British Airways Museum

The Boeing Stratocruiser served with BOAC into the late 1950s because of delayed deliveries of the new Brabazon Types. Air Team Images

Entrepreneurs & Independent airlines

Whilst the 1946 Civil Aviation Act had afforded the State-owned airline corporations a monopoly over scheduled services, there were still potential opportunities for budding post-war aviation entrepreneurs, particularly through the establishment of Independent airlines. These airlines would be able to utilise some of the RAF's huge war-surplus inventory of over 9,000 aircraft, where such aircraft were suitable for conversion for civil use.

Most members of the RAF's 190,000 aircrew in service at the end of the Second World War had no interest in continuing to fly or in becoming aviation entrepreneurs. Their wish was simply to return to civilian life, which, however, would never be the same again. A typical 1945 RAF leaver was Ken Williams, an ex-Lancaster pilot and a former colleague of the Author at Babcock International plc during the early 1980s. Ken appeared quite content with his post-war important, but relatively unglamorous, occupation of running the Babcock Employee Benefits Department. He spoke little of his war experiences and his apparently unexciting later career choice seemed surprising.

However, Ken simply desired the normality and benefits of a steady job. Along with many others of their generation, Ken and his wife had explored post-war Europe, courtesy of the package holiday boom commencing from the 1960s. They loved the dry heat of the Costa del Sol and, upon retirement in 1984, they purchased a Malaga apartment to where the couple relocated in order to spend their final years happily enjoying the sun.

There were many other ex-RAF pilots who, unlike Ken Williams, still wished to continue flying. The new State-owned airline corporations had some vacancies, but the post-war aviation entrepreneurs also generated a flurry of Independent airline formations, providing further opportunities.

Harold Bamberg was a German-Jewish refugee, born in Berlin in November 1923, who had escaped Nazi Germany in 1938 and who had then joined the RAF, aged seventeen. Bamberg established Eagle Aviation in April 1948, initially operating two converted Halifax bombers. Eagle had then acquired further Halifax conversions, together with a number of Avro Yorks, for use on passenger and freight charters and on troop-carrying contracts. Eagle was to grow steadily and was to become a significant force in British Independent civil aviation over the next twenty years.

The entrepreneurial Sir Alan Cobham, who had been knighted for his route-proving efforts in 1926, had continued to promote interest in aviation through his "Flying Circus" and national aviation days. These events had made it possible for the Public to undertake pleasure flights. In the early 1930s, Cobham formed Flight Refuelling Limited to develop in-flight refuelling techniques, which he incorrectly considered had the potential to revolutionise civil aviation (in fact, the major market for in-flight refuelling was and remains for military purposes).

Sir Alan was also an initial shareholder in Skyways, an airline which had commenced operations in 1946 with two new Avro Yorks, together with two Avro Lancastrians. Skyways' initial work was the servicing of the Persian Gulf operations of the Anglo-Iranian Oil Company (today BP) and the airline later operated early tourist flights on behalf of the Sir Henry Lunn Travel Company Limited using four DC-4 Skymasters.

Hugh Kennard, in RAF service in 1940, standing alongside his Jaguar SS90

Wing Commander Hugh Kennard, born in 1918, was the archetypal 1930s RAF officer with a penchant for all things fast. In 1938, he purchased the prototype SS90 Jaguar Roadster, which he then needed to sell in mid-1940 upon the occasion of his marriage. By this time, Kennard was flight commander of No 306 Squadron, a Polish training squadron flying Hawker Hurricanes out of RAF Church Fenton in Yorkshire.

The 1969 film "Battle of Britain" includes a scene in which Squadron Leader Edwards, played by actor Barry Foster, berates his Polish pilots for disobeying instructions during a training exercise. Having sighted a flight of attacking Luftwaffe planes, the Poles had broken formation in order to engage the enemy. At the end of the scene, Edwards announces, to great cheers, that Fighter Command was so impressed by the skills of the

Polish pilots that it had agreed to make the Squadron immediately operational.

The fictional Edwards character would seem to bear a striking resemblance to the real-life Hugh Kennard. In 1946, after completing his successful full-time military career, Kennard employed his leadership and communication skills to become a civil aviation entrepreneur, initially founding Air Kruise based at Lympne Airfield in Kent. Kennard would then be involved in a number of other civil aviation ventures over the following thirty-five years.

The most famous of the post-war British civil aviation entrepreneurs was, without a doubt, Frederick Alfred Laker. Born in Kent in August 1922, Laker had then attended the local Grammar School, leaving early and claiming that he was "not very bright". Laker's interest in aviation is said to have been stimulated by a pleasure flight provided by Sir Alan Cobham's Flying Circus. After leaving school, Laker worked pre-war with Short Brothers Limited in Rochester. During the Second World War, he served with the ATA, where he qualified as a Flight Engineer and learned to fly. Here Laker was also able to gain vital knowledge about the capabilities for civil use of RAF aircraft, many of which would become redundant at the cessation of hostilities.

After leaving the ATA, Laker worked briefly for BEA; however, his entrepreneurial instincts were strong. In 1947, with the assistance of a loan of £38,000 (nearly £2m today) from a "wealthy friend", Laker established Aviation Traders Limited (ATL). ATL subsequently made its main base at Southend Airport, specialising initially in the acquisition and conversion of war-surplus aircraft. Laker's "super-salesman" talents had already facilitated some successful transactions, as evidenced by his ability to contribute around £4,000 (just over £200,000 today) of his "savings" to the ATL project. The "wealthy friend" clearly had confidence in the largely untried twenty-five year old Laker in order to back a venture with such uncertain prospects.

The Berlin Airlift

Despite the initial surge of post-war airline activity and optimism, it soon became apparent that only the strongest Independent airline operators would survive for long. Their continued existence was mostly dependent upon the ongoing availability of sufficient ad hoc freight and passenger charter work. However, external events in Europe were perversely about to provide an important boost for the Independent sector in the form of The Berlin Airlift.

The victorious Allies had split post-war Germany into four zones of occupation: Soviet, American, British and French. Berlin was a particular problem as it was situated deep within Soviet-controlled East Germany (then known as the German Democratic Republic). The City was divided into four sectors, with access from West Germany being by road, rail and canal and by way of an air corridor across the Soviet zone.

The Soviets were intent on taking massive post-war reparations from Germany as compensation for the Nazi's destruction of its people and property. The Americans differed, seeing the rehabilitation of Germany and the distribution of aid to Europe under the Marshall Plan as being essential to the post-war economic recovery of a democratic Europe. In a move designed to prevent the spread of communism whilst also risking the ire of the Soviets, the Americans required those nations seeking to participate in the Marshall Plan to belong to the West.

In early 1948, the Soviets reacted to what they considered were these adverse developments by commencing bureaucratic obstacles to the free movement of people and goods within Berlin. On 5 April 1948, a BEA Viking was buzzed by a Soviet fighter on a flight into West Berlin and crashed, killing all ten people on board, with the Soviets refusing to allow a full crash investigation.

Upon discovering that the Western powers were proposing a Federal West German State with a new currency, the Deutschmark, the Soviets denounced this move as being:

"Against the wishes and interests of the German people and in the interests of American, British and French monopolists".

On 22 June 1948, the Soviets announced the proposed introduction of their own new currency, the Ostmark, into the Eastern zone, which included all of Berlin. Two days later, at 6.00 am on 24 June 1948, the Soviets cut road, rail and canal routes connecting Berlin with West Germany and ceased electricity supplies from power stations situated in the Soviet sector. The more than two million Berliners, together with the Allied military garrison, were now blockaded in the City. The Soviet objective was to oblige the West either to change its policy or to leave Berlin altogether. The Americans considered using force to break through the blockade but decided that it was just feasible to fly in sufficient supplies to meet the City's needs.

On 26 June 1948, the first American C-47 Skytrains flew into Berlin from bases in West Germany and were soon supplemented by substantial numbers of the larger four-engine C-54 Skymasters. The Berlin Airlift had commenced.

The Airlift provided salvation for some of the Independents because the RAF had insufficient suitable, operational transport aircraft to make its required contribution. Consequently, it was necessary to charter all suitable and available civilian aircraft. BEA coordinated this exercise and participated along with other State-owned airline corporations and more than twenty Independent airlines. The Independents collectively provided over a hundred aircraft, mostly comprising Avro Yorks and Lancastrians, together with Haltons and Halifax conversions. The RAF also employed its newly-acquired Handley Page Hastings transports. The blockade was eventually lifted on 30 September 1949, by which time 278,228 flights to the beleaguered City had been undertaken, delivering over 2.3m tons of supplies.

During the Airlift Flight Refuelling Limited and Eagle Aviation had each utilised their Lancaster and Halifax tankers to carry huge amounts of fuel. Skyways had freighted large amounts of supplies with its Avro Yorks, and a small number of Avro Tudor operators, including Airflight, were also able to use their aircraft for freighting purposes. Aquila Airways participated by landing its Short Solent flying boats on Havel Lake and on Berlin's rivers in order to deliver freight during the ice-free months.

At the commencement of The Airlift Freddie, Laker's ATL had available six converted, ex-BOAC, Handley Page Haltons. It leased these aircraft to its associate, Bond Air Services with Laker sometimes flying Airlift missions himself. ATL serviced and maintained the aircraft, received a majority share of the freight charges and supplied converted aircraft to other Airlift participants. Freddie Laker accumulated sufficient funds from The Airlift to pay off his loans and, by its end, he had become a wealthy man.

The Airlift provided much-needed funds for Independent airlines to survive through the lean years ahead. Readers seeking more insight into those dramatic Airlift days are recommended to read "Air Bridge", a 1951 novel featuring a modified Avro Tudor. The book demonstrates the authenticity and powers of description for which its author, Hammond Innes (1913-98), was so well-regarded.

Gas Turbines

As stated earlier, the use of gas turbine engines to power passenger aircraft was the single change that occasioned a huge increase in civil aviation during the second half of the twentieth century and continued into the twenty-first century. The aircraft propulsion produced by the gas turbine engine is a practical application of 17th century scientist, Sir Isaac Newton's third law of motion, which states that "for every force acting on a body, there is an equal and opposite reaction".

For aircraft propulsion by gas turbine engines, the "body" is the atmospheric air which is accelerated as it passes through the engine core and, in the case of today's turbofan engines, also around the engine core. The force produced by the engine to generate this acceleration has an equal effect, in the opposite direction, on the apparatus producing the acceleration. For the gas turbine engine, this apparatus comprises the engine itself.

The opposite force is then transmitted via the engine mountings to the airframe, thereby accelerating the airframe forwards.

Sir Frank Whittle, a brilliant mathematician, using his trusted slide rule

Frank Whittle was born in Coventry on 1 June 1907 to an inventive father who ran a small engineering business. Here, Whittle had developed some practical engineering skills. He resolved to become a pilot, but was initially rejected by the RAF on grounds of his poor fitness and small physique. Whittle persevered and succeeded in becoming a trainee aircraft mechanic at RAF Cranwell in September 1923. It was here that his mathematical genius was first recognised and he was recommended for an officer training course, including flying lessons.

Whittle was required to write a course thesis His subject was "Future Developments in Aircraft Design" in which he commented that "The turbine is the most efficient prime mover known". He then proceeded to argue that the RAF's objective of flying at high levels, at speeds of over 500 mph, was not achievable by current and future developments of propeller engines. What was required, Whittle stated, was a motor jet capable of operating efficiently at higher altitudes due to lower air densities.

In 1929, Whittle sent details of his concept to the Air Ministry, but the information was returned with the comment that it was "impracticable". A fellow RAF officer, who had previously been a Patent Examiner, persuaded Whittle to file a Patent, which he did in January 1930. Whittle then continued his work, publishing a further paper, "The Case for the Gas Turbine". After obtaining top marks at the Officers School of Engineering, Whittle was sponsored to attend Peterhouse College, Cambridge, graduating in 1936 with First Class Honours in Mechanical Engineering.

In 1935, the still doubtful Air Ministry had refused to pay the renewal fees on Whittle's original Patent, which was allowed to lapse. Undeterred, Whittle raised private finance to Patent improvements to his original ideas and to establish Power Jets Limited, commenting that:

"Reciprocating engines are exhausted. They have hundreds of parts jerking to and fro, and they cannot be made more powerful without becoming too complicated. The engine of the future must produce 2000hp with just one moving part: a spinning turbine and a compressor".

As the Second World War loomed, the Air Ministry had then renewed its interest in gas turbines, particularly following news that Nazi Germany was also working on the concept. In early 1938, the Ministry belatedly placed a £5000 (£42,000 today) contract with Power Jets to produce a flyable version of the Whittle engine, the W1X. It also instructed the Gloster Aircraft Company (part of Hawker Siddeley Aircraft) to build the Gloster E.28/39, a simple aircraft for testing purposes. The test aircraft made its first flight on 15 May 1941 and was soon reaching speeds of 370 mph at the height of 25,000 ft, out-performing the latest Spitfires.

The Gloster E.28/39 jet engine test aircraft

In April 1942, the Air Ministry contracted the Rover car company to undertake large-scale production of Whittle engines at its Barnoldswick facility near Clitheroe, Lancashire. The engines were to power the new twin-engine Gloster Meteor fighter.

However, relations between Power Jets and Rover were poor and, in December 1942, a second hugely important meeting in the history of Rolls-Royce took place. It was with the Rover car company and was held at the much less salubrious Swan Hotel, Clitheroe.

Ernest Hives in 1911 test driving a Rolls-Royce Silver Ghost.

Rolls-Royce was represented by its General Manager, Reading-born Ernest (later Lord) Hives, who had commenced his working life at the Charles S Rolls car company. By 1908, at the age of twenty-two, he had become chief test driver for Rolls-Royce. After being appointed General Manager of Rolls-Royce in 1936, Hives had driven a large increase in pre-war Merlin engine production, directing his teams to "Work till you drop".

Stanley Hooker (seated) with Whittle whilst collaborating on gas turbine engines in the early 1940s.

Hives was accompanied by Dr Stanley Hooker, a senior Rolls-Royce engineer and a specialist in fluid dynamics who had been in dialogue with Whittle since early 1940, facilitating Rolls-Royce development assistance to Power Jets. Hooker, the brilliant fifth son of a farm labourer, had won a scholarship to study mathematics at Imperial College, followed by a doctorate in aeronautics from Brasenose College, Oxford.

When previously interviewing Hooker for his job at Rolls-Royce Hives, who was generally unimpressed by academic qualifications, had noted Hooker's limited practical experience with the comment "Not much of an engineer". Hooker soon proved not only that he was very much "of an engineer" but that he was destined to be one of the leading aeronautical engineers of his generation.

Lord Hives, in the 1940s and, by then, Managing Director of Rolls-Royce

Attending on behalf of Rover was its Managing Director, Spencer Wilks, later credited as being the founder of Land Rover, having authorised the first production of the four-wheel drive utility vehicle, which had been designed by his brother, Maurice Wilks. After a short discussion, Rover agreed to trade its Barnoldswick facility, together with the rights to use Whittle's designs, in exchange for the transfer of Rolls-Royce's Nottingham Tank production factory. Rover was also authorised to produce a land-based version of the Merlin (the Meteor), which was the power plant for the Churchill Tank.

The exchange was completed on 1 April 1943, and Rolls-Royce was immediately set to work on developing gas turbines. The company had now adopted the names of rivers for its future gas turbine engines in the place of the bird names previously used for its piston types. Within two years, the Rolls-Royce Welland (later the Derwent), based on Whittle's designs, was being installed in production versions of the Gloster Meteor, the first jet aircraft to be operated by the Allied air forces.

Rolls-Royce was now poised to become a world-leading gas turbine engine manufacturer. In 1946, Hives, by then the newly-appointed Rolls-Royce Managing Director, reported to the Board that;

"There are no new aircraft contemplated or being built which will take the Merlin or the Griffin (the Merlin's successor) or any other piston engines".

The hugely successful Rolls-Royce Dart turboprop powered both the Viscount and a number of other 1960s airliners. Rolls-Royce Museum. The Author

Rolls-Royce's next gas turbine project was the turboprop Dart engine for the proposed Vickers-Armstrongs Viscount and which was also potentially for use in other emerging types. The Dart was to remain in production for forty years, with over 7,000 engines being sold. Another team, headed by Stanley Hooker, was working on the axial flow Avon engine, which first ran in March 1947. Over 11,000 units of Avons for various applications will be produced over the next twenty-four years.

In 1943, the patriotic Whittle accepted Churchill's suggestion to allow Power Jets to be nationalised as part of the National Gas Turbine Establishment. Whittle received a payment of only

£10,000 and retired from the RAF in May 1948 as an Air Commodore. Not a bad achievement for a man who had joined the Service as a trainee aircraft mechanic.

The Royal Commission on Awards subsequently made an ex-gratia payment of £100,000 to Whittle, which, together with a knighthood, was a more proper recognition of his outstanding pioneering work. Post-war, Whittle consulted widely, then moved to the USA in 1976 with his new American wife. A chain smoker, he finally succumbed to lung cancer twenty years later, at the grand age of eighty-nine. In 2002, Whittle was ranked number forty-two in the BBC poll of the 100 Greatest Britons. Like Mitchell and Royce before him, Whittle had made a huge contribution to British aviation and, in his case, also to worldwide aviation.

Two other prominent aeronautical engineers, Barnes Wallis and Neville Shute Norway, also emerged during the Formative Years. They each made their mark on aspects of British aviation, and Annex 1 contains a brief summary of their respective careers and contributions.

Air Regulation

Prior to manned flight, the air was considered to be free, but post-First World War development of civil aviation indicated the urgent need for international regulation of aviation. A series of Air Navigation Acts, commencing in 1919, progressively established a regulatory environment for aviation in the United Kingdom. In the international context, the "Convention Relating to the Regulation of Aerial Navigation" was signed by twenty-seven states on 13 October 1919, also creating the International Commission for Air Navigation (ICAN).

Whilst respecting a state's full and absolute sovereignty over its airspace, the Convention had also recognised the desirability for the greatest freedoms for international air navigation, but consistent with state sovereignty and security concerns. In addition to the safe conduct of air navigation, the Convention also provided for ICAN to establish rules and regulations for matters, including airworthiness certificates and pilot licensing, together with international rules for signals, lights, collision prevention, also including procedures for landing and for ground movements.

In 1927, the Air Transport Committee of the International Chamber of Commerce agreed, at a conference in The Hague, to recognise established airlines as official carriers of the mail. Rules and regulations concerning the conduct of mail services were agreed upon, including the still current requirement for PAR AVION labels to be coloured blue.

Most European airlines during the 1930s were not greatly concerned about the rights to initiate air routes. This was because the majority of their services were for the purpose of connecting their colonies across the globe. Accordingly, there was no need to negotiate traffic rights. However, America had no significant colonies, so its principal overseas carrier, Pan Am, needed to obtain traffic rights to service required worldwide destinations. Juan Trippe was Pan Am's chief negotiator, and, pre-Second World War, he acted effectively as an unofficial US Government representative, conducting direct negotiations for air routes with the various countries concerned.

Post-Second World War and with wide-spread de-colonisation now in prospect, it was clear that this rather ad-hoc situation could not continue. On 1 November 1944, delegates from fifty-four countries met at the Stevens Hotel in Chicago to commence what would be the most significant conference to date on aviation regulation. The objective was to promote the healthy growth of international air travel within an updated and expanded regulatory framework. One of the first successes of the resulting Chicago Convention of 1944 was the establishment of the ICAO as the replacement for ICAN. ICAO became operational in April 1947, following ratification of the Convention by the twenty-sixth country, and in October of that year, it became an agency of the United Nations.

A second success achieved by countries attending the Convention was in reaching an agreement on the **Freedoms of the Air** comprising:

The **First Freedom** which is the right to fly and to carry traffic over the territory of another party to the Convention without landing.

The **Second Freedom** which is the right to land in another party's territory for technical reasons, such as refuelling, without boarding or de-planing passengers.

The **Third Freedom** which is the right of an airline from one country to land in a different country and to de-plane passengers coming from the airline's own country.

The **Fourth Freedom** which is the right of an airline from one country to land in a different country and to board passengers travelling to the airline's own country.

The **Fifth Freedom** which is the right of an airline in one country to land in a second country, then pick up passengers and fly them on to a third country where the passengers then de-planed.

The Fifth Freedom proposal was made by the USA, wishing to have more control over international trunk routes, but was rejected by the other major nations attending the Convention, seeing this proposal as an attempt by the USA to dominate and monopolise much of the world's air traffic.

Bilateral Air Services Agreements to be concluded between individual countries were a third success of the Chicago Convention. The Convention agreed on the key criteria for such Agreements, including a provision for countries to designate their selected carriers to act as the "Chosen Instrument" for routes.

The Bermuda Agreement of 1946 (Bermuda 1) was a Bilateral Air Services Agreement to deal with a number of unresolved matters between Britain and America. The Agreement provided for Fifth Freedom rights and for extensive routes with no arbitrary restrictions on capacity or flight frequencies. Pan Am and BOAC were to be the designated carriers for their respective countries and would be the primary "Chosen Instruments". As a result of Bermuda 1, Pan Am now had Fifth Freedom rights to pick up passengers from London for passage to points east, thereby enabling the airline to launch its round-the-world service in 1947.

Because airline operators had limited involvement in the Chicago Convention, they decided to form a non-governmental organisation of their own in order to deal with the economic aspects of civil aviation. On 19 April 1945, the articles of IATA were approved and adopted.

The purposes of IATA were to promote safe, regular and economical air transport, to foster air commerce, to provide the means of collaboration among air transport enterprises and to cooperate with ICAO. An initial function of IATA, which was later superseded and then dropped, was to coordinate fares and rates between member airlines through periodic traffic conferences. The resulting outcomes were invariably ratified by the relevant governments.

During the formative years of civil aviation, aircraft accidents were fairly frequent although, because of comparatively low speeds and altitudes, they were not always fatal for all of the relatively small numbers of passengers on board. Airlines clearly needed to be appropriately insured. In order to obtain such coverage, there needed to be protection from open-ended liability in the case of damage or loss to cargo or baggage and injury and death to passengers. The Convention for the Unification of Certain Rules relating to International Carriage by Air (the Warsaw Convention) was signed in Warsaw in 1929.

The Warsaw Convention provided for airline liability to be subject to specified financial limits for death or injury to passengers, for loss or damage to baggage and for loss resulting from delays. The Convention was updated by The Hague Protocol of 1955, the basic principle being that air carriers are strictly liable (that is, without determining fault) for proven damages up to specified limits. For compensation sought beyond those limits, the carrier may avoid liability by proving that the accident that caused the injury or loss was not due to its negligence or that it was attributable to the negligence of a third party.

The Montreal Convention, which became effective in November 2003, superseded the earlier Conventions and provides for the payment of proven damages arising from aircraft accidents up to a limit determined by Special Drawing Rights, which limit is currently around $150,000 per passenger.

Passengers today are also entitled to claim compensation from airlines for flight delays or cancellations. There are specific amounts of compensation that can be claimed, depending on the length of the flight and the extent of the delay. Also, individual airlines set out, in their terms and conditions, the relevant details of their particular compensation arrangements.

Part 2- The 1950s

Some of those outstanding personalities who had played notable roles in the Formative Years of British civil aviation passed away during the 1950s. Captain Bill Lawford, the pilot of that historic 1919 first official international flight, died in 1955, followed, two years later, by Captain Alfred Instone, the joint founder of Instone Airline. However, British civil aviation was continuing to move forward and, somewhat unexpectedly, in the early 1950s the British Aero Industry found itself to be a world leader. British-designed and built gas turbines were powering a number of the now emerging new Babazon Types. Some of these aircraft were demonstrating huge advances in performance and passenger comfort over their piston engine contemporaries.

Separately, British Independent airlines were steadily expanding but with many ups and downs along the way. A helpful development had been the Government lifting, with effect from 1 January 1953, of restrictions on the ability of Independent airlines to apply for licences to operate scheduled services. Licences would be granted provided the destinations were not already served by the State-owned airline corporations. The Independent airlines could now be more inventive in making air services for both business and leisure purposes, more accessible to a wider British Public.

The 1950s was also a time of a political and military stalemate between the West and the USSR (Union of Soviet Socialist Republics). The so-called "Cold War" had followed the detonation by the USSR in August 1949 of its first atomic bomb. The result was that both parties now had atomic weapons, and so, thereby, had the capability for Mutual Assured Destruction. During the Cold War, a world divided between capitalism and communism would now live under a constant nuclear threat. An "Iron Curtain" descended over those Eastern bloc countries (Poland, Czechoslovakia, Hungary, Yugoslavia, Bulgaria, Romania and the Baltic territories of Estonia, Latvia and Lithuania) which Stalin, the Russian leader, wished to control as a buffer against perceived future Western aggression.

Britain, war-exhausted and heavily indebted, was also still coming to terms with the reality of its rapidly accelerating loss of Empire. India had gained a chaotic independence, in 1947, followed in the next year by Burma (now Myanmar) and by Ceylon (now Sri Lanka). There was unrest in Malaya and in the African colonies, most of which were seeking independence. In addition, Britain had passed Middle East peace-keeping responsibilities to the United Nations.

In 1952 Farouk, the King of Egypt, had been removed following a military coup, led by General Nasser. There were consequent concerns about the security of the Suez Canal, which was vital to ensure the passage of tankers carrying around two-thirds of Europe's oil and gas.

The British Government had separately previously concluded that the Suez Canal and the area surrounding it (the Canal Zone) no longer had a rationale for the defence of India nor for Britain's access to its rapidly diminishing Empire. Accordingly the 1954 Anglo-Egyptian Act had provided for the phased withdrawal of British troops from the Canal Zone and for the transfer of the Suez Canal Company to Egypt to be completed by November 1968. However, this timescale was pre-empted in the summer of 1956, when General Nasser seized and transferred the control of the Suez Canal Company to the newly formed, Egyptian-owned Suez Canal Authority.

The handsome and charming Sir Anthony Eden, who had supported Churchill loyally during and after the war years, had won the 1955 general election for the Conservatives. However, Eden's health was poor, suffering from abdominal infections following damage to his bile duct during previous gallbladder surgery. He was prescribed Benzedrine, then regarded as a harmless stimulant, but the drug had previously unknown side effects, including insomnia and mood swings.

An increasingly ill Eden decided to support a French Government plan to depose Nasser and it was arranged for Israeli forces to invade Egypt, assisted by British and French troops. Neither the USA nor the United Nations were supportive. Sterling started to lose value and the USA threatened to exacerbate the situation by selling its large holdings of Sterling-denominated bonds. As a result, all military action was rapidly discontinued and the invading forces were promptly withdrawn from Egypt.

The Suez Crisis effectively ended Britain's role as a major world power, together with the political career of Eden early in the following year. The USA's Central Intelligence Agency (CIA), established in 1947, now took on the duties of being the world's policeman with the United Nations, created in 1945, having responsibility for international peacekeeping and security. Britain now had to understand that it no longer needed to play the world's game because it was no longer a major player in world affairs. In December 1962, former American Secretary of State, Dean Acheson, confirmed this new reality by observing in a presentation to the US Military Academy, West Point, that:

"Great Britain has lost an empire and has not yet found a role".

Post-war British Aero Industry

In the post-war years, the British Aero Industry similarly needed to adjust its activities in recognition of the country's changed situation in the world. By the early 1950s, the Industry had been reduced in size from its wartime peak, but it still comprised a significant and important sector of the British Economy, with nearly 180,000 people being employed.

Aviation generally had an increasingly high public profile as was demonstrated, for instance, by the large numbers of spectators attending the 1952 Farnborough Air Show. At that time, Farnborough was exclusively for new British aircraft, and an incredible number of thirty-five new types were on display at the Show. Test Pilots were as well-known to the Public as are today's Formula 1 drivers, although it was an equally hazardous occupation and eighty-two test pilots had lost their lives since 1946.

The Government had concluded that the post-war Aero Industry was too fragmented and that consolidation was necessary to enable Britain to compete effectively in the modern world of aviation and to enable the Industry to keep pace with the sector's increasing technical complexity. These consolidated entities also should be large enough to make the huge financial investments required to bring new projects to fruition. The Government also believed that the United Kingdom's balance of payments position would benefit from reduced volumes of imported, foreign-built aircraft in favour of the home construction and export of new aircraft, particularly civil aircraft, to worldwide customers.

One of the effects of The Cold War was the need to maintain an Aero Industry sufficient to support the defence of the United Kingdom. In 1950, seventy-five percent of the Industry's output was related to Government contracts to service the RAF's capabilities. Not all of these projects would be successful and others would lead to a duplication of effort and to delays. A classic case had been the Air Ministry's 1946 requirement for the development of a new advanced jet bomber. Such aircraft was to be capable of carrying a 4,500kg nuclear bomb over a range of 1,500 – 2,000 miles, at a speed in excess of 500 mph and at a height of 35,000 – 50,000 ft.

Two V Bombers, a Vulcan (left) and a Victor at RAF Gaydon in 1966. Both aircraft would play key roles in the 1982 Falklands War, Operation Black Buck. Air Team Images

Vickers-Armstrongs, Hawker Siddeley's Avro Division and Handley Page, had each responded proposing their Valiant, Vulcan and Victor "V Bombers," respectively. Incredibly, the RAF was allowed to order some of each type of "V Bomber"! The then Air Chief Marshall's justification for this bizarre decision was "to avoid the RAF choosing the wrong one". The "V Bomber" programme produced a significant and continuing revenue stream for the three manufacturers, but it was in stark contrast to the situation today, at a time when the UK no longer produces any large complete civil or military aircraft!

During the 1930s the de Havilland Aircraft Company Limited had grown steadily. In 1940, it acquired Airspeed Limited, which had been founded by Neville Shute Norway in 1931, and there had been huge growth during the Second World War. De

Havilland was now a business employing nearly 40,000 people. In addition to producing its successful small biplane airliners, particularly the Dragon Rapide, de Havilland had also developed the Moth range of two-seater biplanes. The definitive DH.82 Tiger Moth first flew in 1932 and was described as an excellent training aircraft which was "easy to fly, but which was difficult to fly well". Nearly 9000 Tiger Moths were produced, many being built at the Morris Motors Cowley facility, now home to BMW's Mini. Some Moths are still flying today.

Sir Geoffrey de Havilland in wartime with a model of his creation, the highly versatile Mosquito. de Havilland Museum

A twin Merlin powered Mosquito undergoing restoration in 2025 at the de Havilland Museum. The Author

De Havilland had also produced Second World War military aircraft, notably the Rolls-Royce Merlin-powered DH.98 Mosquito. The Mosquito was a multi-role combat aircraft constructed primarily from wood-based products, and it became one of the most successful Second World War aircraft, with well over 7000 being built.

Geoffrey de Havilland had been knighted in 1944 but, in the previous year, the Mosquito's success had been severely tempered, for him personally when John, one of his three sons, was killed in a crash between two RAF Mosquitos. Three years later, on 27 September 1946, the de Havilland family suffered a further crushing blow when another of Geoffrey's sons, Geoffrey de Havilland Jr., was killed when test-flying the DH.108 swept-wing aircraft.

A catastrophic structural failure had occurred when diving from 10,000 ft at near the speed of sound. Geoffrey de Havilland

Jr. had suffered a broken neck as the aircraft experienced severe buffeting during the dive and he was already dead by the time the disintegrating aircraft crashed into the Thames Estuary.

Lady de Havilland never fully recovered from the loss of two of her three sons in these aviation accidents. She later suffered a series of breakdowns and died in 1949. The 1952 British aviation drama film "The Sound Barrier", directed by David Lean, gives some insight into aircraft and gas turbine engine development in the early 1950s. The film tells the fictional story of the aviation magnate, John Ridgefield played by Sir Ralph Richardson, who is attempting to achieve supersonic flight and break the sound barrier. The film is believed to be loosely based upon the de Havilland family's real-life story and includes references to the DH.108 accident together with interesting footage of a number of contemporary de Havilland aircraft, including the Comet 1.

The Government's process, in the 1950s, for dealing with new military aircraft and aero-engine projects differed fundamentally from that operating in America. Beyond the design study stage, such projects were generally not competitively tendered. In America, normal market forces were allowed to operate throughout contracting and manufacturing. In Britain, it was only during the later prototype and production stages that the Government exercised cost controls in the form of either fixed-price or cost-plus production contracts. The British system was intended to enable the manufacturers to make a reasonable return on capital employed in military work, whilst generating sufficient funds for them to self-finance new and potentially high-risk civil aviation projects.

Towards the end of the decade, it became clear that this system was not working satisfactorily and that a number of British aircraft manufacturers were in financial difficulty. The Government then progressively executed a "U" turn in its contracting system and announced its intention, in future, to provide support for approved civil projects in the form of launch aid. It would also encourage and authorise the RAF to order military versions of suitable civil aircraft.

Many years later, in February 1974, the Institute of Economic Affairs published Hobart Paper 57, "A Market for Aircraft", which looked back at the British Aero Industry over the preceding thirty years. The Introduction to the Paper quoted the nineteenth-century philosopher and economist, John Stuart Mill:

"There are some things with which Governments ought not to meddle and other things with which they ought; but whether right or wrong in itself, the interference must work for ill, if Government, not understanding the subject which it meddles with, meddles to bring about a result which would be mischievous".

Hobart Paper 57 argued that the Government had never really understood the intricacies of the Aero Industry and that, overall, its involvement, combined with slow progress in achieving Industry rationalisation, had brought about mischievous results which been unhelpful. We will return to the Paper's findings and conclusions later.

In January 1957, Duncan Sands (MP for Streatham and the son-in-law of Winston Churchill), in his capacity as the Minster of Defence, then dropped his own bombshell in the form of the

White Paper on the future defence of the United Kingdom. The White Paper reflected both the struggling British Economy and recent information about significant progress made by the USSR in its development of ballistic missiles. The study concluded that the UK had no effective defence against such missiles, which could be launched from land bases in East Germany. The much-lauded "V Bomber" force would most likely be mostly destroyed, even before it was airborne, and so was potentially redundant. Further, if the USSR employed land-based missiles in order to deliver its nuclear warheads, then there would be fewer, or possibly no, incoming Soviet bombers to be dealt with by the UK's expensively assembled interceptor fighter force.

The Government resolved to discontinue a number of air defence system projects, particularly for the supply of new manned aircraft, in favour of the UK developing its own missiles. The English Electric P1 "Lightning" supersonic interceptor fighter would survive this change of policy only because its development costs had already been incurred. The Government also made it clear that it required the various remaining participants in the Aero Industry to merge into larger groups. It stated that it would, in future, contract only with such groups.

An initial response to these merger exhortations was the agreement between the Bristol Aeroplane Company and Hawker Siddeley, in 1959, to merge their respective ailing aero-engine businesses; Bristol Aero-Engines Limited and Armstrong Siddeley Motors Limited. The combined operation would be known as Bristol-Siddeley Engines Limited. Further mergers within the British Aero Industry would take place early in the following decade.

Brabazon Types

Responses to the Brabazon Committee's recommendations for the production of seven new civil aircraft types began to emerge in the late 1940s and some of the resulting new British airliners would enter airline service from the early to mid-1950s.

Type 1 was for a very large transatlantic airliner capable of carrying one hundred and fifty passengers at a top speed of 300 mph. The Bristol Aeroplane Company proposed the giant Bristol 167 (known as the "Brabazon"). The Brabazon had a twin-deck fuselage with a length of 177 ft, a 230 ft wingspan and a fuselage diameter of 25 ft. Dimensions which were greater than those of the 1970s Boeing 747 Jumbo jet! Power was provided by no less than eight Bristol Centaurus piston engines, mounted in pairs and driving contra-rotating propellers. The Centaurus was the last in line of Bristol Engines' successful range of radial piston engines. To build the aircraft, Bristol had constructed a new final assembly hall at its Filton site which, at the time, was the largest hangar in the world. It had also been necessary to lengthen and widen the Filton runway.

The prototype Brabazon first flew on 4 September 1949. The Press described the new aircraft as being "the Queen of the Skies", a description more appropriately given, some twenty years later, to the ground-breaking Boeing 747 Jumbo. BOAC test flew the Brabazon and was unimpressed, subsequently showing no further interest. A Brabazon Mark 11 was proposed using Bristol Engine's new Proteus turboprop, but the development of this engine was proving troublesome. On 17 July 1953, following nearly four hundred hours of test flying, the Brabazon was to become an expensive and embarrassing failure. Duncan Sands, who was then Minister of Supply, announced the cancellation of the project after an expenditure of £6m (£206m today)!

A Dan-Air Airspeed Ambassador at Bristol Airport in 1965. Eleven were acquired second-hand by the airline and were operated successfully from the late 1950s until 1971. Public Domain Adrian Pingstone

Type 11 was for a DC-3 replacement, with the specification being split into Type 11A for a twin piston engine airliner and Type 11B for an aircraft using the new Rolls-Royce Dart turboprop engine. This split was made because the Brabazon Committee was still unconvinced about the merits of turboprop power!

Contrary to Ernest Hive's 1946 update to the Rolls-Royce Board, there would still be one new British piston engine airliner. Through its recently acquired Airspeed Company, de Havilland offered the Ambassador powered by two Bristol Centaurus piston engines. The Ambassador first flew in July 1947 and entered service with BEA in late 1951 as the "Elizabethan" class. The Ambassador was an elegant, high-winged aircraft with large windows, providing good passenger appeal; however, it did not succeed as a DC-3 replacement. Just twenty aircraft were supplied to BEA as the only purchaser.

By the late 1950s, Ambassadors had been progressively withdrawn from BEA routes and the aircraft then served the Independent sector for many years. The last commercial Ambassador flight was by the Independent airline Dan-Air, in September 1971, by which time its fleet of second-hand aircraft had flown over ten million miles. Sadly, the aircraft is perhaps best remembered for a tragedy that occurred in early February 1958 and which is described in Annex 2.

Why not a pleasant afternoon out at Heathrow Airport? In early 1958 well-dressed spectators are viewing BEA's growing fleet of Viscounts. Air Team Images

A BEA 1950s Advertising Poster tempting prospective passengers to experience turboprop-powered flight. British Airways Museum.

The way was now clear for Vickers-Armstrongs' response to the Type 11B specification in the form of its turboprop-powered Viscount. The Viscount, with its four Rolls-Royce Darts, first flew in July 1948, and a revised and enlarged version for production, the 700 series, took to the air two years later. The Viscount could carry around fifty passengers at speeds of over 300 mph. BEA placed an order for twenty of the 700 series and, in April 1953, the airline launched the world's first scheduled turboprop service.

The Viscount rapidly caught the Public's attention with its distinctive sound and affording panoramic passenger views from its large ellipse windows. The Viscount offered much superior internal quietness, together with a lack of vibration, when compared with existing piston engine types.

Orders for Viscounts poured in, including from North America, where Trans-Canada Airlines and Capitol Airlines were large early users. In Europe, nearly all of the major European airlines, including Aer Lingus, Air France, Alitalia, KLM and Lufthansa, rushed to purchase. Vickers later offered the 800 series with improved capacity and range. Over its production run to 1963, four hundred and forty-five Viscounts were sold worldwide. BEA operated a large Viscount fleet until its final withdrawal of the type, in 1982, and Viscounts then flew on with many of the Independent airlines.

A British Eagle, ex-BOAC, Britannia and a RAF Handley Page Hastings at Sydney in January 1966. The Hastings was a military version of the Hermes but with a tail wheel undercarriage configuration. Air Team Images.

Type 111 was a four-engine aircraft for "Medium Range Empire" (MRE) routes. The Bristol Aeroplane Company responded in the form of its four Proteus turboprop-powered Britannia. The failure of the Brabazon had been a near catastrophe for Bristol, but some of the learning was relevant for the Britannia and Bristol had also greatly improved its facilities. Further, Stanley Hooker, who had left Rolls-Royce in order to join Bristol Engines in 1948 following disagreements with Hives, was now making better progress with the development of the Proteus turboprop.

Whitney Straight - a Battle of Britain pilot and later Chief Executive of BOAC and Deputy Chairman of Rolls-Royce

The Britannia was envisaged as a Constellation/Stratocruiser replacement, but BOAC's then Chief Executive, Willard Whitney Straight, was reluctant to make a commitment to the aircraft, describing the Proteus as being "an obsolete contraption". Straight, born in New York in November 1912 into the prominent and wealthy Whitney family, was another Trinity College, Cambridge engineering graduate. He had become a naturalised British citizen in 1936 and had then served with the RAF in the Battle of Britain, being awarded the Military Cross.

Straight had left the service in late 1945, with the rank of Air Commodore and he was appointed as BOAC's Chief Executive in July 1947. Straight's connections were valuable, not least his cousin, Cornelius Vanderbilt Whitney, who was the Chairman of Pan Am. This relationship had then helped BOAC's pilots to gain access to Pan Am's Stratocruiser training course in 1949, together with the use of the simulator at La Guardia Field.

Despite Straight's reservations, The Ministry of Supply was determined to keep the Britannia project running and, to do so, it agreed to order three prototypes, the first of which flew on 16 August 1952. Proteus problems were continuing and, in February 1954, the second prototype Britannia suffered an in-flight engine fire. An ensuing electrical fault caused all engines to stop. On-board technicians managed to restart two of the engines, but it was too late to avoid a crash landing in the Severn Estuary. The incident made national news with the helpless aircraft being soon swamped by the rising tide, thereby rendering the alloy structure beyond repair.

The crash did little for the Britannia's reputation. A positive, however, was that the incident helped to thaw difficult relations between Hives and Hooker. Upon hearing of the crash, Hives immediately despatched a Rolls-Royce engineering team to Bristol Engines to assist Hooker in resolving Proteus issues.

The Britannia's Certificate of Airworthiness was awarded late in 1955, by which time BOAC had agreed to order fifteen of the Model 102, with a follow-up order for ten of the longer-range Model 312. In the meantime, the Britannia development delays had made it necessary for BOAC to purchase ten Douglas DC-7Cs, the last in line of the great Douglas piston engine transports. This stop-gap purchase was essential so as to enable BOAC to compete effectively on the North Atlantic routes with Pan Am and with a number of other major airlines that were operating similar equipment.

At the end of 1955, Peter Masefield unexpectedly left BEA, in order to become Managing Director of the Bristol Aeroplane Company, stating that family responsibilities and a significantly increased remuneration package were the reasons for the move. Masefield also had a genuine desire to make a contribution to UK aircraft manufacturing. He immediately set out upon a world Britannia sales tour, at times flying the aircraft himself. Sadly, initial interest from America did not materialise into actual sales because Bristol was unable to offer acceptable delivery dates.

The Britannia, known to the Public as the "Whispering Giant", was an elegant, robust and capable aircraft but its development delays had seriously diminished its commercial prospects. American-designed pure jet alternatives were about to become available, initially in the form of the formidable Boeing 707, which was scheduled to fly in late December 1957. The 707 had four jet engines installed in pods mounted on swept-back wings. It offered a cruise speed of over 500 mph in comparison with the Britannia's cruise speed of around 360 mph. The similar concept Douglas DC-8, with equal capabilities to the 707, was only slightly behind the Boeing aircraft and was due to fly in May 1958.

Despite Masefield's valiant efforts to achieve the one hundred and eighty aircraft sales target, only eighty-five Britannias were built and sold, including over twenty aircraft supplied to the RAF. BOAC's Britannia services commenced in February 1957 and, on December 19 1957, a BOAC Britannia 312 carried out the first-ever non-stop transatlantic flight from London to Canada. Regular Britannia flights to New York were then commenced and were extended, in 1959, to Tokyo and to Hong Kong. The last BOAC scheduled Britannia flight was in April 1965. Britannias then continued to give good service with the RAF until the mid-1970s and with Independent airlines into the early 1980s.

The de Havilland Comet 1 which commenced the world's first jetliner services in May 1952.

Interior of the Comet 1 exhibited at the de Havilland Museum, London Colney. The Author.

Type 1V specified a jet-powered, high-speed transport capable of carrying sixty or more passengers for up to 3000 miles at a cruising speed of 500 mph. The de Havilland Aircraft Company bravely responded with its stunning DH.106 Comet, a potentially world-leading aircraft. The specification was finalised in 1947 and the Comet's first flight was on 27 July 1949 in the capable hands of de Havilland's chief test pilot and famous Second World War night-fighter pilot, John "Cats Eyes" Cunningham. The "Cats Eyes" tag had been wartime propaganda designed to deceive the Nazis into believing that Cunningham had exceptional night eyesight. In reality, it was new secret radar detection techniques which were responsible for the RAF's increasing night-time successes.

The prototype Comet was powered by four de Havilland Ghost turbojets. The Ghost had been the second British jet engine to fly, but de Havilland intended to install the much more powerful Rolls-Royce Avon in production aircraft as soon as these engines became available. BOAC ordered fourteen Comet 1 aircraft, for delivery in early 1952, and the Certificate of Airworthiness was received on 22 January 1952. On 2 May 1952, a Ghost-engined BOAC Comet 1 operated the world's first jetliner flight, with paying passengers, from London to Johannesburg. The jet age had commenced, and the Comet was estimated to be three to five years ahead of its American competitors.

The prototype Handley Page Dart Herald is now exhibited at the Berkshire Aircraft Museum, a stone's throw from the location of the Miles Aircraft factory where the aircraft was designed. The Author

Miles Aircraft factory at Woodley, near Reading was later purchased by Handley Page and is shown here shortly before its demolition in 2024. The Author

Type VA was for a fourteen-seat feeder liner. The Miles Aircraft Company Limited had been extremely successful during the Second World War, producing large numbers of training aircraft. The Miles Aircraft airfield at Woodley had been the scene of the 1934 accident in which Second World War hero Douglas Bader had lost both legs when performing aerobatics. Bader's ensuing life story is dramatized in the 1956 film "Reach for the Sky". Miles Aircraft's response to the Type VA specification was its four piston engine Marathon. However, the aircraft proved to be unsuitable, and only forty examples were completed, which were mostly allocated to the RAF.

By 1947, Miles Aircraft was in severe financial difficulties and Handley Page acquired its aviation assets from the Receiver.

One benefit to Handley Page arising from the acquisition was the Miles design team's HPR.3 Herald, a pressurised forty-four seat, high-mounted wing aircraft. The Herald, an extensive re-design of the Marathon, clearly did not meet the Type VA requirement, but its good flight and performance characteristics made it another potentially suitable contender as a Type 11 DC-3 replacement.

The Herald first flew in August 1955, powered by four Alvis Leonides 14-cylinder radial piston engines. It received a good initial reception, but interest soon switched to the similar concept, Fokker Friendship, but powered by twin Rolls-Royce Darts. Handley Page belatedly realised that turboprop power was essential and it undertook a major re-design. As a result, a twin Dart-engined Herald emerged, but the re-designed aircraft did not fly until March 1958.

Type VB was for an eight-seat replacement for the faithful de Havilland Dragon Rapide. The de Havilland Aircraft Company responded in the form of the DH.104 Dove, a twin-engine, eight to eleven-seater mono-plane which first flew in September 1945. The Dove was a very successful aircraft, with over five hundred examples being manufactured up to 1967. De Havilland also produced nearly one hundred and fifty examples of the similar four-engine DH.114 Heron, with a capacity for up to seventeen passengers.

The DH.114 Heron, big brother of the Dove, which served many regional airlines and which was used as a corporate aircraft for Rolls-Royce well into the 1970s. The Author

The Viscount and the Dove were the only major commercial successes amongst the "Brabazon Types", however the various projects achieved considerable technical innovation and progress. Lord Brabazon passed away on 17 May 1964 without knowing the eventual full outcome of his Committee's recommendations. However, his assessment, some twenty years earlier, that the country would be "manoeuvred off the earth" by American civil aircraft manufacturers was about to be proved largely correct. This situation had arisen despite Government intervention and the best efforts of the British Aero Industry.

The 1950s Comet disasters

During BOAC's first year of Comet 1 operations, in 1952, it carried 30,000 passengers. Flights to Tokyo, Singapore and Sri Lanka were then added to the schedule. The journey time to

Singapore (including stops) was reduced to twenty-seven hours, compared with two and a half days by the previous Argonaut service. The journey time from London to Tokyo was also made significantly shorter and much more comfortable, compared with travelling by Argonaut. Orders for Comets were placed by many airlines, including Pan Am, which wished to purchase the proposed larger and longer-range Comet 3 for transatlantic services.

On 2 May 1953, exactly a year after the first commercial Comet flight, disturbing news was received that a BOAC aircraft, with forty-three people on board, had crashed near Calcutta. A Court of Investigation was convened, which later reported that the Calcutta accident had occurred through structural failure from "overstressing" in adverse weather conditions. No recommendation was made to ground the aircraft and scheduled Comet services continued.

On 10 January 1954, a Comet on the final stage of its service from Singapore to London disintegrated into the Mediterranean, ten miles south of Elba. All thirty-five on board died. Intensive technical examinations commenced and salvage operations began to retrieve wreckage for detailed examination. All Comet services were temporarily suspended, but the relevant Regulatory Authorities allowed BOAC to resume Comet operations on 23 March 1954. Two weeks later, on 8 April, another Comet disappeared shortly after leaving Rome on the last leg of its service to London from Johannesburg. All twenty-one passengers and the crew were lost. Only minimal wreckage was recovered.

The Comet's Certificate of Airworthiness was withdrawn, and the fleet was grounded. De Havilland ceased Comet 1 production immediately, with work continuing slowly on the Comet 2 and Comet 3. This latter aircraft had been ordered both by Pan Am and by BOAC. Meanwhile, the Royal Aircraft Establishment at Farnborough was able to recover the wreckage from Elba and partially to reconstruct the aircraft. High-pressure water tank testing was carried out on other Comet fuselages and a subsequent Public Enquiry determined the cause of the Elba disaster as being structural failure of the pressure cabin due to metal fatigue. It identified a particular failure towards the front of the fuselage around the aperture for the Automatic Direction Finder. Also, the use of the punch-rivet construction technique was considered to have exacerbated the structural problems.

The Enquiry found the basic design of the Comet to be sound and the de Havilland Aircraft Company was absolved from legal responsibility. The situation might possibly have been different in today's much more litigious legal environment.

In March 1955, BOAC ordered nineteen Comet 4s, but the development and extensive testing of this much-modified aircraft was slow, with the Comet 4 not flying until 27 April 1958. The Comet 4s would employ a thicker gauge metal skin, and the square windows would be replaced by oval windows. These changes were made to strengthen the structure and to reduce metal fatigue risks. The Rolls-Royce Avon engines, producing more than twice the pounds of thrust (lbf) of the de Havilland Ghosts, were now available and would be installed as originally intended.

The hand-over of the Comet 4 by Sir Geoffrey de Havilland to BOAC's then Chairman, Sir Gerard d' Erlanger at Heathrow in 1958. A Britannia is in the foreground with a DC-7C in the distance. British Airways Museum.

BOAC inaugurated the first jet-powered transatlantic services with the aircraft in October 1958. However, Pan Am had discontinued its interest in favour of the Boeing 707, which had a longer range and superior operating economics. Pan Am was now about to start 707 transatlantic services, and it would be followed by BOAC, which had also evaluated the aircraft and had ordered fifteen Boeing 707-436s.

The Comet 4 served with BOAC until 1965 and BEA later successfully operated seventeen of the larger capacity, shorter range Comet 4Bs on scheduled European services until 1970. Comets then continued to provide good service in the Independent sector through the remainder of that decade. One hundred and fourteen Comets (including seventy-nine Comet

4s) were produced. In comparison, more than one thousand five hundred American-produced Boeing 707s and Douglas DC-8s were sold. It was these American aircraft which were to dominate long-haul air travel during the 1960s.

The United Kingdom's pioneering venture into jetliner travel, which had previously engendered so much national pride, had transpired to be a huge disappointment. The British civil aircraft industry would never fully recover from the Comet 1 disasters and the Nation would now progressively lose its lead in the development and production of gas turbine-powered passenger aircraft.

Metal fatigue would be a continuing concern for high-performance jet passenger aircraft into the 1960s and 1970s. More than a decade later, in early March 1966, a BOAC Boeing 707-436 disintegrated shortly after leaving Tokyo for Hong Kong. All 707s and the smaller 720 versions, which had flown more than 1,200 hours, were inspected. Twenty-two instances of cracks were found in sixty-three aircraft. BOAC suspended all of its 707 services whilst modification work was carried out before flying resumed under stringent inspection schedules.

New opportunities for Independent airlines

For most of the Independent airlines, the early 1950s were difficult years, with continuing reliance on ad hoc freight and passenger charter work. A new line of business arose, in 1950, with the award of the first trooping contract to Airwork for the carriage of military personnel to Singapore. Airwork was a long-established aircraft servicing and flying training operation which had made a vital contribution to the RAF's war-time training requirements. By the late 1940s, it was in the ownership of shipping companies and had become involved in the airline business, acquiring some of the redundant BOAC Hermes fleet to carry out its trooping contracts. Such contracts provided a useful albeit progressively declining source of income for many of the Independents through the 1950s and the 1960s.

Harold Bamberg's Eagle Aviation was in the process of acquiring BEA's thirty-seven-strong Viking fleet as they were progressively displaced by Viscounts. It now had suitable aircraft potentially available for the operation of scheduled services and so Eagle successfully applied to the Air Transport Advisory Committee (ATAC) to open the first scheduled service by an Independent airline. Its first service was from London (Blackbushe) to Belgrade via Munich, commencing in June 1953. By early 1954, Eagle was operating seven Vikings and was actively applying for additional scheduled service licenses to many other European destinations.

In 1954, the Ministry of Aviation granted permission for airlines to operate limited programmes of a new type of low-fare service. This service was termed "inclusive tour", and it combined air travel with overseas holiday accommodation at a cost substantially below that of each individual component. As far back as the 1850s, **Thomas Cook** had originated the concept of organised group tourism in Europe using bulk purchasing to lower prices. Thomas Cook's early tours were more in the nature of conducted tours for small groups. The new broader and much more widely marketed inclusive tours were to be the forerunner of today's "package holiday" concept.

Harold Bamberg saw the potential of "inclusive tours" for Eagle, which commenced operations on behalf of several tour companies in 1954. Customers included the aforesaid Sir Henry Lunn Travel Company Limited and the Cooperative Travel Service. The far-sighted Bamberg, when he was not working from Eagle's Clarges Street, London offices, conducted operations from his chauffeur-driven car. The car, registered HB100, was equipped with a Dictaphone and a very early mobile telephone. Recognising the business benefits of vertical integration, Eagle later acquired both the Sir Henry Lunn Travel Company Limited and the Polytechnic Touring Association. These two travel companies would be later merged to form Lunn Poly, one of the UK's leading travel agents and subsequently becoming Thomson Travel.

A number of Independent airlines, which were to play significant future roles in British civil aviation, were established in the early 1950s. In 1953, **Derby Aviation** later Derby Airways and, from July 1964 British Midland Airways, was founded by Group Captain Clifford AB. Wilcock an influential Midlands personality and the MP for Derby. Its initial services were de Havilland Rapide flights to Jersey and other destinations, from Burnaston, Derby and from other Midlands locations. DC-3 Dakotas were also operated for freight services, including the transport of engines and parts for Rolls-Royce.

Dan-Air's first aircraft, a Douglas DC-3, is parked outside the Blackbushe Airport Terminal building in the mid-1950s

Dan-Air, a name which would soon become very familiar to post-war airline passengers, was also registered as an airline company in 1953. Davies and Newman, a London firm of shipping brokers, had acted for the defunct Meredith Air Transport and had taken over its DC-3 Dakota in satisfaction of monies owed. Dan-Air, sometimes rather uncharitably but also affectionately, later known as "Dan Dare", commenced operations originally from Southend but moved to London Blackbushe in 1955, with its maintenance base at nearby Lasham airfield. Dan-Air subsequently acquired three Avro Yorks, which soon found profitable work on Ministry freighting contracts to Europe, the Middle East and Singapore. By June 1957 Dan-Air was also operating a pair of Bristol Freighters.

Hunting Air Travel Limited, based at Bovingdon, Hertfordshire, had been created in late 1945 by the Hunting Group of companies which also had shipping connections. By

1953, the company had been re-named **Hunting Clan**, reflecting its close connections with the Cayzer family-owned Clan Line shipping company. In its early years, the airline carried out a wide range of charter activities, operating a small fleet of Avro Yorks, de Havilland Doves and Vickers Vikings.

Silver City Airways was established, post-war, to service the worldwide air transport requirements of the mining industry. In 1948, Captain A G Lamplugh, the head of the British Aviation Services Insurance Company, supported by Air Commodore Taffy Powell, an adviser to the Zinc Corporation, persuaded the Insurance Company's shareholders to set up a subsidiary, British Aviation Services Limited (BAS). BAS then acquired Silver City and also established a second airline, **Britavia**, for trooping flights. BAS later purchased the flying boat operator Aquila Airways.

The longer-established **Skyways** encountered severe financial difficulties during the early 1950s and, in March 1952, it was rescued by the Lancashire Aircraft Corporation (LAC). LAC had operated a fleet of converted Handley Page Halifax bombers in the late 1940s and during The Berlin Airlift and it was now the only remaining Halifax operator. Seeking a replacement, LAC had boldly acquired BOAC's fleet of twenty-three Avro Yorks in May 1951. LAC paid BOAC £137,000 (£5.4m in today's money) for the aircraft, most of which later served with Skyways. David Brown, the Chairman of LAC during the early 1950s, was also Chairman of the David Brown Corporation. The Corporation, amongst its many other interests, also owned Aston Martin. Aston Martin models, to the current day, still bear the initials "DB" in the continuing recognition of the David Brown Corporation's prior ownership.

Freddie Laker - the early years

Aviation Traders Limited continued strongly in business post-war, undertaking a variety of projects. One such project was to facilitate the transfer of a small number of Dakotas from BEA to BOAC. Laker later critically commented that the respective State-owned airline corporation teams appeared unable to manage such a simple deal without the need for an expensive middleman! ATL scrapped redundant RAF and ex-Airlift aircraft and also acquired surplus new Merlin engines, some of which were used to re-engine BOAC's Argonauts.

Freddie Laker was not only a shrewd businessman, but he was also a genuine British aviation enthusiast. He was determined to make some productive use of the much-maligned Avro Tudor, which he considered had the potential for conversion into "Supertraders". Accordingly, ATL purchased all available Tudor airframes. The conversion work was successful, enabling the Supertraders to provide freight and trooping services, including a colonial coach-class passenger service from Stansted to West Africa, until the final withdrawal of the type in 1959.

Laker even designed and produced his own prototype regional airliner. However, the Dart-powered ATL Accountant was later discontinued because Laker recognised that ATL could not hope to compete with similar aircraft now on offer from the larger manufacturers.

By the mid-1950s, ATL's success was such that Laker was able to acquire an airline, the then loss-making Air Charter. Air Charter operated Avro Yorks, Bristol Freighters and later ATL's Supertraders, together with a number of DC-4s and Britannias on a wide range of passenger and freighting charters. One British Government contract involved the delivery of components to the Woomera rocket range in Australia. Laker's simple formula for success in the airline business was to source aircraft as cheaply as possible and then to optimise their operations so as to maximise profitability.

At the end of 1958, Freddie Laker stunned the Independent sector by announcing that he had sold both ATL and Air Charter to Airwork for a reported £800,000 (£17.5m today). In just over ten years, Laker had achieved a huge return on his initial £4,000 investment! Freddie Laker was now an even wealthier man but he was still only in his mid-30s. What would he do next? The answer would not take long to arrive.

In this early phase of his career Laker, the hard negotiator, was always very mindful of the need to maintain a positive cash flow at all times. His golden rule for sales transactions was reputed to be that he would consider most proposals "provided that cash always changes hands in my direction". We will see later in this book that circumstances arising during the later phases of Laker's entrepreneurial aviation career did not always enable him to follow this rule.

The English Channel

The ability to cross the English Channel efficiently and quickly had been an early major benefit delivered by British civil aviation. In the post-Second World War years, there was a continuing focus on the provision of air services across the stretch of water separating the United Kingdom from mainland Europe. BEA, together with the State-owned airlines of other European countries, operated regular scheduled services from airports in the United Kingdom to France and to the major other European destinations. The Government did not allow any direct competition to these scheduled services. However, it was the capabilities of the previously-mentioned, Bristol Freighter which would enable the Independents to provide an alternative type of cross-Channel service.

Silver City Airways undertook cross-Channel feasibility flights with its Bristol Freighters in 1948. It then obtained the approval of the Ministry of Aviation, in January 1949, to commence a vehicle ferry service from Lympne Airport, near Ashford, Kent, to Le Touquet. The service was carried out in conjunction with the French Compagnie Air Transport and was an immediate success. In 1952, Silver City Airways carried over 11,000 vehicles and 27,000 passengers on its scheduled services across the Channel. The larger Series 32 Bristol Freighters later facilitated the carriage of three small cars and twenty passengers, or three cars of any size and twelve passengers.

A Silver City Airways Bristol Freighter flying over Lydd (Ferryfield) Airport in the late1950s.

Customer demand and traffic volumes across the Channel continued to increase year on year, but a constraint was the poor condition of the Ministry of Aviation-owned Lympne airfield. The Ministry repeatedly declined to make improvements, and so Silver City Airways purchased land near Dungeness in order to construct the Lydd (Ferryfield) Airport. By October 1954, Silver City Airways had transferred all of its activities to Ferryfield and over 56,000 vehicles were flown across the Channel during the subsequent year.

The cross-channel successes of Silver City Airways had not escaped the attention of Laker's Air Charter which, in October 1955, announced the opening of a Bristol Freighter vehicle ferry service between Southend Airport and Calais. Services were later extended to Ostend and to Rotterdam. Air Charter also provided a coach-air service from London to Brussels via Southend and Ostend. Air Charter's vehicle ferry services were reorganised in early 1959 to become Channel Air Bridge.

Skyways, under the driving force of its Managing Director, Eric Rylands, also sought to develop cross-Channel opportunities by applying, in 1954, for permission to open a coach-air service initially using DC-3 Dakotas. The Skyways Coach-Air service commenced in the autumn of 1955, with the passengers being transported by coach from Victoria to Lympne and then boarding the aircraft for the flight across the Channel to Beauvais. A French coach would complete the journey to Paris.

Rylands shared Silver City Airways' frustrations with the poor state of facilities at Lympne and he later decided to purchase the airfield. However, it was not until the winter of 1967, following a series of landing accidents attributable to the grass runway, that a concrete runway was laid. In 1972, Dan-Air acquired Skyways Coach-Air, which was then integrated into its domestic operations.

The Independent airlines made good returns from their cross-Channel activities. However, by the early 1990s, there had been progressive improvements in cross-Channel ferry services by sea, together with the subsequent opening of the Channel Tunnel. The result was that car ferry services by air, together with the cross-Channel coach-air services, were progressively discontinued, and they had soon become another distant memory of British civil aviation.

Passenger experiences

In the spring of 1956, the Author's family embarked upon their first-holiday flight, which was from Manchester to Jersey. Our aircraft was to be one of BEA's refurbished "Pioneer class" twin piston engine thirty-two seater, DC-3 Dakotas. Dakotas were still carrying out sterling work for the airline and would remain in service into the early 1960s on shorter routes. The facilities at Manchester's Ringway Airport were basic, to say the least, comprising mostly converted Second World War buildings. The construction of a purpose-built terminal was still some time away.

A BEA Pioneer Class DC-3 Dakota pictured in January 1952. It long outlasted its intended replacement, the Elizabethan Class Airspeed Ambassador, flying alongside. Air Team Images.

Following check-in, the well-dressed passengers, as befitted such a glamorous and exciting occasion, were escorted across the airport apron towards the aircraft. We passed by a number of parked BEA Viscounts and were a little disappointed that one of these new, state-of-the-art aircraft had not been assigned to our flight.

Instead, we boarded our unpressurised Dakota with its tail wheel undercarriage configuration, entailing quite a steep climb up the fuselage in order to reach our allocated seats. To help equalise pressure on ear drums during take-off and landing, the passengers were then offered boiled sweets from the Air Stewardess's selection. The propellers started to turn and the Author looked out of the port window to see a gentleman standing behind the wing, close to the engine and holding a wheeled trolley which was supporting a large cylinder. Unbeknown to us naïve passengers, the individual concerned was an Airport fireman, who was ready with a mobile extinguisher for use in the event of a fire during engine start-up!

Fortunately, there was no start-up incident and the Dakota taxied towards the runway. Traffic was very light and so it was not necessary to queue for take-off in those days; however the aircraft was first steered to a holding area at the head of the runway. The purpose was to "warm up" the engines to ensure maximum efficiency. Modern-day gas turbine engines do not require any such warming-up. We could feel the aircraft straining against its brakes whilst the Captain completed this exercise. At last, we lined up with the runway, the throttles were pushed forward, and the Pratt & Whitney Twin Wasps roared to their full power. The brakes were released and we howled down the runway, lifting off and rising slowly into the grey Manchester skies.

We steadily gained altitude and headed to the south coast and then over the English Channel towards Jersey. The Dakota's Flight Deck was open to the passenger cabin so those passengers seated towards the front could observe most of the pilots' activities. Periodically, the Stewardess would chat with the pilots and would then glide gracefully along the aisle, stopping to pass information to the male passengers, including my father. I eventually asked my father what was happening. His reply was that the pilots were listening to the BBC radio commentary on the Test Match and that the Stewardess was relaying updates on the latest score. It seems to have been automatically assumed that the female passengers would not have any interest in Test cricket!

A Channel Airways Vickers Viking and one of the airline's de Havilland Doves parked at Jersey in the late-1950s

The art deco Jersey Airport terminal building was opened in 1937 and had replaced the "facilities" and runway previously located on Jersey's nearby St Aubins beach. The state of the tides had then determined the timetable for the air services, which had been mostly provided by de Havilland's biplane airliners! The original terminal building is still in partial use today and the Jersey Airlines hangar which once housed the airline's small fleet of de Havilland Herons was demolished only recently. Jersey Airport still retains a pleasant mid-twentieth-century feel, combined with the benefits of the up-to-date facilities provided by its modern terminal extension.

Three years later, in July 1959, the Author's family undertook their first international flight. It was part of an early package holiday purchased from the Manchester office of the aforesaid Sir Henry Lunn Travel Company Limited. Unsurprisingly, the flights were to be provided by Eagle Airways. The destination was the resort of Cattolica, near Rimini on the Italian Adriatic coast. We travelled by train from Manchester to London, gathering with other clients in the late afternoon at the travel company's office near Trafalgar Square. From here, the group was transported by Volkswagen minibuses out of London, along the Great West Road and then down the A30. Our destination was London Blackbushe Airport, then the home of a large number of British Independent airlines.

Pictured at Blackbushe Airport in January 1959 is the Eagle Airways DC-6A which, later that year, flew the Author and his family from the Airport to Rimini on an Italian package holiday. Air Team Images

The Blackbushe Airport Terminal building today, little changed from the 1950s and continuing in daily use for Business aviation customers. The Author

We waited inside the Blackbushe Airport Terminal building for boarding. Outside was the roar of piston engines, as aircraft were prepared for their hard labours during the night ahead. Our four-engine Douglas DC-6A had been purchased by Harold Bamberg during the previous year from the American Slick Airways. The recent loosening of exchange controls meant that those airlines with the funds available could obtain the foreign currency required to acquire a limited number of non-British-produced aircraft.

The DC-6A had been worked very hard over the previous year, accumulating nearly 4,000 hours of flying on trooping flights and on inclusive flights for a number of tour companies. We climbed up the rear steps, looking up at the red tail towering above. We noted that the aircraft was significantly larger than our BEA Dakota of three years previously, although small by modern-day standards, accommodating around seventy passengers.

We flew for three hours across a darkened Europe to our destination, which was a military airfield near Rimini. Here, we were decanted into a hanger and then filed around its two light aircraft occupants towards a very temporary Italian-style Border Control. Having cleared Security we boarded a rear-engined coach which seemed to be smoother and quieter than its front-engine British equivalents. We noted that, instead of the customary British cloth, the seats were vinyl or possibly leather covered.

During the following two weeks, we enjoyed the novelty of almost continuous sunshine, a very rare commodity in those 1950s Manchester overcast, pre-global warming summer days.

Most of the passengers joined the returning aircraft in various shades of red and brown. There was, at the time, only very limited awareness of the dangers of excessive exposure to the sun and minimal availability of effective sun screen!

The flight back to Blackbushe was uneventful, with one very major exception. Approximately an hour into the journey, the pilot activated the "Fasten seatbelts" sign and warned, over the intercom, of turbulence ahead. Moments later the DC-6A hit an air pocket and dropped alarmingly, with a shattering crash, then regaining forward momentum.

We looked nervously through the windows and were relieved to see that the wings and engines were still attached and functioning! The unfettered in-flight meals trolley had been mostly responsible for the noise, as it had hit the aircraft roof and had then descended rapidly back to the floor, with its contents flying in all directions. The two Stewardesses, with insufficient time to secure themselves, had accompanied the trolley on its unscheduled trip. Undaunted and thankfully uninjured, the ladies dusted themselves down, restored order and carried on with their duties, regardless.

The attitude of the Cabin Crew and the skill and resilience of the Flight Crews of those early charter flights can only be admired. After often navigating elderly aircraft across a darkened Europe with limited navigational aids, there was then the challenge and responsibility of landing safely at mostly unfamiliar and dimly lit airfields. Today's jet aircraft are able to fly at speeds of 500 mph or more in clean air at 30,000 ft or higher, well above the weather. Our Eagle DC-6A was churning along at approximately half that speed and height, so turbulence was a fairly regular occurrence.

However, passengers in modern airliners are still advised to keep seatbelts loosely fastened at all times. The rationale for this advice was dramatically demonstrated on 20 May 2024. A Boeing 777-300ER operating Singapore Airlines flight SQ321 from London to Singapore, with two hundred and eleven passengers and eighteen crew members on board, was flying at 37,000 ft over Myanmar's Irrawaddy Basin. Suddenly, the 777 dropped a terrifying 6,000 ft without any warning. One passenger died of a heart attack, and twenty-two others suffered serious spinal cord and head injuries. This incident was a stark reminder that temperature changes, attributable to global warming, can occasion turbulence risks even to modern aircraft flying at high altitudes.

Part 3 - The 1960s

Britain's Economy in the early 1960s remained far from buoyant. Sir Anthony Eden's successor as Prime Minister, Harold Macmillan, had assured the British public in 1957 that "most of our people have never had it so good". However, much of the apparent improvement in living standards had been fuelled by increased domestic debt, including the new and often socially disapproved concept of "hire purchase". Macmillan had also warned of the "Winds of Change" now blowing, particularly strongly in Africa. By the end of the 1960s, Britain would have granted independence or indicated its intention to grant independence to most of its former colonies.

In 1964, a new Labour Government, led by former Oxford Don Harold Wilson, was duly elected. On 24 January 1965, the death of Sir Winston Churchill was announced. Churchill had lived a very dynamic life, convinced in his early years that his time on earth would be short. He did not expect an actual lifespan of ninety years. A strong advocate and supporter of British civil aviation Churchill had been responsible for the Air Navigation Act 1919 and for the formation of the Brabazon Committee.

Manchester International pier in September 1964, where a Channel Airways DC-4 is parked in front of a Rolls-Royce Avon-powered Air France Caravelle. Most spectators are admiring a newly-arrived BOAC Boeing 707 on the other side of the pier. Air Team Images

At Manchester Airport, the 1960s plane spotters were now becoming familiar with the sound of various Rolls-Royce Dart-powered turboprops in place of the previous more distinctive individual notes of piston engine types. The arrival of yet another Dart-powered aircraft at the Airport, usually a BEA Viscount, was becoming somewhat of a bore. Darts also powered the Aer Lingus Fokker Friendships, regularly visiting Manchester, and there was the occasional sight of a Jersey Airlines Dart-powered Handley Page Herald.

One of a fleet of Rolls-Royce Dart-powered Fokker Friendships operated by Air Anglia and its successor, Air UK in the 1960s & 70s.

A BOAC Rolls-Royce Conway-powered Boeing 707 on final approach to Manchester Airport in January 1967 and still exciting large crowds at the Airport. Air Team Images.

BOAC aircraft in the early 1960s were rarely seen at Manchester apart from visits by its Douglas DC-7Cs, now mostly removed from passenger service and some converted to freighters. However, in the autumn of 1960, there was great excitement when BOAC's new Boeing 707-436s commenced weekly calls on their way to New York.

Today, non-travelling members of the Public are actively discouraged from visiting airports. In the early 1960s, crowds of spectators flocked to Manchester Airport and filled, to capacity, the viewing terraces at its newly-constructed terminal facilities in order to see and hear this fabulous new aircraft. Air France's elegant Sud Aviation Caravelles, with their two rear fuselage-mounted Rolls-Royce Avons, were also drawing popular attention as they operated regular services to Paris. To BEA's annoyance, its turboprop Viscounts, previously the main focus of attention, were now beginning to look somewhat outdated.

Enthusiastic plane spotters would often position themselves along a footpath which ran perilously near the east end of the Manchester Airport runway. Here, sometimes uncomfortably close views were afforded of the undersides of landing aircraft as they roared overhead on final approach. Aircraft taking off to the west could be viewed from behind as they commenced their take-off runs before disappearing over a slight hump in the runway. Piston engine types would then slowly re-appear in the far distance, gently gathering height. In contrast, the new jets re-appeared much more quickly, then soaring upwards at what seemed to be meteoric rates of climb. This level of performance from jet aircraft is today's norm and is unexceptional. In the early 1960s, it was considered to be near sensational.

1960s British Aero Industry consolidation

During the 1950s, the output of British aircraft manufacturing had nearly trebled and, by 1960, British manufactured aircraft exports exceeded £100m (nearly £2bn today). Employment in the Industry had also expanded very significantly, to over 290,000 people. The 1960s was to be another period of huge activity and change for the Industry, but not all of its customers were satisfied. One such unhappy individual was Edward Comer Rigg, an officer serving in RAF Transport Command in the early 1960s, who commented to his Service colleagues:

"Gentleman, you must never ever forget that all aircraft manufacturers are thieves and rogues."

Probably lying behind this statement was annoyance at the lack of availability and/or the cost of aircraft spares or servicing. The customer is very much in the hands of the manufacturer once a particular type of aircraft or aero-engine has been selected with regard to follow-up operational and maintenance support. Customers today are still acutely aware of this potential trap and demand appropriate reassurances.

The creation of the British Aircraft Corporation (BAC) in 1960 was a significant step in the consolidation of the British Aero Industry, comprising the merger of the Bristol Aeroplane Company with English Electric (predominantly a manufacturer of military aircraft), Hunting Aircraft and Vickers-Armstrongs. English Electric's brilliant aeronautical engineer, Frederick

William Page (not to be confused with Sir Frederick Handley Page), was appointed as a member of BAC's new senior executive team. Freddie Page had been closely involved in the design of the Lightning fighter and also of the Rolls-Royce Avon-powered Canberra light bomber, which had sold well worldwide, including achieving the rare distinction of being licensed for production in the USA.

English Electric Canberra, designed by Freddie Page and with over 1300 produced. Canberras served the RAF in various roles for more than 50 years. Government Licence AK Benson MOD

Separately, Hawker Siddeley was attempting to rationalise the remainder of the major British aircraft manufacturers. By 1955, the happily re-married Sir Geoffrey de Havilland had ceased day his day-to-day involvement in the de Havilland Aircraft Company. Hawker Siddeley was later able to acquire the company in 1960. Sir Geoffrey, who died in 1965 having enjoyed a well-deserved retirement, saw his business survive within the stronger Hawker Siddeley Group. Here de Havilland employees were able to continue their careers, albeit that the use of de Havilland name would now be discontinued.

As a further part of its consolidation exercise, Hawker Siddeley had also acquired two other British, predominantly military aircraft manufacturers, Folland Aircraft and Blackburn Aircraft. However, the remaining and more difficult major consolidation target for Hawker Siddeley was the Handley Page Aircraft Company, where the septuagenarian Sir Frederick Handley Page was still hugely influential. Sir Frederick had kept the company afloat in the late 1950s by lobbying successfully for the production of a final batch of the Victor V Bomber, with Rolls-Royce also being supportive, seeking to install the Conway, the world's first turbofan engine, into the final Victors.

Sir Frederick could not bring himself to accept what he considered to be Hawker Siddeley's inadequate valuation of "his business" and he was able to convince the other shareholders to refuse Hawker Siddeley's offer. Sir Frederick may have believed that, unlike Sir Geoffrey de Havilland, he had preserved the independence of his company but, in so doing, the Handley Page Aircraft Company would now not survive the decade. Sir Frederick passed away on 21 April 1962, aged seventy-six, after more than fifty years of involvement in British aviation. He was mourned by colleagues, past and present. Despite their differences during his time with Handley Page Transport back in the 1920s, BEA's Lord Douglas described him as "A good man in every way".

As the 1960s progressed and without the presence of its charismatic founder the Handley Page Aircraft Company increasingly lost direction. Work was declining on the Victor and significant costs had been incurred in the development and marketing of the Dart Herald. The Herald was a capable aircraft and featured in a 1962 sales mission supported by Prince Philip, Duke of Edinburgh who sometimes flew the aircraft personally. However, it had achieved sales of only thirty-five aircraft by 1963, compared with the sale of two hundred and forty of its nearest competitor, the Fokker Friendship. Also, the development costs of Handley Page's promising new Jetstream small twin turboprop commuter airliner had more than quadrupled. Further, the British Government was proving true to its word, and little new military business was being directed towards Handley Page.

The Rolls-Royce Dart-powered Avro 748 with, behind, a Fokker Friendship, both operated by Jersey European in the 1980s. Air Team Images

A further threat to Handley Page emerged in 1958 when Hawker Siddeley's Avro Division announced another potential Herald competitor in the form of its new Dart-powered Avro

748. The Avro 748, which first flew two years later, was Avro's attempt to re-orientate itself away from military projects towards civil work and also to regain its confidence following the disastrous Tudor episode. Prototype 748s were regular sights over Stockport in the early 1960s as they were test flown from Hawker Siddeley's nearby Woodford assembly facility and test airfield.

The Government declined any significant involvement with the Herald beyond authorising BEA to lease three aircraft in the early 1960s for service on its Scottish routes. The Minister of Aviation, Peter Thorneycroft, refused to allow the RAF to purchase Heralds in favour of ordering thirty-seven Andovers, the military version of the Avro 748. The eventual total sales of the Herald amounted to just fifty aircraft compared with the production of three hundred and eighty-one Avro 748s until 1988, including licensed manufacture in India. The Herald flew on with a number of Independent airlines, with its last passenger service being operated by British Air Ferries in 1987. A Herald series 400 freighter of Channel Express, the predecessor of today's Jet2.com, operated the final flight of the type on 9 April 1999.

By the late 1960s, the main hope for Handley Page's survival lay in an anticipated Government order for the conversion of a number of redundant RAF Victor bombers to aerial refuelling tankers. Some of the out-of-service Victors were already parked at Handley Page's Radlett facility awaiting confirmation of the order. Such confirmation was never received with the Government announcing that it had accepted an alternative conversion proposal from Hawker Siddeley. The Victors were then flown up to Avro at Woodford.

This contract loss proved fatal for the Handley Page Aircraft Company which, in August 1969, entered voluntary liquidation. Another great name of British civil aviation had reached a sad end. The Liquidator disposed of the remaining assets.The Jetstream development was passed to Scottish Aviation, which then successfully pursued the project. Events might have been so different if Hawker Siddeley's 1960 offer had been accepted.

The Government's decision to enforce Industry consolidation had also received early vindication by an incident in 1960 involving the downing of an American U2 "Spy" aircraft from high altitude. The U2 affair and the subsequent repatriation of its pilot, Gary Powers, in exchange for the Russian spy Rudolf Abel, is dramatized in the excellent 2015 film "Bridge of Spies", where Sir Mark Rylance plays Abel, and Tom Hanks takes on the role of the negotiator, American lawyer James Donovan.

This further improvement in the USSR's surface-to-air (SAM) missile technology and capability was another shock to both the American and British governments. The main implication for Britain was the Government's decision progressively to transfer responsibility for Britain's nuclear deterrent from the V Bomber force to the Royal Navy's nuclear-powered submarines, carrying Polaris missiles. It was considered that the V Bombers were now unacceptably vulnerable to high-level missile attacks. The V Bomber force was progressively wound down, but certain elements would yet have their moments of glory in the 1982

Operation Black Buck missions, which are summarised in Annex 3.

Short Brothers Limited was already, by the 1960s, a primarily British Government-owned organisation and so did not feature in the 1960s consolidation. The company had relocated from Rochester to Belfast in 1948, having produced well over 2000 of its Second World War, Bristol Hercules engined Sterling Bombers. During the 1960s and 1970s, Short successfully contributed to British civil aviation in the form of its Skyvan, which was developed into the Short 330 and 360 short take-off and landing regional passenger aircraft. Around three hundred of the 330/360 versions were produced up to the early 1990s, serving widely throughout the world and with a number of British regional airlines. In 1989 Short Brothers was bought by Canadian-owned Bombardier and was later sold on to Spirit AeroSystems, an American-owned aero-structures manufacturer.

The USSR's enhanced SAM missile capability also posed a significant threat to the Canberra aircraft. A replacement for both the V Bombers and the Canberra was considered to be essential. The Ministry of Supply specified a supersonic, all-weather aircraft which would be capable of delivering nuclear weapons both over a long range at a high level, at Mach 2+, and also from a low level, at Mach 1.2. The aircraft should have a short take-off and landing capability or possibly be capable of vertical take-off and landing. This was a most stretching specification, to say the very least!

On 1 January 1959, the Ministry announced that a contract had been placed with Vickers-Armstrongs, working with English

Electric, to develop an aircraft to be known as the TSR-2 ("Tactical, Strike and Reconnaissance, Mach 2"). BAC adopted the contract, with Bristol Siddeley being selected to supply a developed version of the Vulcan's Olympus engine. The TSR-2 flew on 27 September 1964, and twenty-four further test flights followed over the next six months.

In early 1965, the new Labour Government reviewed the behind schedule and struggling TSR-2 project and, in the Chancellor's budget speech of 6 April 1965, it was cancelled. The TSR-2 prototypes were immediately scrapped, presumably to forestall any attempts to resurrect the project. The Minister of Defence, the avuncular Denis Healey, commented that:

"The trouble with the TSR-2 was that it tried to combine the most advanced state of every art in the field. The aircraft firms and the RAF were trying to get the Government on the hook and understated the cost".

As a TSR-2 replacement, the Government announced its intention to order the American F111. This proposal was not eventually pursued and instead, it was then proposed to acquire four hundred McDonnell Douglas F-4 Phantom combat aircraft to serve both the Fleet Air Arm and the RAF. Around half of the aircraft structure and equipment was to be produced by the British Aero Industry, including a developed version of the Rolls-Royce Spey engine, with re-heat to increase its thrust. The additional costs of the work sub-contracted combined to treble the unit cost of the aircraft. As a result, only one hundred and seventy Phantoms could be afforded!

Within the aero-engines sector, Bristol Siddeley acquired the de Havilland Engine Company Limited in 1961. This de Havilland subsidiary had been created in 1944 when de Havilland had absorbed the engineering consultancy business of Frank Halford. Halford had been responsible for the design of most of the previous engines for de Havilland's aircraft, including the Gipsy range of piston engines which were installed in the Dragon Rapide and in a number of other de Havilland types. In the same year Bristol Siddeley had also absorbed the aero-engine division of Blackburn Aircraft.

Bristol Siddeley had hoped to supply large numbers of Olympus engines for the TSR-2 and so the cancellation of the project was a serious blow. By early 1966, rumours were circulating of interest from America's Pratt & Whitney in acquiring Bristol Siddeley, working in conjunction with the French aero-engine company SNECMA, a collaborator on the Olympus 593 Concorde engine project. Bristol Siddeley had also signed an agreement with Pratt & Whitney and SNECMA in order to market Pratt & Whitney's new advanced technology JT9D turbofan in Europe.

Fearing the creation of a large, internationally resourced competitor on its very doorstep, Rolls-Royce quickly moved to acquire Bristol Siddeley. Its owners, BAC and Hawker Siddeley, negotiated hard, and the acquisition was agreed upon for an eye-watering £63.6m (£950m in today's money), including the transfer to Rolls-Royce of Bristol's twenty percent shareholding in BAC. Rolls-Royce had previously purchased the engine manufacturer, D Napier & Son Limited, from English Electric, and so it had now become the sole British aero-engine manufacturer. The consolidation of the British Aero Industry was largely completed, but would it be sufficiently extensive to ensure future world competitiveness?

State-owned airline corporations' woes

In 1955, BEA moved all of its operations from Northolt to Heathrow. A number of hangars had been erected at Heathrow, the largest of which, for Pan Am, had been pre-constructed and shipped in from the USA. Long-range radar monitoring was now centred at the airport, with British airspace divided into five controlled flight information regions. However, BEA was still significantly loss-making and BOAC was only marginally profitable, struggling to maintain services because of aircraft shortages due to its problems with both the Interim and Brabazon Types.

The Air Transport Licensing Board (ATLB) was established in 1960, assuming the activities of ATAC. To add to the State-owned airline corporations' woes, the Independent airlines were now able to apply to the ATLB for licenses to operate on all routes, on an equal basis. BEA and BOAC made strong efforts to retain their current routes' exclusivity by objecting strongly to these multiple licence applications.

Equally annoying for the corporations was the fact that the Independents were often the only available purchasers for their superseded aircraft, such as Ambassadors, Argonauts, Constellations and Vikings. Many of these aircraft still had reasonable service lives ahead of them. Also, BOAC was now introducing its Boeing 707-436s, displacing the expensively acquired and introduced turboprop Britannias, which were being readily snapped up by the Independents for use on their newly-acquired scheduled routes and to fly increasing numbers of inclusive tours. BOAC's Comets would also soon filter down to the Independents, together with BEA's Viscounts, as the second generation jets were introduced by the State-owned airline corporations.

Gerard d' Erlanger had been knighted in 1958 but sadly died in 1962, aged just 56. After leaving BEA, he had then chaired BOAC during the period 1956-60. D'Erlanger had been criticised, somewhat unfairly, on the grounds that his merchant banking connections with a number of ventures in the Independent airline sector might have occasioned conflicts of interest. However, d' Erlanger would be long remembered for his vital contribution to the ATA during the Second World War and for his positive involvement in many aspects of pre and post-war British civil aviation.

BOAC Chairman, Sir Matthew Slattery on the Comet 4 Flight Deck in 1960. His forthright views were not always welcomed by the Government. British Airways Museum.

D' Erlanger's replacement at BOAC was Rear Admiral Sir Matthew Slattery an appointment which attracted some Industry criticism because, although Sir Matthew had previously chaired aircraft manufacturing companies, he had no previous airline experience. However, Sir Matthew was not afraid to speak his mind about British aviation matters. At his first BOAC Press Conference, he revealed that the Government had authorised the building of a supersonic airliner "more or less regardless of the economic consequences" and further commented that;

"I am probably getting old, but I don't want to fly to New York in two and a half hours. I rather look forward to six hours away from the telephones and perhaps a quiet snooze on the way."

Later, when presenting BOAC's 1961/62 results and on being questioned about the prospects of the proposed supersonic airliner, Sir Matthew responded;

"I don't want a supersonic transport at all. It is not going to lower fares or generate new traffic. I think it is going to be an infernal nuisance".

Sir Matthew's assessments would transpire to be prophetic as circumstances later evolved, but they were certainly unwelcome hearing to a Government which had just appointed him to an important public sector role. This was particularly true when France and the United Kingdom were about to commit to a major investment in the Concorde project! Sir Matthew would later pay a personal career price but, together with BOAC's capable Chief Executive, Basil Smallpeice, he now set about tidying up BOAC's finances.

The publication of BOAC's Accounts for the year 1962/63 came as an embarrassment and huge shock to the Government, showing a massive accounting loss of £64m (around £1.1bn today)! Sir Matthew explained that more than half of the loss was attributable to the "rationalisation of the aircraft fleet", with Accounting Principles having required the writing down of aircraft book values.

The failures and disappointing performances of some of the Interim and Brabazon Types had necessitated the 1950s expensive purchases of Constellations and Stratocruisers and their prolonged operation pending the delayed arrivals of new British-produced aircraft. There had also been the enforced 1956 purchase of the ten Douglas DC-7Cs at a cost of $4m each (broadly equal to the $50m required today to acquire a ten years old, second-hand, Boeing 787 Dreamliner).

Many of BOAC's aircraft had served insufficient operational lives to allow their full costs to be amortised in the normal manner and so this additional write-off had therefore been necessary. The Accounts also included the costs of the more recent development flying of the new Vickers-Armstrongs VC10. The Government refused Sir Matthew's request to write off BOAC's significant accumulated financial deficit, whilst later allowing his successor to do precisely that!

The situation at BEA was not much brighter, although it had been able to report that it had carried more than 3.8 million passengers during 1960. However, the airline was still demonstrating some very antiquated views, as evidenced by the following appalling mid-1960s Management statement:

"We do not employ girl pilots because we don't think they do the job as well as men, and many people would not be prepared to get on a plane if they knew a woman was at the controls. We know of no big international airline that employs women pilots on any scale."

BEA seems to have completely ignored the competence and excellent wartime service of female pilots with the ATA. Thankfully, the Independent sector was considerably more enlightened. A number of female pilots were employed, particularly at Dan-Air, where Yvonne Pope became a Captain of its Avro 748 fleet in 1970, often flying with Marilyn Booth as her First Officer. Pope later became Britain's first female Captain of a jetliner on 16 June 1975, when she commanded a Dan-Air BAC One-Eleven on its flight from London Gatwick to Heraklion.

Pictured here at Southend in July 1971 is an Invicta International Vanguard. Invicta operated the type's last passenger service in late 1975. Creative Commons Attribution - Richard Vandervord Collection.

BEA, in accordance with the Government-imposed "buy British" policy, had signed a contract in 1956 for twenty Vickers Vanguards, powered by the new Rolls-Royce Tyne turboprop and capable of carrying up to one hundred and thirty-nine passengers over short/medium range routes. However, the aircraft and its engines had suffered development delays and it did not enter BEA service until March 1961. The Vanguard was intended to operate as an "Airbus" for what was forecast to be a growing number of Economy Class passengers. However, passenger preference was in favour of travelling on pure jets, especially the previously-mentioned Rolls-Royce Avon engined Sud Aviation Caravelles, now operated by many European airlines. To remain competitive on its European routes BEA had found it necessary to follow the pure jet route by purchasing its fleet of Comet 4Bs.

Heathrow August 1963. BOAC Comet 4 and Britannia 312. By now, both aircraft already superseded on N Atlantic routes by the Boeing 707, an example of which is parked behind. Air Team Images.

The Vanguard had been too tightly designed around BEA's specific requirements and so just forty-four aircraft were built, with the only other purchaser being Trans Canada Airlines. This was not the only time that the commercial prospects for a new British airliner would be severely diminished by over-specification to meet the requirements of a single domestic customer. Vickers-Armstrongs had also taken insufficient account of the emerging economics of civil aircraft production. Specifically, new airliner projects were viable only if realistic minimum sales targets could be achieved.

The fact that it did not make commercial sense for the State-owned airline corporations to order British-produced aircraft simply to enable the manufacturers to achieve their minimum sales targets was reflected by the following words of Sir Richard

Nugent when Chairman of a Commons Select Committee reviewing BOAC:

"Is it really practicable in 1964 to build a national aircraft for a national airline? Should we not look forward to international cooperation in construction?"

One aircraft which had managed to slip through the net was the Armstrong Whitworth AW.660 Argosy, the last aircraft to be produced by Hawker Siddeley under the Armstrong Whitworth name. The first Argosy had been the 1930s passenger aircraft operated by Imperial Airways but the new Argosy, which first flew in January 1959, was a specialised cargo aircraft for both civil and military use. The Argosy was powered by four Rolls-Royce Dart turboprops, and BEA ordered five series 200 aircraft to operate its freight-only services. These services were not profitable, and the aircraft were displaced, from 1969, by Vanguards withdrawn from passenger service and converted by ATL to "Merchantman" freighters. A total of eighty Argosy aircraft were built, including fifty-six for the RAF, and the type remained in civil use until the early 1990s.

Second Generation British jets

Sir Richard Nugent's comments came too late to stop the work that was already well underway on no less than three Government-backed, second generation jet airliner projects, comprising the Vickers-Armstrongs (BAC) VC10, the Hawker Siddeley Trident and the BAC One-Eleven.

The VC10 had been conceived as a long-range airliner capable of operating to and from destinations with "hot and high" airports and with shorter runways. BOAC's Boeing 707-436s were considered to be oversized and underpowered for these previously mentioned Medium Range Empire (MRE) routes. The VC10, with its four powerful rear-mounted Rolls-Royce Conways and a high-lift wing, was designed to perform well from the airports servicing such routes.

Gatwick May 1970. A BUA Vickers VC10 shows the extended loading door which was specified and designed by Freddie Laker when Managing Director of the airline. A Caledonian Boeing 707 is parked behind. Air Team Images

Heathrow August 1974. A British Eagle Viscount passes by a BEA Vanguard. Behind are parked an Eagle Britannia, a BEA Trident and, at the top right, a twin-boom AW Argosy freighter. Air Team Images.

BAC estimated that eighty sales were needed to achieve break-even, later reducing this figure, believing incorrectly that it would be able to lower manufacturing costs by re-using items from the Vanguard production line. The underlying reality, however, was that the commercial prospects of the VC10 were diminishing as rapidly as were Britain's declining colonial involvements. The importance of the MRE routes was reducing and the newly-independent states were recognising that the superior operating economics of the Boeing 707 and of the Douglas DC-8 meant that future international air services would mostly be carried out by these aircraft. Airport facilities consequently required improvement and runways were being lengthened. These changes were further reducing the rationale for an airliner with the VC10's short-field capabilities.

In January 1958, BOAC had indicated its intention to order thirty-five VC10s, for delivery in 1965, with an option to purchase an additional twenty aircraft. It was the biggest potential order ever for a British civil aircraft. BAC announced that there would also be a stretched Super VC10, which could carry over one hundred and eighty passengers over a range of 4000 miles. However, by the early 1960s, BAC was experiencing financial problems in its civil aircraft business. In June 1960, the Government felt compelled to step in and to provide support for the VC10 project by ordering five aircraft for the RAF. The RAF would eventually receive a total of fourteen new VC10s.

Sir Matthew Slattery's appointment as BOAC's chairman had, predictably, not been renewed. His successor, in late 1963, was the more youthful Sir Giles Guthrie, a pilot and a successful businessman. Sir Giles commenced his period of office with the statement:

"Whether you are running an airline or any other commercial business, the principle remains the same – to achieve revenue and watch overheads".

In May 1964, Sir Giles, having assessed the state of affairs at BOAC, advised the Minister of Aviation that BOAC's favourable operating experience with its Boeing 707-436s was questioning its need for the VC10. So, at the very time that the BOAC Marketing Department was producing a film extolling the undisputed virtues of the VC10 (the film is still available in British Airways' in-flight entertainment offering), its Chairman was proposing to the Minister that BOAC should not order the Super VC10. Instead, BOAC should purchase additional Boeing 707-436s, a proposal which created a political and Industry furore.

Now in full focus was the underlying conflict, which had been rumbling for some time, between the interests of State-owned airline corporations and those of a Government-directed, civil aircraft industry. In an uneasy comprise, BOAC eventually agreed to order seventeen Super VC10s, with most of the remaining aircraft, scheduled for production, being allocated to the RAF.

Another day at the office! Chief BAC Test Pilot GR"Jock" Bryce is followed by Brian Trubshaw (later Chief British Test Pilot of Concorde) after the first flight of the VC10 in 1962. No flying suits, crash hats or iPads in sight!

The standard VC10 entered service with BOAC in April 1964, with the Super VC10 making its first flight a month later. Despite the troubled background, BAC had produced a great-looking and highly capable aircraft with state-of-the-art avionics and having a huge appeal to both passengers and crews. It had clean swept-back wings with its four Conways mounted neatly in pairs on each side of the rear fuselage. Internal noise levels were lower than the Boeing 707 and the Douglas DC-8, together with the smaller risk of engine ground debris ingestion.

Passengers enjoyed the attractive interior layout and quietness, whilst pilots preferred the aircraft's flying characteristics. British Prime Minister Margaret Thatcher was a VC10 fan, always specifying the aircraft to transport her on her overseas visits. However, there were few other purchasers for the VC10 and only fifty-four aircraft were built before the production line closed in early 1970. Never again would Britain be involved in the production of a large, long-haul, complete civilian airliner.

The Super VC10 operated successfully with BOAC on the North Atlantic routes until high ground noise levels ended all VC10 civilian operations in April 1981. The RAF then acquired the remaining airframes and operated its VC10s for many years as personnel/ VIP transports with some aircraft being later converted to aerial tankers to replace time-expired Victor tankers. The VC10 tankers served usefully in the 2003 Iraq war and the last RAF VC10 flight was in September 2013. Although a commercial failure, the VC10 eventually completed a useful operational life of over fifty years.

Heathrow October 1974. A line up of British Airways Tridents. Air Team images

The Hawker Siddeley Trident, originally the de Havilland DH 121, was a medium-range airliner powered by three Rolls-Royce Spey engines. In January 1962, John "Cats Eyes" Cunningham, by then Hawker Siddeley's Chief Test Pilot, took the Trident on its first fight. Two of the engines were rear-mounted on each side of the fuselage, with the third located beneath the tailplane. The estimated £55m (£1.5bn today) launch costs were supported by up to fifty percent of Government aid.

The Trident was developed to a BEA specification, which was varied numerous times. The aircraft had thereby joined the earlier Vanguard by falling into the trap of being an aeroplane "designed exclusively for one customer that has potentially a much wider scope". BEA's Chairman, Lord Douglas, confirmed this folly in 1962, commenting:

"BEA's hopes lie with the Trident... It is the very last word in subsonic jet transport and is specifically designed for our particular network. "

In the late 1950s, de Havilland had extended an invitation to Boeing to send a Technical team to Hatfield, presumably to share the latest knowledge. Boeing's subsequent 727 trijet airliner, which commenced operations with the US Eastern Airlines in 1964, was strikingly similar in concept to the Trident but was far more flexible and was not designed around any particular airline's specific requirements. The resemblances between the two aircraft did not extend to later sales statistics. Boeing was able to sell over eighteen hundred 727s, in comparison to the sale of only one hundred and seventeen Tridents, BEA and China being the only significant purchasers.

BEA operated three marques of Tridents from the late 1960s with a total fleet of sixty-seven aircraft. The final version, the slightly shorter range Trident 3, was able to accommodate up to one hundred and forty passengers. The Trident had a reputation amongst pilots as a "ground gripper" and so, as a typically pragmatic British solution, the take-off performance of the Trident 3 was assisted by using its Rolls-Royce RB162 auxiliary power unit as a booster engine. The Trident had also successfully trialled auto-landing technology, enabling it to operate in poor visibility conditions. However, noise regulations spelled the early end of Trident's service life in Europe in late 1985.

A British Airways One-Eleven 500 series at Heathrow in January 1984 with its noisy Rolls-Royce Spey engines now hush kitted. A Concorde is parked behind. Air Team Images

The BAC One-Eleven was a Hunting Aircraft design, adopted by the newly-created BAC, for a short to medium range eighty seat airliner to be powered by two rear-mounted Rolls-Royce Spey engines. The prototype first flew in August 1963 but, two months later, the development programme experienced a tragic setback when an aircraft crashed after its elevators had locked in high-stress trials. All on board were killed, including BAC's senior test pilot, Mike Lithgow. Despite this incident, the development programme was successfully completed. In complete contrast to the Trident, the One-Eleven was not designed to meet the specific needs of any particular customer, and it attracted worldwide interest. In the USA, American Airlines placed an order for thirty aircraft.

BEA, initially tardy in its interest in the One-Eleven, later ordered the stretched 500 series in January 1967. The airline eventually operated a fleet of over forty One-Eleven's until its withdrawal of the type in 1993. The One-Eleven was a successful project by the standards of those days, achieving worldwide sales of two hundred and forty-four aircraft, well above the break-even level. However, sales interest slowed significantly in the early 1970s as sales of the competing Boeing 737 and Douglas DC-9 twinjets rapidly caught up, supported by compelling financial deals from their well-resourced American manufacturers.

The 1965 Plowden Committee of Enquiry into the Aircraft Industry had determined that British aircraft production costs were significantly higher than those of their American counterparts. This disparity stemmed from shorter production runs, which were, in part, due to the fractured European market. The previously-mentioned 1974 Hobart Paper 57, "A Market for Aircraft", later argued that post-Second World War British Government aviation sector policies had brought about costly results to the taxpayer because of:

1) Mistakes in project selection with large associated cancellation costs.

2) Duplications (such as the previously-mentioned V Bombers project) and delays due to the Aero Industry taking on too many projects in relation to its scarce technical resources.

3) Significant escalation of development costs, sometimes being five times or more than the first estimates.

4) Excessive profits being made on military projects in some instances despite the system of fixed price or cost-plus Government contracts.

In comparison with the USA, the British Aero Industry had taken longer to design, develop and deliver similar products and its productivity had been inferior. Further, the large costs to the State of aviation projects involved a substantial "sacrifice" of Government spending in many other areas, including schools, hospitals and roads. The Paper also cast doubt on whether the balance of payments argument for the support of British civil aircraft projects was as strong as Governments had suggested and commented that other industries could have made an equal or larger contribution. The Paper also quoted the Minutes of Evidence to a 1972 Trade and Industry Department Committee, when a Treasury official had stated:

"It is probably right to say that the particular aircraft projects that have been supported are projects which, if we were looking at them afresh, we would not support – most of them not at all".

The Paper's proposals for a future British Aero Industry were first, that the Government should acquire military aircraft from the least-cost source of supply and second, that it should cease to offer financial assistance for civil aircraft projects. The Government should also reduce its involvement in the airline sector where, the Paper commented that, previous effects had been "market-displacing" by limiting the role of the Independent sector rather than the intended "market-improving" effect.

It was acknowledged that the implementation of these proposals would result in a smaller British Aero Industry, but it would be more efficient and internationally competitive, specialising where it had a competitive advantage. Such a reduced-scale Industry would no longer undertake major projects but would participate as a sub-contractor in international consortia.

In 1969, the Chairman of BEA, Sir Anthony Milward, had already recognised the reality of the commercial aircraft manufacturing situation by commenting that the British Aero Industry had reached a critical point when:

"If Britain does not build a new generation jet transport, her chances of remaining in the manufacturing race are very slight. BEA will be forced to buy American equipment and, by 1985-90, its whole fleet would be American."

We know now that Britain did not build a new generation of jet transport aircraft and that the current British Airways fleet and those of the other British airlines, with some small exceptions, is comprised entirely of aircraft produced by either American or European consortium aircraft manufacturers.

Varying fortunes for the Independents

The adverse political, economic and market trends in the early 1960s were of particular concern to the Independent airline sector. The need for services to former colonies would most likely decline, together with a reduction in trooping contracts. Most potential passengers had limited funds available for overseas travel, a situation further exacerbated by the Government's decision, in 1967, to introduce a restricted £50

Overseas Travel Allowance (£1,000 today) in order to support Sterling.

In this environment, some of the Independent airlines were clearly at serious risk. Air Safaris another post-war start-up and now involved in the inclusive tour market was particularly exposed together with the more recently formed Overseas Aviation. Overseas was financially over-extended, having increased its Argonaut fleet with the purchase of a number of aircraft from Trans-Canada Airlines.

Together with many of the other Independent airlines, Air Safaris and Overseas Aviation were now aspiring to take up the opportunities for new routes by way of making appropriate licence applications to the ATLB. However, the ATLB was cautious, requiring confirmation as to on-going financial viability before granting new licences.

The ATLB's position was justified when Overseas Aviation filed for liquidation in August 1961. It was further vindicated at the end of October 1961, when Air Safaris also ceased operations and entered into liquidation with debts of over £500,000 (nearly £14m today). In the case of Overseas Aviation, a substantial amount was owed to Rolls-Royce in respect of unpaid overhaul charges for Merlin engines. A number of the Argonauts were flown to the Rolls-Royce facility at Hucknall, Nottinghamshire, where their Merlins were removed and then cannibalised for spares. This exercise provided some reimbursement towards the amounts owed.

Elsewhere, the positions of other major Independents were as follows:

British Eagle

Harold Bamberg had successfully led Eagle Airways through the 1950s. However, in July 1960, it was announced that the Cunard Steamship Company Limited had acquired a 60% interest in the airline. In line with previous moves by other shipping companies Cunard had decided to make an investment in the rapidly growing business of civil aviation.

Cunard's shrewd Chairman, Sir John Brocklebank, had fully recognised the risks to Cunard's business of the growing popularity of air travel on the North Atlantic routes. These risks were confirmed when official statistics in August 1960 reported that air traffic across the North Atlantic had increased by nearly a quarter over the previous year. 778,000 passengers had chosen this method of transport, compared with a decline of 14%, to only 635,000 passengers, travelling by sea.

The price for Eagle was rumoured to be £1m (£29m today). Bamberg had agreed to sell in the hope that the newly-named Cunard-Eagle Airways Limited, now with the benefit of a strong financial backer, could be developed as an effective competitor to the State-owned airline corporations. Bamberg joined the Cunard Steamship Board, from where he believed he would have the authority and financial support to achieve a substantial expansion of Cunard-Eagle's fleet and route network.

Eagle Airways had been active in the late 1950s in setting up subsidiary companies in Bermuda and in the Bahamas. To BOAC's annoyance, Eagle had then served USA East Coast destinations from these two locations. Cunard-Eagle now further increased the pressure on BOAC by using its Britannias, some of which were ex-BOAC aircraft, to develop competing services on the London to Bermuda route. In 1961, Cunard-Eagle applied to the ATLB for permission to operate on the prime London-New York route in competition with BOAC. Somewhat surprisingly, permission was granted and Cunard-Eagle then ordered two Rolls-Royce-powered Boeing 707-436s to operate these services, commencing in 1962. BOAC successfully appealed this permission and Cunard-Eagle then had a major problem in the form of two very expensive but potentially redundant new Boeing 707s!

Shortly afterwards, in June 1962, Cunard, presumably concerned at BOAC's successful licensing appeal, announced a dramatic U-turn with the formation of a new company, BOAC-Cunard Limited. BOAC would hold 70% of the shares, with the Cunard Steamship Company holding the balance. This operation was to be completely separate from Cunard-Eagle, whose Bermudan services were to be transferred to BOAC-Cunard. BOAC also agreed to take over the order for the two Boeing 707-436s.

Bamberg was, not unreasonably, furious at what he considered to be this "stab in the back" and it is hard to disagree. The days of Cunard-Eagle were now limited and, on 14 February 1963, Bamberg repurchased the Cunard shareholding. The name British Eagle International Airlines was adopted in August of that year, but the airline was now confined initially to developing its services for domestic and European routes. British Eagle also took over the route network of Starways, an airline founded in 1948 and which had taken its name from its initial purpose of transporting show business personalities to their Blackpool summer shows. During 1966,

British Eagle supplemented its Britannias with a growing fleet of One-Elevens and by the end of that year, British Eagle had carried just short of one million passengers on its services.

In September 1966, BOAC announced its acquisition of the Cunard shareholding in BOAC-Cunard. This airline's activities would now be absorbed by BOAC. BOAC had thereby effectively eliminated an emerging competitor on international routes and there had been no apparent benefits to Cunard. Over the following fifty years, the trend of crossing the North Atlantic by air would continue unabated, with air travel today being the undisputed choice for both business and leisure.

Harold Bamberg's battles and ambitions were far from over. He decided to resume British Eagle's international route ambitions and applied to the ATLB for permissions to operate services from London to New York, the Bahamas, Bermuda, Jamaica and Hong Kong. In anticipation of being awarded these routes, Bamberg repeated past history by placing an order for two new Boeing 707s. The first aircraft was handed over at the end of 1967, but the licence applications had not yet been determined, so it became necessary to lease this aircraft to Middle East Airlines.

In early 1968, British Eagle also acquired two Boeing 707-138Bs from the Australian airline Qantas. These aircraft were intended for use on inclusive tour flights to the Caribbean and to supplement the One-Elevens on the European summer inclusive tour programme. However, the year did not start well for British Eagle with the cancellation, in March, of its trooping and Australian migrant contracts. The introduction, the previous year, of the restricted Overseas Travel Allowance was another difficulty, together with the ongoing devaluation of the British pound. British Eagle suffered summer programme cancellations of over £1m (£22m today).

In October 1968, British Eagle closed its Liverpool base with four hundred jobs being lost. Bamberg managed to negotiate ongoing financial support, but this lifeline was suddenly withdrawn when the banks learned that BOAC had secured the revocation of British Eagle's inclusive tour licence for the proposed Caribbean operations. On 6 November 1968, British Eagle announced a cessation of all operations, with two thousand five hundred employees being made redundant. The company entered liquidation with around £5.5m of debts (£120m today). Rolls-Royce again headed the list of trade creditors with £630,000 (£14m today) owing in respect of unpaid overhaul charges.

Bamberg claimed that the revocation of the Caribbean licence was further evidence of the Government's protectionist attitude towards the State-owned airline corporations. However, sadly, he had now lost his last battle. Eagle was consigned to Independent airline history, having done so much to develop post-war British civil aviation. Sir Anthony Milward, then BEA's Chief Executive, commented;

"There will not be any crowing at BEA that British Eagle has disappeared".

Despite voicing these apparent sympathies, BEA immediately applied for many of Eagle's route licences.

Harold Bamberg (centre) in later life at Blackbushe in 2012. Creative Commons Attribution WyrdLight.com

Harold Bamberg never established another airline, but he could look back with some pride on his twenty years of airline achievement. Starting with two converted Halifax bombers, Eagle had ended its operations with an all-jet fleet of twenty-five aircraft. Bamberg remained active in business aviation with an agency for Beechcraft aircraft and later claimed that he had sold a thousand of them. Bamberg retired in the early 2000s to breed race horses at his Surrey estate and he died in September 2022, just short of his ninety-ninth birthday.

Some ten years previously Bamberg had been guest of honour at the unveiling of a notice board at Blackbushe Airport commemorating those Independent airlines which had once operated from the Airport. Commercial aviation passenger services had ceased from Blackbushe, following the enforced move to Gatwick in 1960. Don Bennett had then re-emerged, acquiring the majority of the aerodrome which he reopened in October 1962 as a general aviation facility focussing on business and private aviation. Blackbushe Airport continues to serve successfully in this role today.

The newly-opened Gatwick Airport in 1960, with two parked DC-3 Dakotas. A somewhat quieter scene than today!

British Midland

During the early 1960s, British Midland had commenced regional services with a fleet of six Handley Page Heralds together with running an inclusive tour programme using five Argonauts which it had acquired following the 1961 failure of Overseas Aviation. On 1 October 1964, the troubled, Manchester-based scheduled and charter airline, Mercury Airlines, was purchased and, in the following year, British Midland moved its base to the East Midlands Airport at Castle Donnington. Scheduled operations were steadily increased using a fleet of second-hand Viscounts. An important recruit from Mercury, then only in his mid-twenties, was Michael Bishop, it's former, very capable, ground handling manager. Bishop was soon to become the General Manager of British Midland.

On the morning of Sunday, 4 June 1967, Manchester plane spotters listening in on their VHF radios to Manchester Airport Air Traffic Control would have heard the exchanges with Captain Harry Marlow, the pilot of a British Midland Argonaut, G-ALHG. The aircraft was returning from Palma de Mallorca with eighty-four people on board and it was in difficulties. Marlow had already called a landing overshoot and, whilst circling in preparation for a second attempt, engines three and four of the Argonaut had suddenly cut out. The pilots could not feather engine three and, with the propeller continuing to windmill, the aircraft was becoming uncontrollable.

In his final terse response to Air Traffic Control, Marlow stated that the Argonaut was unlikely to complete the remaining five miles to touchdown. The following brief moments must have been terrifying for its passengers as the Argonaut continued to lose height before crashing into Stockport town centre.

Marlow's piloting skills had enabled him to locate the only small open area in central Stockport and so there were no casualties on the ground. Twelve people were rescued from the wreckage of the Argonaut, including Marlow, but the First Officer was amongst the dead. A subsequent investigation determined fuel starvation as being the cause of the accident, due to a previously undiagnosed flaw in the fuel system. A contributory cause was considered to be the tiredness of the Flight Crew, who had been on duty for over thirteen hours. Further, the internal bracing bars separating the seat rows were inadequate in strength, which resulted in many injured passengers being trapped and dying inside the burning aircraft.

Apart from the tragic loss of life, the accident was a huge setback for British Midland and the remaining Argonauts were immediately withdrawn from service. Three One-Elevens, which had been acquired for use on inclusive tour services, were later sold. Bishop, who was promoted to Managing Director of the airline in 1972, had concluded that British Midland did not have the scale to compete effectively in that market. The focus would now remain on providing domestic and close European scheduled services. In addition, a number of Boeing 707s originally intended for use on Affinity Group charters would now be "wet-leased" to other airlines under Aircraft, Crew, Maintenance and Insurance (ACMI) contracts. This line of business was successfully continued until 1984.

British United Airways

In the autumn of 1956, Airwork, by now part of the British & Commonwealth Shipping Group (B&C), had taken the first significant step towards consolidating the British Independent airline sector with its purchase of Transair, an airline operating Dakotas and Viscounts, mostly on trooping and charter flights. After acquiring Freddie Laker's businesses in late 1958, Airwork then undertook another consolidation move on 1 July 1960 by merging its airline activities with Hunting Clan. The new combined airline was named British United Airways (BUA) by what were, by then, its mostly shipping company owners. BUA commenced operations in early 1960 and it also included Morton Air Services, a regional short-haul airline, together with a Helicopter division under the supervision of Alan Bristow.

The BUA directors now had the task of finding a suitably qualified and experienced Managing Director. Such individual needed to have appropriate sector experience, with a proven track record of entrepreneurship. There was one outstanding candidate. Frederick Alfred Laker, now refreshed following his short break, was duly appointed to the role and he set to work with his customary drive and enthusiasm. In addition to a helicopter fleet, BUA started life with forty-three fixed-wing aircraft, comprising some ageing Dakotas, DC-4s and DC-6s, together with the Bristol Freighters of Channel Air Bridge and a reasonable number of turboprop Britannias and Viscounts.

The BUA Board resolved to develop the airline primarily as a scheduled services operator and applied to the ATLB for a large number of domestic and international, short, medium and long-haul scheduled licenses. The objective was to establish a scheduled routes network with sufficient critical mass to achieve financial viability by 1965. Freddie Laker recognised, from the outset, that state-of-the-art jet aircraft were needed to operate this proposed network. Accordingly, he continued his support for the British civil aircraft manufacturing industry by placing an order, on 9 May 1961, for ten of the second generation One-Eleven twinjets.

BUA was the first purchaser of this new medium-range airliner and it has been said that Laker personally conducted the negotiations with BAC and with its engine supplier, Rolls-Royce. In early 1974, as a new member of the Rolls-Royce Commercial Departmental Legal Team, the Author was allocated the tedious task of reviewing the Departmental filing system and then archiving older files. One of the said older files was the BUA One-Eleven engine supply agreement which, upon reading, confirmed Laker's personal involvement in the Rolls-Royce negotiations.

Taking advantage of Rolls-Royce's need to find customers for the new Spey engine, Laker had negotiated a number of small but important changes to the normally sacrosanct Rolls-Royce Standard Warranty. The Warranty clarified Rolls-Royce's obligations in the event of an engine defect, but, critically, it also purported to exclude or restrict other liabilities. Colleagues in the Commercial Legal Team could not recollect any previous changes having been made to the Warranty. On behalf of BUA, it was clear that Laker had driven the best possible deal with Rolls-Royce and it is probable he had done likewise in the airframe negotiations with BAC.

BUA purchased Jersey Airlines in 1961, thereby acquiring the six Handley Page Heralds that the airline had ordered in the previous year. A further significant transaction in 1961 was the merger of BUA with British Aviation Services (BAS), which added the considerable route networks and aircraft fleets of Britavia and Silver City Airways.

Pictured at Liverpool in January 1966, this BUA Carvair was one of a number of DC-4 conversions by Freddie Laker's Aviation Traders Limited. The resulting aircraft was suitable for car ferrying and for carrying abnormal loads. Air Team Images.

Laker then reorganised BUA, consolidating Channel Air Bridge with Silver City's car ferry services in order to create British United Air Ferries (BUAF). BUAF became interested in a then-current ATL project, which involved the acquisition of cheaply available Douglas DC-4s and converting them into an aircraft to be known as the ATL Carvair. ATL produced twenty-one Carvairs, which were sold worldwide. In 1962, BUAF introduced Carvairs to its car ferrying services. The 1964 James Bond film, Goldfinger, shows Auric Goldfinger, together with his vintage yellow Rolls-Royce, boarding a BUAF Carvair for a flight to Switzerland. Bond follows with his Aston Martin DB5 on the next flight.

In May 1963, BUA commenced a rail-air-rail "Silver Arrow" cross-Channel service between London and Paris. Laker, using his remarkable negotiating powers, had persuaded the French authorities to build a spur from the main railway line to Le Touquet Airport in order to make this service viable! BUA passengers were now able to board an SNCF train at the Airport, which took them direct to the Gard du Nord in the centre of Paris. Also, at this time, British United Island Airways was also created to provide second-level UK domestic services.

Laker further supported the British civil aircraft Industry with a BUA order for two VC10s for its proposed longer-haul services. The first aircraft was delivered in September 1964 and was displayed at the Farnborough Air Show before setting off on an eight-day route-proving exercise. Freddie Laker was aboard the VC10, accompanied by a borrowed Rolls-Royce Silver Cloud. Laker had negotiated with BAC to install a large loading door on BUA's VC10s. The purpose of taking the vehicle was said to be to demonstrate the aircraft's combined passenger and freighting abilities.

The first of BUA's One-Elevens arrived in April 1965, and scheduled services with the type were commenced immediately. Air Holdings was now BUA's holding company, with 90% of its shares held by B&C and the balance by Eagle Star Insurance. However, by this time, Freddie Laker had decided he was not made for corporate life. Laker left BUA at the end of 1965, after five very active and dynamic years, during which time he had, doubtless, enjoyed setting BUA on its future course. However, Laker's career as a serial aviation entrepreneur still had some very considerable way to run, as we will see later in this book.

Caledonian

Adam Thomson was born into humble Glaswegian origins in 1927. He joined the Fleet Air Arm at age 17, subsequently qualifying as a pilot. After demobilisation, Thomson decided on a career in civil aviation and became a Captain with Britavia.

However, like Freddie Laker, Thomson had wider entrepreneurial ambitions. In mid-1961, in partnership with a former BEA Steward, John de la Haye, Thomson raised $54,000 ($420,000 today) from investors in order to charter a Douglas DC-7C from the Belgian State airline, SABENA. The new Caledonian Airways commenced operations with this aircraft in late November 1961. Thomson was Deputy Managing Director, and Caledonian's initial flights were a series of long-haul charters on behalf of its main investor, the Overseas Visitors Club.

Disaster struck on 4 March 1962 when Caledonian's DC-7C, flying a charter from Africa to Luxembourg, crashed on take-off, with the loss of one hundred and eleven lives. The casualties exceeded those of the 1950 Llandow Tudor incident, thereby becoming the worst accident in British civil aviation history. At this early stage in its existence, Caledonian Airways was now facing a bleak future. It had no operational aircraft, and the Overseas Visitors Club founder had taken fright and was now seeking an immediate exit. Thomson moved quickly to form Aviation Interests (Thomson) Limited in order to acquire the said majority shareholding. A replacement DC-7C was leased from SABENA, with that airline also providing assistance with maintenance and crew training. Despite objections from BOAC, Caledonian obtained ATLB permission to continue its African routes. During the summer of 1962, it also operated charter flights from Gatwick to Canada.

Caledonian made further progress in 1963 after successfully applying to the American Civil Aeronautics Board for permission to operate closed "Affinity Group" charter flights from the United Kingdom to the United States. This application succeeded despite strong objections from Pan Am and TWA. Many inclusive tour flights were carried out during 1963, and by the summer of 1964, Caledonian was growing strongly with a fleet of four DC-7Cs, together with three Britannia 312s, which it had acquired as BOAC had disposed of its remaining fleet.

Pictured at Manchester in January 1964, this Caledonian DC-7C is an ex-BOAC aircraft, one of the ten purchased as a stop-gap measure in 1956. Air Team Images.

By 1968, Caledonian Airways was operating Boeing 707s from Gatwick to New York, Los Angeles, Singapore and other destinations, primarily on "Affinity Group" charters. On one occasion during the late 1960s, Adam Thomson was present at an aircraft financing negotiation in New York when he received a message that one of the pilots of a Caledonian flight from New York to Bermuda had been taken ill. Thomson was advised that he was the nearest qualified pilot. Sighting the opportunity of early exiting a possibly tedious meeting, Thomson duly headed for the airport, where a uniform was awaiting him in the aircraft's cockpit. He donned the uniform and co-piloted the aircraft to Bermuda.

Later, when modestly relating this incident, Thomson ended with the words: "So I flew the damned thing. And I loved it". Caledonian Airways would proceed to play an important role in the Independent airline sector in the United Kingdom during the 1970s and 1980s.

Few other senior airline executives, with the possible exception of Willie Walsh, the Chief Executive of British Airways and later of IAG from 2005 -2020, would have been willing or able to take up such a challenge. Like Thomson, Walsh had started flying in his late teens, in his case as a trainee with Aer Lingus, then rising to Captain in its Boeing 737 fleet before moving into the commercial side of the business. After retiring from IAG Walsh later became the Chief Executive of IATA.

Monarch

In June 1967, the Cosmos Tours Group decided to form an in-house airline to operate its inclusive tour programmes from 1968 onwards. Monarch Airlines was established with its operational and engineering base at Luton airport, and the new airline commenced services using the two ex-BOAC Britannia 312s, which Caledonian Airways had phased out in favour of its Boeing 707s. During the 1968 season, Monarch carried just over 250,000 passengers, and by the summer of 1970, the airline was operating eight Britannias for Cosmos package holiday flights.

Up until the late 1980s, interested passengers were, with the Captain's permission, welcome to visit airliner Flight Decks. In the summer of 1970, the Author had an opportunity to chat with a Monarch Britannia Flight Engineer in the course of a package holiday flight to Naples. As the ageing whispering giant proceeded gracefully over the Alps in the fading evening light, the Flight Engineer commented that he expected "Brits" to continue in Monarch service for at least another five years.

In actuality, Monarch management was already actively seeking a Britannia replacement for the 1972 season in the form of a fleet of Boeing 720s, a shorter range, smaller capacity version of the Boeing 707. Monarch then progressively withdrew its Britannias from passenger services, retaining some for freighting flights until late 1975. The Flight Engineer's prediction was therefore mostly correct and hopefully he was able to continue his career. However, during the following decade, vastly improved avionics and systems would progressively phase out all Flight Deck positions other than for the two pilots.

Skyways/Euravia/Britannia

In the early 1960s the financial position of Skyways had again deteriorated after it had unsuccessfully transferred some of its Hermes aircraft for use on services between Nassau and destinations in Florida. The Hermes had proved unpopular with the mostly American passengers, and huge losses had been incurred. By mid-1962, Skyways had withdrawn from this involvement, and its remaining aircraft now comprised just three potentially under-utilised, ex-BOAC Lockheed Constellations.

Euravia had been started in early 1962 by three experienced airline professionals, including Captain TED "Ted" Langdon, who was also the owner of a travel company named Universal Tours. The new airline had acquired a small fleet of Constellations from the Israeli airline EL AL. In September 1962, it agreed to purchase the remaining assets of Skyways. This acquisition excluded Skyways Coach-Air Limited, which, as previously mentioned, had been established, in 1958, as a completely separate company to carry out cross-Channel coach-air operations and which was later acquired by Dan-Air. By the summer of 1963, Euravia was operating a fleet of eight Constellations and was solely but extensively involved in the inclusive tour business.

In mid-1964, Euravia negotiated the purchase of some of BOAC's redundant Britannia 102s, which had been stored at Cambridge Airport. The first Euravia Britannia flight took place in December 1964 under the newly adopted name of Britannia Airways. This name would soon become very familiar to package holiday customers. Britannia Airways subsequently withdrew its Constellations and operated an increased fleet of five Britannias. In April 1965, Britannia Airways and Universal Tours were acquired by the Canadian-owned Thomson Organisation. Britannia Airways was now destined for significant growth, using the latest Boeing 737-200 aircraft, and it would act as the "in-house" airline for Thomson Travel, a major future UK package holiday provider.

Part 4 - The 1970s

The 1970s opened in a similar fashion to the previous decade with new civil aviation legislation. This time it took the form of the Civil Aviation Act of 1971, which came into force in August of that year. The Act created the Civil Aviation Authority (CAA), as had been recommended by the 1969 Edwards Report "British Air Transport in the 1970s" prepared by Sir Ronald Edwards, a Professor at the London School of Economics. The CAA then assumed the functions of the Air Registration Board, which had previously regulated British civil aviation.

The CAA is still fully operational today, and its many responsibilities include the issue of pilots' and aircraft engineers' licences, the regulation of security standards and the operation of the Air Travel Organisers' Licensing Scheme (ATOL) in conjunction with ABTA – The Travel Organisation, formerly known as the Association of British Travel Agents and first established in 1950. The ATOL scheme is particularly effective in protecting sums of money paid by customers to travel companies for package holidays, should there be a company failure, and it also provides for the reimbursement of additional hotel costs and for the provision of flights home.

Southend Airport Control Tower at the commencement of the 1970s. Viscounts of Channel Airways, together with a variety of car ferries, can be seen, parked on the apron.

Economic conditions in the early 1970s continued to be challenging for British Independent airlines. An early casualty was Channel Airways, which had been established at Southend Airport in 1947 by another post-Second World War aviation entrepreneur, Squadron Leader RJ "Jack" Jones, when he was still a serving officer at RAF Brize Norton. Channel had taken up residence when the Airport opened and had then expanded steadily with a fleet of Dakotas and Vikings before purchasing a number of ex-BEA Viscounts. In September 1966, Channel Airways supported the One-Eleven programme by placing an order for four 400 series aircraft. The airline then demonstrated its further confidence in British second generation jets by announcing, in October 1967, an order for five Trident 1s, although only two aircraft were actually delivered.

In early 1970, the award of a large three years inclusive tour contract had encouraged Channel Airways to purchase five of BEA's low-utilised Comet 4Bs, now being displaced as BEA introduced its Tridents. Channel paid £2m (£41m today) compared with the current cost of well over £100m to buy five, broadly equivalent, second-hand Airbus A320s.

Sadly, by early 1971, one of the Channel Airways' Tridents was standing engineless at Stansted, having been partially cannibalised for spares, an action which had been necessary to keep the other Trident flying. At the end of the season, Channel was forced to sell both of its Tridents to BEA. This sale could not save the airline and a Receiver was appointed on 1 February 1972. So another, once significant, British Independent airline was now aviation history.

Wide-bodied passenger aircraft

The Boeing 747 "Jumbo"

An important event had taken place across the North Atlantic in early 1965 when Pan Am's Juan Trippe accepted an invitation from William Allen, the President of the Boeing Corporation, to join him on his boat, the Wild Goose, for a weekend fishing trip in the Puget Sound, near to Seattle in Washington State. Characteristically "talking shop" over the weekend, Trippe advised Allen that Pan Am needed to replace its ageing Boeing 707s and Douglas DC-8s with an aircraft with two and a half times their capacities and with thirty percent lower passenger-mile operating costs. It is believed that Trippe asked Allen, "Would you build it if I bought it?" to which Allen responded, "Would you buy it if I built it?"

In April of the following year, Juan Trippe enlivened the Boeing Corporation's fiftieth-anniversary celebrations with the announcement of a Pan Am order for twenty-five of Boeing's proposed new 747 Jumbo-jets at a price of $525m ($3.8bn today). The Boeing Corporation had just taken the biggest commercial gamble in its history in agreeing to produce this huge new aircraft.

The Corporation then proceeded to purchase a site at Everett, fifty miles north of Seattle, in order to construct a facility which was large enough to accommodate the Jumbo production line. Boeing also commenced design work with the aero-engine manufacturer, Pratt & Whitney, to produce, for the Jumbo, its proposed new, high-bypass, turbofan engine, the JT9D.

By September 1968, twenty-five other airlines, including BOAC, had ordered Jumbos. The aircraft's first flight took place on 9 February 1969 with its four JT9Ds mounted on wing pylons and with its distinctive short upper deck accommodating the Flight Deck and a small passenger compartment. The Jumbo commenced airline service in 1970 and could carry over four hundred passengers, with a three-four-three seat configuration in Economy Class, effectively transforming international air travel by tripling future passenger capacity.

More than 1500 Jumbos would be subsequently sold in numerous variants, and the aircraft would remain in passenger service for over fifty years. Its life was shortened only by the 2020 Covid-19 pandemic, after which most airlines re-launched services with the latest twin-engine wide-bodies in the place of four-engine aircraft.

The McDonnell Douglas DC-10

In the late 1950s, the Douglas Aircraft Company had been criticised for its slowness in producing its DC-8 competitor to the Boeing 707. Now, towards the end of the following decade, the proud company was determined to redeem itself. It decided to work with American Airlines to develop a smaller, wide-bodied, aircraft which would compete with the Jumbo on similar long-range routes, but with the ability to operate from shorter runways. Douglas merged with the McDonnell Aircraft Corporation, in 1967, and this merger created a much financially stronger McDonnell Douglas.

The merged Company pressed on with the DC-10 project as a trijet, single-deck, wide-bodied, passenger aircraft. American Airlines followed up its initial interest with an order for twenty-five DC-10s. United Airlines went further, ordering thirty aircraft with options for a further thirty.

The maiden flight of the DC-10 took place on 29 August 1970, powered by the American General Electric Company's CF6, high-bypass, turbofan engine, which had been designed to compete with the JT9D. During an intensive subsequent DC-10 testing programme an outward-opening cargo door blew out in the course of ground tests. This failure resulted in the de-pressurisation of the aircraft and the collapse of the main cabin floor.

The incident then led to a dispute between McDonnell Douglas and its fuselage sub-contractor, Convair, concerning appropriate remediation work. Twelve months later, Convair sent a formal memorandum to McDonnell Douglas, expressing concerns about the adequacy of the proposed re-design and rectification work and stating that, without further modifications, it considered there was a serious risk of the loss of an aircraft.

Despite these issues, unmodified DC-10s entered commercial service with American Airlines a year later, closely followed by the DC-10s of United Airlines. The aircraft was configured to carry around three hundred passengers, with eight across seating in Economy Class, over a range of more than 3,500 miles. On 12 June 1972, an American Airlines DC-10, flying over Ontario, Canada, lost a cargo door. The aircraft de-pressurised and the main cabin floor collapsed, damaging the control lines, but the pilots were able to make an emergency landing. The US National Transportation Safety Board investigators recommended modifications, but no airworthiness directive was issued.

On 3 March 1974, a lightly loaded DC-10, operated by Turkish Airlines, called in at Orly Airport, Paris, on its way from Istanbul to London. A large group of England Rugby Union supporters, who had attended the Five Nations game against France, were stranded at the airport due to a strike by British Airways ground staff at Heathrow. Two hundred and sixty-one additional passengers, including most of the supporters group, joined the Turkish Airlines flight. The DC-10 had left Paris for London and was climbing to its flight level of 23,000 ft when the rear left cargo door blew off. All control lines were severed, and the DC-10 entered into a terrifying, seventy-seven-second-long dive with the pilots being helpless to recover control. The aircraft reached a speed of nearly 500mph before crashing into Ermenonville Forest, killing all three hundred and forty-six passengers and crew on board. 20,000 body parts were recovered, with only one hundred and eighty-eight bodies being identifiable. This was the worst crash in aviation history at the time.

A sub-committee of the US House of Representatives immediately investigated this appalling incident. An airworthiness directive was belatedly issued, requiring mandatory door modifications, and there were no other DC-10 accidents attributable to cargo door failures. Significant passenger litigation followed against McDonnell Douglas, and the aircraft's reputation was badly damaged.

There was a further incident on 25 May 1979 when an engine and pylon assembly of an American Airlines DC-10 swung upwards over the left wing. The aircraft stalled and crashed with the loss of all two hundred and seventy-one people on board and two people on the ground. The Federal Aviation Agency (FAA) promptly grounded all DC-10s from US airspace. The ban was lifted upon discovery that the cause was unrelated to previous incidents and was due to defective maintenance work by American Airlines. However, this serious crash further damaged the DC-10's reputation.

Production of the DC-10 continued until 1989, with three hundred and eighty-six aircraft being sold, after which it was superseded by the improved McDonnell Douglas MD11, two hundred examples of which were produced. The MD11 is still flying today, with a number of freight carriers including FedEx, which currently operates twenty-five aircraft and is likely to retain the type in service until the end of the decade.

Despite these high-profile accidents, the DC-10/MD11's safety record over its service life is broadly comparable with that of similar-era passenger jets. However, there were implications for British civil aviation in the 1970s because many passengers refused to fly on the aircraft which Laker Airways had selected to operate its innovative new Skytrain service.

The Lockheed Tristar

The Lockheed Corporation had developed a strong military aircraft business during and post-Second World War. It was now seeking opportunities to repeat the success of its 1950s Constellation piston engine civilian airliner. Lockheed decided to re-enter the civil aviation market with a wide-bodied airliner with a three-engine (trijet) configuration similar to that of the DC-10. Such configuration was chosen for the same reason; the FAA prohibition on twin-engine commercial jets from flying more than thirty minutes from an airport. Trans-oceanic flights by twinjets were consequently impossible, but the use of trijets would satisfactorily address this issue.

In contrast to McDonnell Douglas's conservative approach to the design of its DC-10, in re-using established DC-8 era technology wherever practicable, Lockheed adopted advanced technology for its new jet airliner, which was to be known as the Tristar. In particular, it had chosen the new Rolls-Royce RB211 turbofan as its power plant, which offered lower noise emissions, improved reliability and higher efficiency. The prototype Tristar flew on 16 November 1970, but its development programme was then delayed during the following year, primarily due to difficulties in engine supply from Rolls-Royce. TWA and Eastern Airlines were launch customers for the Tristar, and Delta Airlines later became the largest operator.

The Tristar and DC-10 were broadly similar in external appearance, the main difference being that the Tristar's third engine was mounted within the rear fuselage and was fed through an S-duct. The DC-10's third engine was mounted above the fuselage, at the base of the tail, for simplicity and for more economical construction. Lockheed claimed that the reduced drag and improved stability of the S-duct system, together with the reduction in empty aircraft weight, outweighed its disadvantages. Many observers considered the Tristar to be more pleasing to the eye than the DC-10.

Between 1968 and 1984, Lockheed produced two hundred and fifty Tristars, but despite its questionable safety reputation, the DC-10 progressively gained a sales advantage, partly because Lockheed was slow in producing higher capacity and longer-range variants of the Tristar. This task was not assisted by delays in the availability of the more powerful RB211-524 engine. British Airways was a purchaser of the longer-range Tristar 500, but Tristar sales fell far short of Lockheed's break-even target of five hundred units.

In 1984, Lockheed concluded its Tristar programme and withdrew from civil aircraft production. British Airways sold its Tristar 500s to the RAF in the early 1980s but successfully operated its remaining eighteen Tristars for the remainder of that decade. The RAF also purchased three ex-Pan Am aircraft and successfully employed its fleet of Tristars as both aerial tankers and passenger/freight transports until they were finally withdrawn from service in March 2014.

The Second Force Private Sector airline

The Edwards Report had recognised the difficult economic conditions facing Independent airlines and so it proposed the creation of a "Second Force" Private Sector airline. This new airline would be financially and managerially sound and would operate a state-of-the-art, long-haul fleet, including wide-bodied aircraft and supersonic transports. The Government would transfer certain routes, primarily in Africa, from BOAC to the new airline.

Having suffered progressive intrusions by the Independents into its mainstream business during the 1960s, BEA had concluded in 1969, "If you can't beat them, join them". Accordingly, it created BEA Airtours in order to service the inclusive tours market. BEA Airtours commenced operations from Gatwick in March 1970, and its initial aircraft comprised seven Comet 4Bs recently made redundant from BEA's scheduled services by the arrival of Tridents. These aircraft were soon joined by a further two displaced Comets. BEA Airtours also negotiated the purchase, from BOAC, of seven of its higher capacity Boeing 707-436s, which were now at the end of their service lives with the airline. The very reasonable price paid for the 707s, which arrived over the period 1971-73, was £4.3m (around £90m today) and the deal included spare engines and a large inventory of other spare parts.

BEA Airtours started to poach business from the Independents. BUA lost a large inclusive tour contract and B&C, under the direction of the Cayzer family, now decided the time had arrived for the shipping group to lay down the burden of its increasingly troubled airline. Although Laker had driven consolidation and efficiencies in the early and mid-1960s by replacing BUA's piston engine types with a mixed all-jet fleet of Viscounts, VC10s and One-Elevens, significantly more expenditure was now required. More new aircraft would cost £60m. A further £25m was needed for improved ground services and to provide adequate working capital for BUA.

Sir Nicholas Cayzer decided he was not prepared to authorise investment on this scale so he looked around for a suitable purchaser. BEA was approached but agreement could not be reached on price. A provisional agreement was subsequently made for BOAC to acquire BUA. The fiery Labour politician and President of the Board of Trade, Roy Mason, gave his preliminary approval to the transaction but "on the understanding that there were no prospects of a merger with another Independent airline", as had been the Edwards Report's recommendation.

The reality was that such alternative prospects did, in fact, exist. An Adam Thomson-led Caledonian Airways team had been discussing a possible merger with senior members of BUA's management for some time. When this information reached Roy Mason, he considered that he had been misled. He promptly withdrew his approval of the BOAC transaction "until the situation has been clarified".

The situation was duly clarified when successful negotiations were concluded by Caledonian to acquire BUA for £12m (£240m today). The transaction was completed on 30 November 1970, and it also included the transfer of the three new One-Eleven 500 series, which B&C had previously intended to lease to BUA. British United Air Ferries and British United Island Airways were not included in the transaction and the ownership of these two airlines remained with B&C for the meantime.

It is difficult to understand how the proposed acquisition of BUA by BOAC could possibly have been consistent with the Edwards Report's recommendation for the creation of a "Second Force" Private Sector airline. However, it would certainly have served to eliminate a well-resourced competitor to the State-owned airline corporations and to have avoided any forced transfer of routes!

Adam Thomson (second left) celebrates a success in 1972 with members of his BCal Sales and Marketing team. British Caledonian

To crown a successful year, Adam Thomson was nominated "UK Businessman of the Year" in 1970. The new airline, with the initial name of Caledonian/BUA, started life with thirty-one jet aircraft and with four thousand four hundred employees. On 1 November 1971, British Caledonian Airways was adopted as the name for Britain's new Second Force Private Sector airline.

The New British Airways

During 1970, BEA's annual turnover had reached £126m (£2.4bn today). Lord Douglas had retired in 1965 and he had died four years later. Under his guidance, BEA had become a leading world airline, both commercially and technically. His successor as Chairman, the capable Sir Anthony Milward, was able to boast, in 1969, that BEA was profitable and that twenty percent of all European passengers were flying on the airline. However, rumours continued about a possible merger of the two remaining State-owned airline corporations, a step not favoured by the respective senior management teams of BEA and BOAC. A merged airline would have only one Chairman and one Chief Executive and many other senior positions would be duplicated and so potentially eliminated.

Henry Marking had originally joined BEA in the 1950s in a temporary role as an Assistant Solicitor. He was later appointed Company Secretary and he became BEA's Chief Executive in 1964. Marking succeeded Sir Anthony Milward as Chairman in early 1971 and, shortly after his appointment, commented on the persistent merger rumours to the effect that:

"There will always be misguided people in this world who, from time to time, try to raise this old thing. It comes up every so many years, but one has learned to discount it."

A newly-arrived BOAC 747-100 at Heathrow in September 1972. Behind is a Pan Am 747 dwarfing the Pan Am hangar, which was once the largest building at the Airport. Air Team Images.

Whilst Marking may have discounted "this old thing", others in the Government and in the Civil Service had certainly not. The Civil Aviation Act of 1971 also included provisions creating the British Airways Board under the chairmanship of David Nicolson, a specialist in corporate planning. The stated purpose of the Board was to oversee both BOAC and BEA. However, there was a clear intention to effect a subsequent merger.

At BOAC, the first of fifteen of its Boeing 747 Jumbos was scheduled for delivery in April 1970. A Pan Am aircraft had undertaken the first commercial Jumbo transatlantic flight on 12 January 1970, arriving at Heathrow with three hundred and sixty-three passengers on board. However, BOAC Jumbo operations were delayed until April 1971 because of a British Airline Pilots Association (BALPA) dispute with BOAC over pay levels for flying this new aircraft. BOAC pilots refused to attend training in Seattle until the dispute was settled.

There was also more widespread industrial relations unrest in the two State-owned airline corporations in the early 1970s concerning both engineering staff and pilots. On 18 June 1972, a BEA Trident crashed shortly after take-off from Heathrow, killing all one hundred and nine passengers and a crew of nine. The flight recorder indicated that the leading edge droop slots had been retracted too early, causing the aircraft to lose lift and stall. Immediately before the flight, the now-deceased Captain had been involved in heated discussions deploring industrial action. His speech on the matter, which had been prepared for a later meeting, now had to be delivered posthumously.

In January 1973, the Secretary of State for Trade & Industry accepted a British Airways Board recommendation that, with effect from 1 April 1974, BEA and BOAC would be merged to create a new public corporation. The name of British Airways would now be revived, some thirty-five years after the previous late-1930s airline had been absorbed into BOAC. The merger also included BEA's affiliates, Cambrian Airways and Northeast Airlines (formerly BKS Air Transport). The new British Airways would have the most comprehensive route network in the world, extending to half a million miles. It would serve two hundred destinations in eighty-four countries with the world's largest passenger fleet of two hundred and twenty aircraft.

In the late 1970s a British Airways Trident 1 is parked alongside an RAF Lockheed Hercules transport. Behind is a BA Jumbo with a VC10 taking off in the background. British Airways Museum.

The forthcoming 1974 "Oil Crisis" would provide some early challenges for the new public corporation, and critical decisions needed to be made on fleet replacement and on aircraft sourcing. In this context, Sir Anthony Milward, in his farewell comments as BEA Chairman in January 1971, had confirmed his earlier views when making the largely correct forecast that:

"BEA will probably never be able to buy another British aircraft".

Rolls-Royce - disaster and recovery

Rolls-Royce had a huge military aviation involvement during the Second World War but, at the conclusion of hostilities, the company had only a small presence in civil aviation. By the early 1960s, following the acquisition by Hives and Hooker of the Whittle gas turbine designs and production facility, it held 50% of the civil aviation aero-engine market outside the USA. However, during the late 1950s, the strong sales of Avon and Dart engines had started to slow and their 1960s replacements, the Tyne turboprop and the Conway and Spey turbofans, were now not selling quite as well. Rolls-Royce Management recognised that radical decisions were required, if the company was to retain a significant presence in the world aero-engine market.

In the early 1960s, Rolls-Royce had commenced work on the RB178, a two-shaft advanced technology engine. It was intended as a replacement for the Conway engine and to be suitable for long-range subsonic aircraft and also as the power plant for projected third generation British jets. However it was becoming clear that there would be no such new British civil aircraft projects.

Rolls-Royce then focussed its efforts on presenting the RB178 to Boeing for its new Jumbo, but the engine was rejected because Boeing had already committed to work with Pratt & Whitney on the development of the JT9D. In early 1966, Rolls-Royce cancelled the RB178 and announced the launch of an Advanced Technology Engine (ATE) family featuring a triple, concentric shaft architecture, together with a structurally integrated power-plant nacelle and with a range of thrusts from

10,000 to 60,000 lbf. This configuration facilitated the fitting of a huge front fan, directing eighty percent of the airflow around, rather than through, the engine core.

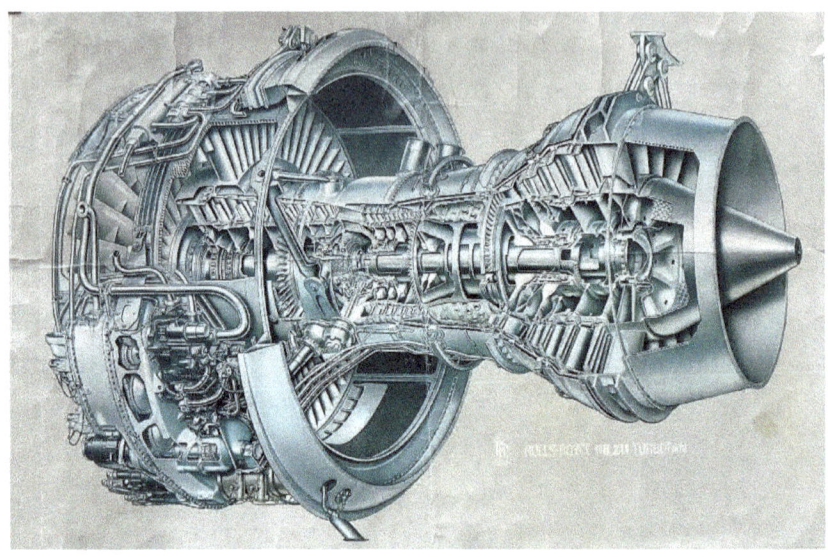

The 1970s Rolls-Royce RB211, high-bypass, turbofan. The large front fan drove the majority of the air intake around rather than through the engine core.

Rolls-Royce proposed an engine from its ATE family, the RB207 producing 47,500 lbf, to power the forthcoming twinjet Airbus A300. Airbus Industrie declined the proposal, refusing to adopt a completely new engine. Instead, it specified what it considered to be the lower-risk American General Electric CF6 turbofan engine.

Rolls-Royce then cancelled the RB207 in favour of the RB211, a scaled-down engine, which would produce 33,260 lbf at take-off. This engine was forecast to have a better power-to-weight ratio than the competing American Pratt & Whitney and GE large turbofan engines, resulting in operational advantages for customers.

Some such advantages would be derived from the fitting of a huge carbon fibre (Hyfil) front fan, resulting in considerable weight savings over conventional Titanium steel fans. The target was to achieve engine certification by the end of December 1970 with a budgeted price of just over $500,000 per engine (around $4m today). By way of comparison a current Trent 1000 for the Boeing 787 Dreamliner, is reputed to cost more than $20m and even higher for one of the latest XWB engines for the Airbus A350.

A serious setback occurred to the RB211 project in July 1967, with the sudden death from a brain haemorrhage of Rolls-Royce's Chief Engineer, Adrian Lombard, aged just fifty-two. Dr Stanley Hooker later described this loss in the following terms:

"It was all too obvious that the Derby engineers, normally proud and self-confident to the point of arrogance, had slid from bad to worse when their great leader, Lombard, had been so suddenly plucked from them in 1967. His death left a vacuum which nobody could fill".

Rolls-Royce had offered the RB211 both to McDonnell Douglas and to Lockheed for their wide-body projects. In early 1968, American Airlines had proposed that its DC-10s would be powered by RB211s, but there was strong American political and industry resistance. McDonnell Douglas then substituted the General Electric CF6.

As a consequence the only "show in town" now remaining for the RB211 engine, in which a huge financial investment had already been made, was the Lockheed Tristar. Rolls-Royce focussed its sales efforts on Lockheed with over two hundred visits being made across the water. The Managing Director of Rolls-Royce's Aero-Engine Division, David Huddie, personally conducted negotiations, having taken up six months' temporary residence in the USA.

In early 1968, following Lockheed having secured its launch orders for the Tristar from Eastern Airlines and from TWA, Rolls-Royce was able to announce, on 29 March 1968, Britain's biggest-ever export order. It was for a total of five hundred and forty RB211s, comprising one hundred and fifty Tristar ship sets, plus ninety spare engines. The price was $350m ($2.73bn today), with deliveries to Eastern Airlines commencing in the summer of 1971.

Huddie was knighted for his efforts later in 1968, and the focus now switched to manufacturing the engines to specification and to time. Ominously, during final negotiations, Lockheed had refused Rolls-Royce's request to increase the engine price in order to reflect additional production costs whilst also specifying an increase in the thrust level to 40,600 lbf.

As identified by Hooker, the underlying engineering situation on the RB211 development programme was not good. Also, Rolls-Royce Management was grappling with the rationalisation and integration of the expensive and defensive 1966 Bristol Siddeley acquisition. The business had been found to be barely profitable and significant stock write-offs relating to redundant and unsuccessful engines had been necessary. Rolls-Royce's Balance Sheet had been further strained by the write-down of the Bristol Siddeley acquisition goodwill, which had comprised one-third of the price. Further, at the Bristol factory, the Olympus 593 development costs for Concorde were mounting, but there was no clarity as to the future sales potential of this engine.

On 21 July 1970, in what, then unknown to him, was to be his final Chairman's Statement, Sir Denning Pearson had reported to the Rolls-Royce Annual General Meeting a reduced turnover during the previous year. In relation to the RB211 project, Pearson stated that further Government support was required for its ongoing development and that related funding talks were in progress with the Ministry of Aviation Supply. Pearson argued that the competing American large turbofan engines, whilst not receiving launch aid as such, were benefiting from significant indirect US Government support in the form of pre-payments on contracts for military aircraft using these new engines.

Pearson also highlighted cash pressures in the business but reported that Rolls-Royce had secured additional finance in the form of a £20m loan (£390m today) from the Industrial Reorganisation Corporation (IRC). The first instalment of £10m had already been drawn down, and the second instalment would be paid by the IRC before the end of the year, subject to a satisfactory report from the Chartered Accountants, Coopers, on the company's finances.

The mounting financial crisis had been further compounded by a most concerning event which had happened two months previously concerning the RB211 project. A number of degradation issues concerning the Hyfil carbon fibre front fan had already been identified in development, but the situation reached a crisis point when the fan of the test engine failed final bird ingestion tests. These tests involved the firing of chicken carcasses at the engine at high speeds in order to simulate a bird strike. The RB211 team had reluctantly decided that this growing level of vulnerability was unacceptable; consequently there was no alternative other than to replace the Hyfil fan with a more robust but heavier Titanium fan. Such a change would occasion additional costs and potential delays and would also endanger some of the perceived competitive advantages of the engine.

In September 1970, Rolls-Royce provided an update on the RB211 project, reporting that development costs had risen to £170.3m, an amount which was double the original late 1960s estimates. In November 1970, at the Government's insistence, Pearson was replaced as Chairman by Lord Cole, a highly experienced businessman who was the recently retired Chairman of Unilever. Lord Cole had taken on the role only upon the Government agreeing to provide additional RB211 support. He barely had time to settle into his new job before the Board received the Coopers' Report. To the Board's shock and horror, the Report concluded that there was no basis for the payment of the balance of the IRC loan. Despite the promised additional Government funding, Rolls-Royce was now facing the biggest crisis since its formation and was projected soon to exhaust its remaining cash resources.

Even more concerning was the news that the delays and additional costs affecting the RB211 programme meant that the production cost of each engine would now exceed its contracted selling price. The Lockheed contract, so triumphantly announced just two and a half years previously, would now be loss-making, with further substantial penalties arising from likely late engine deliveries.

Even the commercially astute Rolls-Royce Deputy Chairman, Whitney Straight, a member of the Board since 1955 and who had been very critical of its 1945 decision to sell Derwent and Nene engines to Russia (which engines had been copied to power the MiG-15 fighters deployed against the USAF's Sabres in the 1950 Korean War), had not foreseen such a dire situation.

The company had fallen into a terrible trap. A frenetic two months followed, when all feasible options were analysed. On 4 February 1971, the Board reluctantly concluded that there were, in fact, no such feasible options. There was no escape, and it issued the following short and stark statement:

"It is no longer possible to continue with the present contract. Rolls-Royce has therefore called in the Receiver".

*This Rolls-Royce internal memorandum, dated 1 February 1971
and addressed to the Author's father-in-law, evidences the
desperate efforts which were made over the preceding weekend
to save the RB211 project*

Shock waves reverberated throughout the United Kingdom, where Rolls-Royce employed 80,000 people as the Country's fourteenth largest employer. The impact was felt particularly strongly in Derby, where a quarter of the employees worked, with Rolls-Royce being the major direct employer. In addition, many other local firms were closely associated with its fortunes. Queues rapidly formed outside branches of the Derbyshire Building Society as desperate local people sought to withdraw their cash deposits in fear of losing not only their jobs but also their life savings!

The British aviation industry, some twenty years after the 1950s Comet disasters, was now facing another major crisis. The

Receivership posed a particular problem for the newly elected Conservative Government, led by Edward Heath, which had adopted a policy of not supporting failing industries known as "lame ducks". However, Rolls-Royce was a high-technology company with strategic importance as a major United Kingdom defence supplier.

The Government considered that some form of rescue was essential and, in May 1971, it announced the formation of Rolls-Royce (1971) Limited to acquire the aero-engine business from the Receiver and to take on a renegotiated RB211 supply contract with Lockheed, on terms which restored its viability. The Receiver followed up separately by realising the remaining assets for the benefit of the creditors, including the disposal of the original car manufacturing business, the Diesel Engine Division and the company's twenty percent shareholding in BAC.

The terms of the re-negotiated RB211 supply contract included a 50% price increase and a delivery timescale reasonably achievable for the new company. Lockheed installed a team of engineers at Derby in order to monitor engine build and testing on a day-by-day basis. The team was led by Lockheed's Head of Propulsion, Walt Sheehan, who had previously been involved in the Spirit of America's successful November 1965 attempt to set a new land speed record of over six hundred mph. Lockheed itself was now also in financial difficulty, but its determined President, Daniel J Haughton, kept his nerve and obtained US Government loan guarantees sufficient to enable the Tristar programme to continue.

An RB211 production engine as supplied for on-wing service. Rolls-Royce Museum, the Author

The Board of Rolls-Royce (1971) Limited consisted of just seven members, including Dr Stanley Hooker, who had been coaxed out of retirement in 1970 to assist Rolls-Royce with resolving the difficulties on the RB211 programme. Hooker had thereby returned the 1954 favour extended to him by Ernest Hives, who had died in 1965, in providing the Rolls-Royce team to assist Bristol Engines with the Proteus problems. Hooker had finally achieved his long-held ambition of becoming the Rolls-Royce Technical Director. He was able to persuade a number of other retired senior engineers to return to the company and join him in the task of ensuring that the RB211 could meet the revised price, delivery and performance specifications.

The Tristar prototype flies over a Rolls-Royce facility on 5 June 1971. It later landed at East Midlands Airport where thousands of Rolls-Royce employees were queuing to inspect.

The prototype Tristar, in its Eastern Airlines livery had been displayed at the 1971 Paris Air Show. Over 10,000 Rolls-Royce employees were gathering at East Midlands Airport, on the following day, 5 June 1971, waiting to view the elegant aircraft with its three RB211s proudly displaying Rolls-Royce logos. It was widely recognised across the Nation that the rescue of the RB211 project had been essential to enable the continuation of a company which was critical to both its Economy and its Defence.

In retrospect, the composition of the Rolls-Royce Board in 1970 fell well short of modern-day corporate governance standards. Sir Denning Pearson held the positions of both Chief Executive and Chairman. Today's standards disapprove of Chief Executives succeeding as Chairmen, let alone allowing one individual to perform both roles! Also, many of the Directors, like Whitney Straight, had been Board members for well in excess of the nine years, after which current corporate governance deems such individuals to be no longer independent. The Rolls-Royce Board had no women members, and a number of Directors were either retired or were currently serving as senior executives.

It has also been said that the Receivership occurred due to the predominance of engineers at senior management levels in the company and that Rolls-Royce was weak commercially. There might be an element of truth here, but a subsequent report by Inspectors appointed by the Department of Trade and Industry confirmed that the failure encompassed a range of difficulties, although the immediate cause was the drain on the company's resources, arising from the RB211 venture. The DTI report stated, in relation to the RB211 contract, that:

"The terms ultimately negotiated meant a commitment for Rolls-Royce which placed at hazard its continued existence".

The Inspectors allocated much of the blame to Pearson and Huddie personally, commenting that they had:

"Failed properly to discharge the responsibilities of stewardship which rest upon the directors of a public company".

The Receivership and events leading up to the disaster took a heavy personal toll on Huddie, who suffered a serious breakdown and left the company in late 1970. David Huddie was a brilliant engineer with First Class Honours in Mathematics and Economics from Trinity College, Dublin and he was a man who had dedicated most of his career to Rolls-Royce. With his health later restored, Huddie became a senior research fellow at Imperial College, London where he used his wide experience of Industry to design courses, which prepared engineers for management roles.

Given Lockheed's strong negotiating position in the late 1960s, it is highly unlikely that it would ever have accepted an engine supply contract without binding delivery, price and performance guarantees. Rolls-Royce had arrived at a vulnerable point in its existence, in the early 1960s, and the RB211 programme had been "make or break". Sadly, it had proved to be the latter.

Sir Kenneth Keith (left) and Dr Stanley Hooker during a mid-1970s Rolls-Royce sales trip to China

In 1972 Lord Cole was replaced as Chairman by merchant banker, Sir Kenneth Keith. Educated at Rugby School, Keith had qualified, pre-war, as a Chartered Accountant with the leading firm, Peat Marwick. During the Second World War he served with distinction as a Staff Officer in England and France, rising to Lieutenant-Colonel and being awarded the Croix de Guerre. In 1946 Keith joined the largely moribund financial firm, Philip Hill, and immediately set about a series of mergers, culminating in the creation of Hill Samuel, in 1965, with Keith as its CEO and Deputy Chairman. Through hard work, merit and aggression, Keith's widely-recruited professional staff had then created a diversified financial services firm, termed "The Whale of Wood

Street". By the early 1970s, Sir Kenneth was turning his attentions to British Industry. At Rolls-Royce, here was an opportunity to apply his professional skills and City experience towards the recovery of a great British name.

Sir Stanley Hooker died from prostate cancer at the age of seventy-six in May 1984. He had been knighted ten years previously and had been recognised by many Institutions for his brilliance, including the award of an Honorary Professorship in Aeronautical Engineering at Beijing University. Sir Kenneth Keith commented after Sir Stanley's death;

"I always thought Stanley was a near-genius. He was very, very clever and a very good engineer."

With typical engineering precision, Sir Stanley had managed to put off death until the day before the publication of his autobiography, which was, of course, entitled "Not Much of an Engineer".

"Sir Kenneth Keith successfully steered Rolls-Royce (1971) Limited through the challenging post-Receivership years, retiring in 1980. He then continued to live a very full professional and personal life; dying in his home county of Norfolk on 1 September 2004, the day after his eighty-eighth birthday and two years after celebrating his fourth marriage!

Rolls-Royce (1971) Limited subsequently made a major success of the RB211 and, without this engine, it is highly probable that there would, today, be no Rolls-Royce Trent or XWB engines powering many of the world's large airliners. Also, it is more than likely that Britain would have no involvement whatsoever in the production of aero-engines.

Working at Rolls-Royce

Rolls-Royce (1971) Limited expanded its Commercial Department in the early 1970s, and the Author was one of three young lawyers who joined the Department's Legal Team in that period. The first few days were spent attending an RB211 familiarisation course for which the attendees received a certificate, fortunately without taking any form of examination! The initial impressions were of a company still recovering from the traumatic events of early 1971. Many long-standing employees had departed, but old attitudes were at times evident. For example, at the 1974 Business Update given by the Managing Director of the Derby Engine Division, the Group Function employees present were advised by a member of the Personnel & Administration Department that they were attending;

"Because even those of us who work in Group need to know something about what is happening in the Business".

Since "Group" comprised a major cost centre and was actually generating no income other than by way of a limited amount of technology licensing, there could be no doubt that "those of us who work in Group" were entirely dependent upon the "Business" for our wages and benefits. The Legal Team had this consideration totally front of mind in our day-to-day activities. However, Management appeared to think that others required appropriate reminders!

Rolls-Royce Management was concerned about the power of the Engineering Unions, a fear which was demonstrated by a seemingly innocuous contract for the bulk supply of hand-held digital calculators from the American Digital Equipment

Company (DEC). In early 1975, the Author and a Legal Team colleague were summoned to the office of the Purchasing Director in order to receive instructions on this proposed transaction. We were initially baffled at the Director's repeated insistence on maintaining strict confidentiality. We later discovered that the issue was possible Union objections.

Following a number of clandestine visits to DEC, the contract was concluded, and the sinister objects were delivered. Management's fears about objections proved to be unfounded, with the large majority of Rolls-Royce engineers taking up the use of these newfangled devices with great enthusiasm. Just a few individuals declined, determined to stave off, for as long as possible, the obsolescence of their long-trusted slide rules!

The company's engineers were now making steady progress in achieving the contracted thrust levels from the RB211. Also, the Government had provided launching aid for the higher thrust RB211-524 engine proposed for installation in the projected longer-range Tristar and to be available to power the next batch of Boeing 747s, some of which had been ordered by British Airways for service from early 1977.

Although the previous attempts to secure the RB211 as an engine option on the Jumbo had failed, here was a second opportunity to agree terms with Boeing. If there had been mistakes with the Lockheed Tristar engine supply agreement, then Rolls-Royce was determined to avoid a repetition with Boeing. In the first quarter of 1974, Bob Young, a partner in the New York law firm of Gilbert Segal and Young, effectively took up temporary membership of the Commercial Department Legal Team. With Bob's assistance and doubtless at horrendous expense, the Boeing supply agreement was successfully concluded.

An RB211-524 powered BA Jumbo climbs out from Heathrow in April 1982. A Concorde, VC10 and two Boeing 707s are parked below at the British Airways Engineering base. The Author.

A Pan Am Tristar at New York JFK in April 1982, next stop Chicago. Some of Pan Am's Tristars were later purchased by the RAF. The Author

The RB211-524 engine proved to be a popular Jumbo choice with many airlines and it was an engine option for the 747-400 series, which entered service in 1989. Advances in avionics and control systems had now eliminated the need for Flight Engineers and so the latest Jumbos had provision for just the two pilots. On 9 February 2020, an RB211-524 powered British Airways 747 400 broke the New York-London subsonic airliner speed record, making the crossing in a Jetstream-assisted four hours fifty-six minutes. This was five minutes faster than the record, which had been set forty-one years earlier by a BOAC VC10.

Rolls-Royce's relationships with Boeing were now good and Boeing made a number of presentations to the company on its future airliner concepts. To non-technically-minded lawyers these concepts appeared to be mostly comprised of a series of tubes of varying lengths and diameters, with each wing boasting a single high-bypass ratio large turbofan. It was certainly not a very enticing future prospect for the plane spotters of the era, who were still accustomed to seeing and hearing a variety of distinctive shapes at airports and in the sky.

However, to the disappointment of many of today's plane spotters, Boeing's assessment of the future airliner market has subsequently been proven to be correct. The twin wing-mounted engine configuration is now the widely adopted standard for all medium to large-sized passenger aircraft. The 7X7 "tube" later became the very successful, single-isle Boeing 757, and its wide-bodied, two isles, contemporary tube mock-up evolved into the equally successful Boeing 767. Both had two large, wing-mounted, turbofan engines.

One of Rolls-Royce's other prominent customers in the early 1970s was the British Independent airline, Court Line, previously known as Autair, which had commenced fixed-wing flying operations in 1960. It was acquired in April 1965 by the London shipping company of a similar name and was based at Luton.

Court Line initially operated small numbers of second-hand Airspeed Ambassadors and Handley Page Heralds on a limited number of scheduled services but, in October 1969, it changed its focus to inclusive tour work, acquiring a fleet of eight One-Elevens. Seventy per cent of their passenger capacity was contracted by Court Line's closely associated tour company, Clarksons Holidays, and over half a million inclusive tour passengers were carried during the 1969 summer season.

On 1 January 1970, Court Line announced that seven new One-Eleven 500 series aircraft were being acquired and that the One-Elevens would be painted in one of three pastel liveries, green, orange or pink, with matching Cabin Crew uniforms. Court Line had also acquired a seventy-five per cent interest in Leeward Islands Air Transport and had invested significantly in hotels in the Caribbean.

On 17 August 1972, the airline entered into a further massive financial commitment by announcing an order for five Lockheed Tristars. The first two aircraft, also displaying the new pastel liveries, were to be delivered in April 1973 and would thereby provide welcome support for the Rolls-Royce RB211 programme. The Tristars would carry up to four hundred passengers for short-haul inclusive tour work, although they were large aircraft to fill and were not ideally suited for destinations which had limited passenger facilities. The Tristars were much better matched to the provision of long-haul charter and package holiday services, particularly to the Caribbean, and using a three hundred-and-fifty passenger configuration. These services commenced in November 1973.

Court Line however, was still heavily dependent on Clarksons Tours for its passenger supply and the arrival of the Tristars coincided with the disturbing discovery that the tour company was on the verge of bankruptcy. In early 1974, Court Line decided it had no alternative other than to step in and buy Clarksons. It also purchased another customer, the struggling Horizon Holidays Group.

Bookings for the 1974 season however remained weak, due to the general poor economic outlook, and airlines throughout the world were also being affected by the 1974 Oil Crisis. The crisis originated in October 1973 when Arab members of the Organisation of the Petroleum Exporting Countries (OPEC) adversely reacted to a decision by the USA to re-supply Israel with arms to enable it to continue the 1973 (Yom Kippur) Arab-Israeli war. Oil shipments to the USA and to other countries supporting Israel in the conflict were limited by OPEC and, in some cases, were stopped. The embargo was lifted in March 1974, but OPEC had now realised its potential leverage over the world price-setting mechanism for oil. The Organisation embarked upon a programme to increase OPEC member incomes by progressively increasing prices.

Oil supply and pricing would now be a volatile and uncertain factor for the future planning of Aero-Industry production and airline services. Court Line found itself with significant potential excess aircraft capacity, with the Oil Crisis dramatically increasing its operating costs.

The Government was advised of Court Line's parlous position and intervened by taking over its shipping interests. This transaction proved insufficient to save the airline and, on 15 August 1974, all Court Line operations were ceased and the airline was placed into liquidation. At the time, this was the worst airline collapse in British civil aviation history, leaving 50,000 holidaymakers stranded abroad. The airline was a member of ABTA and so the ATOL scheme provided rescue flights, but 150,000 people had lost their planned holidays and 1100 former Court Line employees were put out of work.

Rolls-Royce was, once again, a significant unsecured creditor. However, a number of Court Line's Spey engines were in the process of overhaul at the East Kilbride facility. The standard Rolls-Royce Overhaul Agreement provided for a right of lien over customer property in respect of unpaid charges. The Commercial Legal Team in Derby advised Management that it should exercise these rights and retain the engines until outstanding charges had been paid. A slightly different Law of Delict applied in Scotland and so, a few days later, the Author accompanied an ashen-faced Rolls-Royce Credit Control Manager on a British Midland Airways Viscount flight to Glasgow. The poor man was clearly fearing that his world was about to end unless we could achieve a result in recovering at least some of the Court Line debt.

The purpose of the visit was to attend a conference with Senior Scottish Counsel in order to receive advice on how to proceed under Scottish law. We emerged from the expensive event still not exactly clear on the effects of the mysterious Law of Delict. Returning the next day to East Midlands Airport, flying on Rolls-Royce's de Havilland Heron an ageing member of the company's very modest corporate fleet, was a most pleasant experience, cruising at around 5,000 ft over the Scottish lowlands and North West England and then descending gently over the Midlands.

Back in Derby, despite the continuing lack of absolute legal clarity, it was decided to proceed on the basis of "possession being nine-tenths of the law". We retained the engines and, soon afterwards, received an irate call from the BAC Commercial Department complaining that Rolls-Royce's behaviour was "obstructing its efforts to place Court Line's One-Elevens with other operators". Our response was that we would be delighted to complete the overhaul work and then release the engines, provided, however that BAC paid all outstanding charges. No reply was ever received. We did not recover the debt, but Rolls-Royce retained the engines, which were then profitably used to expand Rolls-Royce Leasing Limited's fleet of engines available for hire.

A Court Line L1011 Tristar, at Luton in January 1975, displaying one of the airline's pastel liveries and now awaiting a new owner, following Court Line's collapse during the previous summer. Air Team Images

The two Tristars, which had already been delivered to Court Line, sat expensively and unproductively at Luton airport for several months. They were eventually acquired by Hong Kong-based Cathay Pacific Airlines, thereby initiating a Rolls-Royce relationship with Cathay Pacific as an important future major customer. The Court Line Commercial Director, Roland Heeks, joined Rolls-Royce as a Commercial Executive, in which role no doubt his inside knowledge of airline operations was much valued.

Whilst the One-Eleven had achieved good initial domestic and international sales success during the late 1960s, customer interest in the aircraft began to fall off in the early 1970s. The One-Eleven 500 series had not sold in North America and the competing Boeing 737 and Douglas DC-9 aircraft were offering customers more operational and financial flexibility. The One-Eleven's Spey engines would ultimately infringe forthcoming noise abatement regulations and it was becoming clear that no apparent suitable successor engine would be available within a reasonable timescale.

In 1975, an unlikely opportunity to prolong the life of the One-Eleven arose in Romania, where the dictatorial President, Nicholae Ceausescu, wished to boost the Romanian aviation industry and earn Western foreign currency. In response, the British Government had originated the ROMBAC project, supported by a number of London banks. The project proposed the transfer of the One-Eleven 500 series production line to Romania, together with licensed production of the Spey engine. Negotiations were to be initiated between BAC, Rolls-Royce and the Romanian National Industrial and Aeronautic Authority (CNIAR) for the production of an aircraft to be known as the ROMBAC, some of which would be acquired by Romania's Tarom Airlines, an existing One-Eleven operator.

The Rolls-Royce ROMBAC team leader was a tall and impressive thirty-two year old Senior Contracts Manager. Gordon Page was another Cambridge-educated engineer and he was a rising star within Rolls-Royce. Page had, unusually, decided to follow a career within the Commercial Department, rather than in Engineering and he had achieved his already quite senior position through talent and ability. He also had immaculate Industry credentials as the eldest son of the aforementioned Freddie Page, a senior director of BAC and destined to become the first Chief Executive of British Aerospace. Freddie Page was knighted in 1979 and he later served as the Chairman of British Aerospace until 1982.

The members of the Rolls-Royce ROMBAC team, including the Author as Legal Adviser, gathered at Heathrow on a dismal, wet morning in February 1975 for their flight to Bucharest. We boarded the rather drably appointed Tarom One-Eleven. The flight was notable only by a disturbingly tight manoeuvre executed by the aircraft on its final approach to Brussels, where it was scheduled to collect further passengers. We wondered if the pilots were on secondment from the Romanian Air Force!

We arrived at Bucharest Airport where some equally drably dressed lady cleaners were awaiting the aircraft. Having navigated Immigration, we were directed towards two Russian-built Zim taxis which then transported us at high speed into central Bucharest. For the second time that day, we thought that our lives might be at risk!

We checked in at the Bucharest Intercontinental Hotel for a two-week stay and attended CNIAR's office promptly the following morning at the designated time of 9.00 am. We were served small cups of Turkish coffee before the belated arrival of the Romanian negotiators. Discussions then commenced, with a lunch break from 1.00 pm, after which we were required to return promptly, at 3.00 pm, for a second session continuing to around 6.00 pm. For security reasons, we were instructed not to discuss the negotiations in our hotel rooms and so most evenings were spent quietly playing cards when, annoyingly, Gordon Page frequently came out as the winner.

The remainder of the visit followed an intense similar pattern, except that each morning session commenced with a review of the previous day's discussions. The parties' recollections of what they respectively believed to have been agreed invariably differed significantly and so most mornings were spent putting the record straight, before any further progress could be made!

Towards the end of our visit, we attended a very convivial reception at the British Consulate, an event well supported by sales teams from Hawker Siddeley, offering the HS125 Business jet, and from BAC, with the One-Eleven. Fortunately the BAC team appeared to have forgotten about our clash in the previous August over the Court Line affair. Also present were many other British suppliers and agents, including representatives of Britten-Norman, which was setting up a production line in Romania for its very successful BN-2 Islander aircraft.

The reception was well underway when it was suddenly interrupted by the sound of crashes and associated breakages. An unfortunate member of the Consulate staff, apparently having over-indulged on Her Majesty's hospitality, had fallen backwards, colliding with the Consulate's extensive collection of potted plants and shrubs. The now comatose individual was discretely removed by Security, and what remained of the previously immaculate display was re-arranged. The incident was rapidly forgotten and the merriment then continued unabated.

We did not see the unfortunate individual again during our visit and, following two weeks of gruelling negotiations, we were relieved to be homeward bound aboard the much more welcoming British Airways Trident, enjoying our complimentary scotch and dry gingers. Back in Derby we had little to report other than a surprise CNIAR confirmation, at one of our final meetings, that "of course Romania would be buying hush kits" for any Spey engines it ordered. This addition implied a large uplift in the potential contract value and so was a welcome development for Rolls-Royce Management.

Many negotiating visits to CNIAR followed, and the ROMBAC agreement was not signed until 9 June 1979. The first ROMBAC aircraft flew in late 1982, by which time UK production of the One-Eleven had ceased. Only nine ROMBACs were eventually manufactured and so, despite the efforts expended over a long period, only a comparatively small return was achieved.

Ceausescu was overthrown during the 1989 Romanian Revolution, and he and his wife were executed by firing squad on 25 December 1989. Gordon Page continued his successful career with Rolls-Royce but left in the early 1990s to become Chief Executive of Sir Alan Cobham's Flight Refuelling Limited. The name Cobham plc was adopted in 1994 in honour of its founder, and Gordon later became Chairman.

Under his leadership, until 2013, the company expanded its aviation activities widely. Cobham was controversially acquired by the American company Advent, in 2020. Despite pre-acquisition assurances, within three years, the company had been broken up and all UK manufacturing had ceased. Sir Alan, who died in October 1973, would have been sad at this disappointing outcome for the company which he had established nearly ninety years previously.

Being fortunate enough to be a member of the Rolls-Royce Commercial Legal Team during the 1970s was a rewarding experience with excellent training in contract drafting and negotiation skills. The Rolls-Royce Contracts Manual was of particular assistance and it served as a valuable reference document for many years after leaving the company. Opportunities for significant promotions for lawyers at the company were limited and most recruits eventually moved on to roles elsewhere However we had appreciated and enjoyed making our small contributions towards helping Rolls-Royce restore its former prominence as a world-leading aerospace group.

On 4 May 2004, exactly one hundred years after the meeting of the "unlikely pair", large numbers of past and present Rolls-Royce employees once again gathered at Donnington Park/East Midlands Airport, this time to attend the Rolls-Royce centenary celebrations. The Airport was closed to commercial traffic for the day in order to accommodate static exhibits, together with flying displays by many Rolls-Royce-powered aircraft.

This Virgin Atlantic Boeing 747-400, pictured at Heathrow in September 2004, is similar to the aircraft, which, earlier that year, performed thrilling aerobatics at the Rolls-Royce centenary event. Air Team Images

In the late morning, heads turned upon hearing the approach from the east of a large four-engine aircraft. The unexpected star of the show was about to make its dramatic appearance in the form of a Rolls-Royce RB211-524 powered South African Airways, Boeing 747-400. The giant, nearly 400-tonnes aircraft made a thundering, high-powered, low-level pass over the runway, then climbed out sharply to the right in order to commence its first circuit.

Vehicles, which were still queuing to access the Airport car parks, were rapidly abandoned as their occupants rushed to the nearest vantage points. Together with the thousands already admitted, they were about to witness possibly the most thrilling display of aerobatics ever performed by a large passenger aircraft. The Jumbo continued to circuit the airfield, each time with tighter and higher climb-out turns, then swooping down for its next runway pass. During the turns, the aircraft appeared, at times to the enthralled watchers, almost to be standing on its wing. No one other than the pilots could possibly have been on board and with anything moveable being securely bolted down.

On completing its last runway pass, the pilot further turned up the power settings on the RB211-524s in order to commence a final, stunning, high-powered spiral climb-out from the airfield. The Jumbo was almost out of sight before it gracefully resumed its normal flying attitude and then gently returned to its day job of safely transporting large numbers of passengers between Africa and various international destinations!

The display was a brilliant celebration of more than twenty-five years of service of the RB211-524 in the Jumbo, together with a tremendous demonstration of the aircraft's capabilities, facilitated by the awesome power of its Rolls-Royce engines. Those who had survived the 1971 disaster were particularly proud to have been present and, through their service with the company, to have made their contributions towards this amazing and memorable event.

Airbus Industrie

Airbus Industrie, which was the original Airbus consortium, was created in 1970, following the correct recognition across Europe (the conclusion also reached by the authors of the 1974 Hobart Paper 57) that multi-national collaborative projects were the only solution to address a fractured European market for passenger aircraft. This collaboration was necessary to reduce aircraft unit costs to match those of the American manufacturers. The consortium comprised some impressive European aero-industry participants, including France's Aerospatiale and Matra, together with Daimler Benz, Dornier and Messerschmitt Bolkow-Blohm of Germany and Spain's CASA. Hawker Siddeley was also a participant as the designer and supplier of the wings for Airbus aircraft.

The proposed launch of the wide-bodied Airbus A300 twin-engine aircraft had become feasible because of a recent critical change in ETOPS (Extended-range Twin-engine Operations Performance Standards), which had increased, from sixty to ninety minutes, the time allowed for twin-engine aircraft to operate from the nearest airport. This major change now enabled twin-engine, long-range aircraft to operate over the North Atlantic, the Bay of Bengal and the Indian Ocean. The A300 was capable of carrying up to two hundred and fifty passengers and presented a number of advantages to airlines, including lower fuel consumption, over their existing three and four-engine aircraft. The A300 first flew in October 1972 and it entered service with Air France in May 1974.

The British Government had initially supported the A300 venture, but this support was conditional upon the installation of Rolls-Royce engines in the aircraft. The decision by Airbus Industrie, to reject the RB207 and to specify the General Electric CF-6 instead had occasioned the British Government to withdraw from the project. However, Hawker Siddeley's enlightened Managing Director, Sir Arnold Hall, decided that his company should stay involved. Hawker Siddeley then invested considerable amounts in tooling to manufacture wings for

Airbus aircraft at Broughton in North Wales, where de Havilland had once produced Mosquitos and Comets.

Sir Arnold, born in 1915, was another brilliant Cambridge-educated engineer who had been Director of the Royal Aircraft Establishment at Farnborough during the Comet 1 disasters. He had then joined de Havilland as Technical Director, subsequently becoming the first Managing Director of Bristol Siddeley Limited and then Managing Director of the Hawker Siddeley Group. Sir Arnold served as Chairman of Hawker Siddeley until the Group's aviation activities were absorbed into British Aerospace in 1977.

Sales of the A300 progressively grew and over eight hundred aircraft, including the lower capacity A310 version, were produced until 2007, significantly outselling both the McDonnell Douglas DC-10/MD11 and the Lockheed Tristar. British Airways never purchased the A300, having belatedly committed itself to the Tristar.

After its formation in 1977, British Aerospace took a twenty percent shareholding in what had then become the Airbus consortium. Airbus work was now also being carried out at the former Bristol facility at Filton and was broadened to include the production of landing gear and fuel systems.

Airbus has subsequently become a formidable competitor to Boeing, with Rolls-Royce belatedly becoming an engine supplier to Airbus, commencing from the 1980s. In 2006, BAE Systems, British Aerospace's successor, concluded that it was not prepared to fund its share of the significant cash injections into Airbus, which were anticipated to be required to produce the giant A380 and also the new A350 which was being developed to compete with Boeing's 777 and its proposed 787 Dreamliner. BAE Systems then sold its shareholding to EADS, the majority owner of Airbus, for €2.75bn (£1.9bn).

BAE Systems had correctly assessed the A380 situation because production was terminated in 2021 after a total of two hundred and fifty-one A380s had been built, not reaching the break-even level of two hundred and seventy units. However, the A350 has been a very successful aircraft and is proving to be an effective competitor with and a successor to many of the Boeing 777s now in service.

The longer-established A330, developed from the A300, also remains a good worldwide seller. Amongst the world's A330 operators is the UK's Air Tanker consortium, which operates fourteen A330 Voyagers to provide the RAF's air refuelling and Troop/VIP transport capabilities. The A320 family of short and medium-range passenger aircraft, successfully launched in the late 1980s, has also continued its stunning success, particularly during the last two decades.

Laker Airways & Skytrain

After leaving BUA at the end of 1965, Freddie Laker wasted little time in resuming his entrepreneurial career. He funded aircraft deposits of £200,000 (£4.8m today) and with further backing from some new but, again undisclosed "wealthy friends", he established Laker Airways. The new airline initially operated two ex-BOAC Britannia 102s on ad hoc charter flights from Gatwick, together with contract work for other airlines. For Laker personally this was a difficult time. He was suffering the tragedy of his first son dying in an accident in the sports car which he had given to him for his seventeenth birthday. Also, the first of his four marriages was on the rocks.

A Laker One-Eleven, one of five of the type acquired by Freddie Laker in the late 60s/early 70s in order to fly package holiday customers to European hot spots.

Despite his personal difficulties, Laker resolutely carried on with the development of Laker Airways. Applying all of his twenty years of Industry knowledge, he showed no interest in operating scheduled domestic flights in favour of focusing Laker Airways' efforts on inclusive tour work. Laker maintained his previous view that new aircraft were essential for a successful airline operation and promptly placed an order with BAC for three One-Eleven 300 series aircraft, the first of which was delivered in February 1967.

Much of Laker Airways' passenger capacity for the 1967 summer season was contracted to Lord Brothers Travel. Later that year, Laker acquired Liverpool-based Arrowsmith Travel and, during the 1967 summer season, inclusive tour flights were carried out for both travel companies by Laker's Britannias and One-Elevens, flying from Gatwick, Liverpool and Manchester. Laker Airways could not initially afford a new all-jet fleet, and so, in January 1969, it replaced the Britannias with the two Boeing 707-138s which had previously been operated by the now-defunct British Eagle. The Boeings were fitted out in a 158-seat configuration, and Laker Airways then secured licences to operate Affinity Group transatlantic charters.

Two of the fleet of One-Elevens, purchased by Freddie Laker when Managing Director of British United, are parked at Gatwick in December 1972. An under-employed DC-10 is awaiting the start of Skytrain

Laker Airways also applied to the ATLB for permission to operate a no-reservation service from Gatwick to New York, initially using its 707s. The determination of this application was delayed, pending the setting up of the new CAA, but permission was eventually granted in October 1972, provided that the services were operated from Stansted rather than from Gatwick.

In January 1973, Laker Airways was designated as an Atlantic carrier. Preparatory work then commenced for the future introduction of Freddie Laker's brainchild, the Laker Airways' "Skytrain" service. With typical optimism, Freddie Laker had already placed an order for Douglas DC-10 Series 10 aircraft to operate this new innovative service. Two DC-10s arrived in November 1972 and, as a temporary measure awaiting the US State Department approvals, they were used for ad hoc charters and on the summer inclusive tour programme.

In 1973, the much abused "Affinity Group" rules were replaced by new simplified "Advanced Booking Charters". This change enabled Laker Airways to improve the utilisation of its DC-10 fleet, which soon numbered three aircraft, but operations were still at a low and uneconomic level. In July 1975, Peter Shore, Labour's Minister of Trade, delivered a potentially fatal blow to Skytrain by revoking Laker's licenses, stating that, because of the Oil Crisis and potential over-capacity, the Government would not allow British airlines to compete with British Airways on the Atlantic routes.

A period of legal challenge followed and Britain renounced Bermuda 1 in July 1976 on a number of grounds, including that it did not enable BCal, as the British "Second Force" airline, to operate the scheduled services from Gatwick to Houston and to

Atlanta, which routes had been awarded by the CAA some years earlier. The Government also reversed its previous position and now required Laker Airways to be included in the new Agreement to enable it to initiate the Skytrain service between London Stansted and New York.

The replacement Bermuda II Agreement was signed in July 1977. It enabled BCal to commence its licensed international services from Gatwick including also a service to Dallas/Fort Worth. The Agreement also provided that, where an American airline was competing with BCal, Gatwick was to be nominated as that airline's London gateway airport. The United Kingdom designated Laker Airways as a second UK flag carrier on the New York route and also on the Los Angeles and Miami routes. Peter Masefield, who had been knighted in 1972 and who was Deputy Chairman of BCal at the time, complained, in July 1976, that insufficient advantages had been achieved for British air transport under Bermuda II. He stated that the principle of fair and equal opportunity had been undermined.

Skytrain had now been cleared for take-off and, at a very late stage, the Regulators also agreed that the service could be operated from Gatwick. The first Skytrain service left Gatwick on 26 September 1977 with the three hundred and forty-five seat DC-10 carrying two hundred and seventy-two passengers to New York.

Gatwick 25 September 1977. After years of frustration, Freddie Laker, with a DC-10 behind him, is celebrating on the day before the first flight of Skytrain. Mirrorpix

Freddie Laker had succeeded, at last, in his ambition of bringing low-cost international travel to the general public. The one-way, no-frills Skytrain fare was £59 (£390 today). This price does not appear to be dramatically low when compared with the Economy Class fares applicable to flights in today's highly loaded super-efficient aircraft. However such fares were a major reduction from those being charged at the time by the traditional North Atlantic carriers. Services were being operated by those carriers at load factors of below fifty percent, meaning that half of their daily flights across the North Atlantic were effectively empty.

British Airways reacted immediately, offering a Skytrain-style service to New York, but with guaranteed seats and a meals and drinks service, at £149 return (£1,200 today). This fare was significantly below its pre-Skytrain fare levels. Laker now had more DC-10s on order and with ambitions to extend routes to other destinations, including Florida and the West Coast of the USA. After such a long and tedious build-up, surely the way ahead for Laker's Skytrain would now be clear and without further difficulties?

Concorde

Despite BOAC's Sir Matthew Slattery's early 1960s unsupportive comments concerning the need for and the prospects of a supersonic airliner, the British and French Governments had proceeded to sign a treaty on 29 November 1962 for the development of such an aircraft. The estimated cost was £70m (£1.8bn today), and a market was predicted for three hundred and fifty aircraft. Contracts were placed with BAC and with Sud Aviation for the production of six prototypes, with construction to commence in February 1965. Rolls-Royce at Bristol was working with SNECMA to develop the Olympus 593 engine to power the aircraft.

The mighty Olympus 593 developed initially, by Bristol Siddeley, for Concorde from the Avro Vulcan bomber engine. Rolls- Royce Museum. The Author.

In 1968, the Society of British Aircraft Constructors (now the ADS Trade Association) boasted that, in addition to the work being carried out at BAC at the Filton factory and at Rolls-Royce, there were over three hundred sub-contractors working on the project and that: "Virtually every major town in Britain has one or more factories contributing to Concorde."

This magnificent aircraft was rolled out at Toulouse in late 1967. An early potential Anglo-French conflict was avoided by the British accepting the French name, Concorde" on the basis that the "e" represented England, Excellence, Europe and Entente (Cordiale). Concorde first flew on 2 March 1969, but it was not until the end of 1975 that it received its French and British Certificates of Airworthiness. In March 1968, Anthony Wedgewood Benn, then Minister of Technology and also a Bristol MP, had reported to the House of Commons that the costs of the Anglo-French supersonic programme had risen substantially. By early 1976, the projected development costs were estimated to be a massive £1.5 – 2.1bn (£10 – 14bn today).

External factors had certainly been unhelpful, with the 1974 Oil Crisis dramatically increasing fuel prices. Another very material development had been the establishment of the US Environmental Protection Department (EPA) by President Richard Nixon in December 1970. An early EPA document concerning future aircraft noise standards would later be used by the Port Authority of New York and New Jersey to support legislation designed to impose revised noise limits, effectively banning Concorde flights into its airports.

In response, Gerald Kaufman, the newly appointed British Minister of Industry, claimed that, whilst Concorde noise was greater than that of the 747 Jumbo, it was:

"Broadly comparable with the Boeing 707 and DC-8 types, which make tens of thousands of flights a year in and out of New York and Washington".

Kaufman had conveniently overlooked the fact that these first generation jets were being phased out by the quieter second generation wide-bodies. Also, he did not have the Author's awareness of living conditions close to the John F Kennedy Airport.

In the summer of 1969, following a ten-week stay in the USA, courtesy of a Laker Airways Affinity Group charter, a cash-strapped Author had gratefully accepted the offer of last weekend accommodation at the Long Island family home of an American student acquaintance. A fine home, but conversation there was all but made impossible as first generation jets continually roared overhead on their final approaches to JFK. The noise was ear-shattering and the entire house appeared to tremble. Noise pollution was most definitely an issue.

A further setback arose from an international law determination that supersonic flight was suitable only for ocean-crossing routes, in order that sonic booms did not affect populated areas. The US, Indian and Malaysian governments promptly ruled out supersonic flights over their countries. The focus was then placed on obtaining consent for Concorde to fly on the prime routes across the North Atlantic to New York and Washington, DC. The crossing time would more than halve that of the current subsonic airliners. After much time and effort, the American Secretary of State was persuaded to grant limited permission for Concorde flights into New York and Washington Dulles Airport for a trial period of sixteen months.

Despite legal appeals, two Concordes of British Airways and Air France respectively touched down at Washington Dulles on 24 May 1976, after flights of just under four hours from London and Paris. The era of commercial flights across the North Atlantic by Concorde had at last commenced.

Concorde viewed from the A4, making its final approach on return to Heathrow from New York in the late 1980s. The Author

Sales efforts had initially resulted in non-binding reservations and options being registered for the purchase of around one hundred Concordes by the world's then top international carriers. This interest had rapidly evaporated as the problems and uncertainties had mounted, leaving just British Airways and Air France as the only two remaining potential Concorde operators, each with seven aircraft. However, Concorde was now in successful operation, in contrast to the rival Russian Tupolev Tu-144, which never flew passengers after a prototype disintegrated following a catastrophic structural failure when being demonstrated at the 1973 Paris Air Show.

Concorde in mid-career and now operating profitably. The aircraft here is ready for boarding at Heathrow Terminal 4 on 5 June 1989. The Author

Concorde memorabilia from the late1980s.

Concorde continued to fly for more than twenty-five years, so well into the Modern Era of British civil aviation, but we will complete its story in this section. British Airways established successful Concorde services on the routes to New York and Washington. Ticket prices were expensive, with passengers being mostly celebrities and top business executives for whom, apparently, the shortest travel time possible was their key priority.

The Author became an unexpected Concorde passenger on Monday, 5 June 1989, after receiving a previous late Friday evening call to make an urgent return trip to New York. The trip was necessary because he was the only available signatory of documentation required for a time-critical business sale transaction. The company's travel office was shut over the weekend and so the Author needed to book his ticket direct. After a phone call with a most courteous British Airways assistant, in the course of which the Author was relieved of £4,425 (nearly £14,000 today), a Concorde open return ticket to New York was duly acquired. Every source of available personal finance had to be accessed in order to raise the required funds.

Concorde departed from Heathrow Terminal 4 promptly at 11 am on the following Monday morning and swooped down three hours later over Long Island. As the Captain powered up the four thunderous Olympus 593s to enable the nose cone to be lowered in preparation for landing, the Author's thoughts flashed back to his noisy weekend on Long Island, some twenty years previously. It was difficult not to sympathise with the residents below, who were attempting to go about their daily business, but clearly struggling with the significant noise pollution overhead.

The Monday morning meeting at the Manhattan offices of a large New York law firm continued all day and through the night, with expensive American lawyers rushing self-importantly from meeting to meeting. The documentation was eventually finalised and signed as dawn broke. No time for sightseeing but just sufficient to scramble back to JFK to catch the return Concorde flight. A fellow passenger on board was the Author's former boss and the then Chairman of British Airways, Lord King of Wartnaby (see Part 5).

During the 1990s, British Airways and Air France had increasingly recognised that their low-utilised Concorde fleets could be hired out for occasional charter flights. On 25 July 2000, a chartered Air France Concorde, operating Flight AF4590, thundered down the runway at Paris Charles de Gaulle airport, carrying one hundred German tourists and a crew of nine bound for New York JFK. The fifty-four year old pilot, Christian Marty, was an Air France veteran with over 13,000 hours of flying experience. He was at the zenith of his career, having achieved the status of Captain within the prestigious Concorde fleet.

That fateful morning, Concorde was heavily loaded with fuel and, due to a maintenance error, a critical wheel spacer was missing from the left-hand main undercarriage. As a result, during the take-off run, Captain Marty was fighting to keep Concorde on the centre line, and the aircraft was struggling to gain speed. At 185 mph, Concorde struck debris on the runway, bursting the right front tyre of the left-hand undercarriage bogie and sending a large chunk of rubber flying into the underside of the left wing. The resulting shock wave ruptured the number five fuel tank and ignited fuel started to gush from the aircraft. It was too late to abort the take-off. The aircraft lifted off but engines one and two had lost power. The undercarriage could not be retracted, and Concorde was unable to climb or accelerate.

The aircraft stalled, crashing into an airport hotel, killing all on board, together with three people on the ground. This terrible event shocked the aviation industry and the world, after so many years of accident-free Concorde flying. Concorde services were suspended, but it was determined subsequently that it was still a fundamentally safe aircraft. Modifications were possible to secure its operational future, including improved electrical controls, Kevlar-lined fuel tanks and burst-proof tyres.

Concorde operations were resumed on 7 November 2001 but economic conditions were unfavourable. The wide-bodied aircraft now operating so successfully on long-haul routes were capable of achieving three times more passenger miles per gallon of fuel than Concorde, which guzzled two tonnes of expensive fuel, simply during start-up and then in the process of taxiing to the take-off runway. Also Concorde was, by this time, the only remaining aircraft type in the British Airways fleet which required a three person Flight Crew, including provision for a Flight Engineer.

The Paris disaster remained a negative consideration for many prospective passengers. Air France and British Airways then decided that the era of supersonic passenger flights was over, at least for the meantime. The last British Airways

Concorde flight took place on 26 November 2003, Air France having ceased flights in the previous May. Richard Branson attempted to secure a Concorde for Virgin Atlantic, but British Airways decommissioned the fleet to be dispersed to various locations to serve as static exhibits. Once described by Flight magazine as being "one of aerospace's most ambitious but commercially flawed projects", the Concorde saga had finally reached its end.

Part 5 - The Modern Era
(The 1980s to the current day)

The Modern Era already extends to well over forty years and here is a summary of some of the key events during that period:

1982 – Laker Airways collapses with massive debts. Sir Freddie Laker retreats to Grand Bahamas, vowing to sue those IATA airlines who he claims have conspired to put him out of business.

1984 - Richard Branson's Virgin Atlantic Airways rents a single 747 Jumbo from Boeing and commences transatlantic services from Gatwick to New York- Newark.

1987 – Lord King of Wartnaby crowns six years at the helm of the previously loss-making British Airways with its successful flotation. In the same year Government-owned Rolls-Royce also returns to the Stock Market, sixteen years following the 1971 Receivership.

1988 - The Government abandons its Second Force Private Sector airline policy. British Caledonian Airways is acquired by British Airways. BCal's founder, Sir Adam Thomson, is disgusted at the turn of events and declines an invitation to join the British Airways Board.

1989 – Pan Am Flight 103 is destroyed by an on-board terrorist bomb over Lockerbie. Two years later America's once trail blazing flag carrier files for insolvency.

1992 – Richard Branson sells Virgin Music and allocates the proceeds to fleet modernisation at Virgin Atlantic and to the pursuit of a libel action against British Airways and Lord King personally.

1993 – British Airways and Lord King agree to an out-of-court settlement with Richard Branson and with Virgin Atlantic. The European Commission, as part of its creation of the "Single European Market", follows the USA model and removes all barriers to a free aviation market in Europe.

1995 – Stelios Haji-Ioannou borrows £5m from his father and starts the low-cost airline EasyJet, with its first flights from Luton to Glasgow taking place in November of that year.

1997 – The Boeing Corporation merges with McDonnell Douglas creating, together with Airbus, an effective duopoly over the world manufacturing of medium to large-sized passenger aircraft. Diana, Princess of Wales, dies in a Paris car crash. The future King Charles 111 flies to Paris on a BAE 146 of the Queen's Flight in order to recover her body. A deeply shocked British Nation is plunged into mourning. Hong Kong, Britain's last remaining significant colony, is returned to China.

1999 – British Aerospace merges with Marconi Electronic Systems and adopts the name BAE Systems. Two years later, it closed its remaining civil aircraft business.

2001 – Worldwide civil aviation was temporarily halted by the 11 September "nine eleven" attacks when airliners hijacked by Al-Qaeda terrorists were flown into the Twin Towers of the World Trade Centre in New York and into the Pentagon in Washington DC. Nearly ten years later, on 2 May 2011, the Al-Qaeda leader, Osama bin Laden, is tracked down to his hide-out in north Pakistan, where he is assassinated by US Navy SEALs working in conjunction with the CIA.

2008 – The US/EU Open Skies Agreement comes into force, enabling every US and EU carrier to operate in every US and EU city. Heathrow Terminal 5 opens as the new home for British Airways.

2010 – IAG is formed by the merger of British Airways and the Spanish flag carrier, Iberia. IAG subsequently acquires the remaining operations of British Midland (BMI) from Lufthansa and then purchases both the low-cost Spanish airline, Vueling and Aer Lingus.

2017 – Monarch Airlines becomes insolvent after many years of struggle, reflecting the impact of the low-cost operators and the trend away from "package holidays". Two years later, the Thomas Cook Group filed for insolvency and its in-house airline ceased operations.

2020 – Aviation worldwide is brought to a grinding halt by the Covid-19 pandemic. Airline fleets are parked up throughout the world. Rolls-Royce teeters on the brink of insolvency in a situation reminiscent of the late 1970s crisis. Engine Flying Hours, now vital for revenue generation at aero-engine manufacturers, would take four years to return to their pre-Covid-19 levels.

2022 – Civil aviation now commences a steady recovery. Most four-engine jets are withdrawn from passenger service in favour of the latest twin-engine aircraft. Airbus and Boeing re-commence new aircraft deliveries, but orders have out-paced production and supply chain capacities.

2023 - The United Kingdom's National Air Traffic Control System is corrupted by the filing of a single faulty flight plan on 28 August. More than 700,000 passengers are disrupted. Jet2.com surpasses Germany's TUI to become the UK's largest air tour operator.

2024 – Emirates, Etihad and Qatar (collectively known as the ME-3), together with Turkish Airlines, with their state-of-the-art aircraft, have become the major force in worldwide civil aviation. Civil aviation's dependence on digital technology is further demonstrated by a defective software update at cyber security provider CrowdStrike on 19 July, which occasions the cancellation of five percent of flights worldwide.

2025 – Heathrow Airport is shut down for twenty four hours, on 21 March, following a fire at a nearby electricity sub-station. 1350 flights are cancelled (of which 700 were British Airways) affecting around 300,000 passengers. Airlines incur significant costs and a Government enquiry is launched to ascertain culpability and to ensure future improved resilience at UK airports.

Last farewells

By the commencement of the Modern Era, the number of post-war British Independent airlines then still operating was much reduced. All but one of these gallant survivors, together with some more recent start-ups, would now progressively be saying their last farewells to British civil aviation. Here is how their various operations came to an end:

British Caledonian had re-trenched during the Oil Crisis and had then resumed transatlantic services in October 1977, as had been permitted by Bermuda II. By now BCal had replaced its VC10s with Boeing 707-320C aircraft and had followed Laker Airways in ordering the DC-10 for its long-haul services. The first two DC-10s arrived in early 1977 and were used successfully, initially on BCal's West African and South American routes. For the financial year 1977/78, BCal reported a pre-tax profit of £12.2m, together with the introduction of the first employee profit-share scheme for a British airline.

BCal focussed its efforts on the provision of scheduled services from Gatwick, a strategy favoured by the Government which was seeking to improve the utilisation of the then loss-making Airport. To encourage the use of Gatwick, the Government introduced the London Air Traffic Distribution Rules, which obliged airlines without an international service from Heathrow prior to 1 April 1977 to operate any future services from Gatwick. The side-effect of the Rules was to advantage those airlines already established at Heathrow, such as British Airways and Pan Am.

*. A British Caledonian DC-10 is enjoying the snow at Glasgow Prestwick Airport in January 1987. British Airways continued to operate the type following its 1988 take-over of the airline.
Air Team Images.*

By the early 1980s, BCal was operating a fleet of eight DC-10s on its long-haul services and, in 1983, it became the first non-French airline to order the new narrow-body Airbus A320 with an order for seven aircraft with three options. This was a very important order for Airbus in its efforts to challenge the effective duopoly then enjoyed by Boeing and McDonnell Douglas for the worldwide supply of medium to large-sized civil aircraft.

However, a combination of external events in 1986 occasioned a disastrous year for BCal. Pre-tax profits of £21.4m in the previous year had reversed into a £19.3m pre-tax loss, reflecting revenue reduced by around £80m. There was a general reluctance to fly long-haul because of American bombings of Libya in retaliation to a 1986 terrorist attack on a Berlin nightclub when two Americans had been killed and seventy-nine injured. Further, the world's worst nuclear accident had taken place at Chernobyl, in the USSR, and there had been a devaluation of the Nigerian currency, seriously affecting returns from BCal's West African routes. Perversely, a decline in the oil price, normally good for airlines, had reduced the number of oil industry-related passengers who were flying on BCal's premium services.

In response to its growing difficulties, BCal had engaged unsuccessfully, in early 1986, with the International Leisure Group (ILG) concerning a possible merger with its rapidly growing airline, Air Europe. BCal also commenced an asset disposal program, selling two DC-10s and six hotels and executing the sale and lease-back of its fleet of short-haul One-Elevens. The imminent privatisation of British Airways was seen to be a threat to BCal's existence as the UK's second-largest international airline. British Airways already had over eighty percent of scheduled UK airline capacity and occupied a dominant position at Heathrow.

BCal proposed the transfer of a large number of routes from BA, together with their associated staff and infrastructure, in exchange for the payment of £200-250m. BCal stated that the only alternative was the move of its scheduled operations to Heathrow. The British Airways Chairman, Lord King of Wartnaby, described this proposal as a "smash and grab raid" and made it clear to the Government that he and the British Airways Board would resign if there was any enforced transfer of routes. The Government then requested the CAA to review the UK's airline competition policy.

Although the CAA's ensuing report broadly endorsed BCal's proposals, the Government's priority was the successful flotation of British Airways and it eventually agreed only to a limited transfer of routes, specifically services to Saudi Arabia. The Government also required BCal to return its South American routes, together with a number of unused licences. These changes took effect in mid-1985 and BCal then also commenced a Gatwick-New York service using second-hand 747 Jumbos.

British Airways had been successfully floated in early 1987, with the share offering being eleven times over-subscribed. It was now keen to acquire BCal's routes and thereby achieve the further economies of scale required to compete with the major American airlines. It also wished to ensure that BCal did not fall into the hands of a foreign competitor.

On 16 July 1987, Lord King and Sir Adam Thomson (who had been knighted in 1983) announced, at a joint press conference, that British Airways had agreed to buy BCal for a price of £237m. ILG made a counter-bid, which was rejected by BCal because it considered its Air Europe subsidiary to be essentially an incompatible charter airline with no significant synergies arising from a merger.

ILG successfully referred the British Airways offer to the Monopolies and Mergers Commission. The October 1987 Stock Market crash then intervened, as a result of which BCal held merger discussions with both British Midland and the Scandinavian airline SAS. British Airways adopted an aggressive strategy, employing a range of arguments, including one that, since SAS was fifty percent owned by the Danish, Norwegian and Swedish governments, a SAS take-over of BCal would effectively be the backdoor nationalisation of a significant player in Britain's air transport industry. Such a step would be contrary to the Conservative Government's policy of the internal privatisation of the civil aviation industry. British Airways also threatened that it would apply to the CAA for the revocation of BCal's licences. The grounds were that relevant Bilateral Air Services Agreements required that any airline claiming UK flag carrier status must be substantially owned and controlled by British nationals.

Following this barrage, BCal's shareholders considered themselves effectively compelled to agree to a revised British Airway's offer of £250m. BCal ceased to exist on 14 April 1988, and its assets were rapidly disposed of, with the exception of the DC-10s which British Airways elected to operate. Also, the newly-arriving Airbus A320s were gratefully received by British Airways for operation from Heathrow. The European Commission also acted to restrict the number of "slots" available at Gatwick to British Airways to enable other airlines to launch competitive services from the Airport.

Sir Adam Thomson, clearly disappointed with the Government's cavalier abandonment of its Second Force Private Sector airline strategy and upset at how his airline had been battered into submission, decided to leave the Industry. He later completed his business career with a number of directorships, including being Chairman of the Institute of Directors for three years from 1988. In retirement, he wrote the aptly named "High Risk: The Politics of the Air", a topic of which he had had considerable direct personal experience. Sir Adam then continued to enjoy his modest lifestyle and died in 2000, aged seventy-three.

British Air Ferries (formerly British United Air Ferries) **(BAF)** and **British Island Airways** (formerly British United Island Airways) **(BIA)**, as previously-mentioned, were excluded from the 1970 sale of British United Airways to Caledonian Airways and remained, for the meantime, in the ownership of B&C. However B&C soon off-loaded BAF, in October 1971, to TD "Mike" Keegan, another post-war aviation entrepreneur who, amongst many other projects, had negotiated the 1960 sale of the five ex-Overseas Aviation Argonauts to British Midland. Keegan also owned Stansted-based Transmeridian Air Cargo. In 1951, he had been one of the three founders (being the "K") of BKS, an airline which had been absorbed into BEA in 1967.

BAF was still operating a number of Carvairs, together with an ageing fleet of Bristol Freighters. Its last car ferry service from Southend was performed on 1 January 1977. BAF then acquired three Handley Page Dart Heralds in order to build up a network of scheduled services. BAF's informal but effective style of operations was illustrated, when the Author was told by a BAF pilot acquaintance that, in early 1979, he had been unexpectedly called in to meet Mike Keegan. The pilot was informed that he was to be appointed as the Herald fleet Training Captain. Keegan's rationale for this choice was that, since the pilot had previously flown turboprop Viscounts with Iraqi Airways, then: "You must know all about Darts"!

An early 1980s line up of time-expired British-built airliners at Southend Airport, now being dismantled by BAF for spares. The Author

BAF's scheduled operations were transferred to BIA at the commencement of 1979, with BAF continuing with charter and oil industry support work. BAF acquired eighteen ex-BEA Viscounts in 1980, but Keegan then progressively exited from the business and what remained was placed into administration in 1988. The company emerged a year later, adopting the name British World Airways, and it operated the Viscount's last passenger flight on 18 April 1996, forty-three years after the aircraft's first commercial service with BEA.

Amongst the invited passengers on that final flight was Sir Peter Masefield. After leaving the Bristol Aeroplane Company at the time of the creation of BAC, Masefield served as Chairman of the British Airports Authority between 1965 and 1970. In addition to being Deputy Chairman of BCal, he was also

President of the Royal Aeronautical Society. Masefield died aged ninety-one in February 2006. British World was badly affected by the post-nine-eleven Industry downturn and it ceased trading in December 2001.

BIA operated steadily through the 1970s and then merged with Air Anglia to form Air UK. In April 1982, Peter Villa, the former BIA Managing Director, acquired the charter operations of Air UK in order to create a new British Island Airways, which was subsequently floated on the Stock Exchange.

BIA operated a number of One-Elevens before they were replaced in the late 1980s by the more capacious and efficient MD-83's

The new BIA then boldly acquired four new twin-jet McDonnell Douglas MD-83s (a medium-sized airliner developed from the DC-9) to operate inclusive tour services alongside a small fleet of One-Elevens. The MD-83s had lower operating costs than the Boeing 737-200s of other charter airlines. After initial success, economics tightened towards the end of the 1980s and there were unsuccessful merger discussions with Air Europe. The First Gulf War and resulting recessionary conditions in the United Kingdom occasioned a nearly 40% drop in the package holiday market and the new BIA ceased operations on 9 February 1991. The last remnant of this brave venture is still visible to passengers when departing from the west runway at Gatwick. Near to the Airport perimeter and used for training purposes, is the derelict fuselage of one of the BIA MD-83s.

An Air UK Rolls-Royce Tay-powered Fokker 100 at Dusseldorf in May 1993. The aircraft did not sell in sufficient volumes to stave off Fokker's bankruptcy three years later. Air Team Images

By 1995, the Dutch airline, KLM, was holding a 45% shareholding in Air UK and it became its sole owner two years later. B&C's mostly unsuccessful post-war foray into British civil aviation had now reached its end. Air UK was re-named KLM UK but found life increasingly difficult as competition emerged from the low-cost carriers. Routes which served Amsterdam were transferred to KLM Cityhopper. Other routes were taken on by KLM's own low-cost carrier, Buzz, which airline was itself subsequently sold to Ryanair in 2003.

British Midland had continued successful scheduled operations during the 1970s, primarily with Heralds and Viscounts and had later selected the McDonnell Douglas DC-9 as their replacement. This decision disappointed some of those Derby-based Rolls-Royce Contracts Officers who had been convinced that their close neighbour would be compelled to revert to the One-Eleven with its two Rolls-Royce Spey engines. Perhaps it was their previous occasional unhelpfulness, when leasing Dart engines to support British Midland's Viscount operations, which had not assisted good relationships.

In 1978, Minster Assets decided to sell its shareholding in the airline. Michael Bishop, with the assistance of a Californian entrepreneur, raised £2.5m to complete a management buy-out. Bishop complained that: "I had to borrow the money from an American citizen". He stated that he had not been able to secure finance closer to home because: "Most venture capitalists want a return of forty percent to make up for their other failures, and they want an exit strategy".

East Midlands Airport, May 1980. A British Midland DC-9 with two Viscounts in the distance. Immediately behind is a Boeing 737-200 of Orion Airways, which became part of Britannia Airways in early 1989. Air Team Images

British Midland's annual passenger numbers in 1980 exceeded one million. A further breakthrough was achieved in October 1982 when the CAA granted the airline licences to fly, in competition with British Airways, on the key domestic routes from Heathrow to Glasgow, Edinburgh and subsequently to Belfast. These services, operated initially by DC-9s, included a full in-flight service, which compared favourably with the no-frills shuttle services then offered by British Airways. British Airways rapidly lost market share and commissioned a Report from expensive consultants for advice on how to address the situation. Their somewhat predictable recommendation was to

270

introduce an upgraded "Super Shuttle", which included a full breakfast, hot drinks and a free bar service!

The abolition of the aforementioned London Air Traffic Distribution Rules, in 1991, was beneficial to British Midland by enabling it to increase its take-off and landing slots at Heathrow. The Diamond Club frequent-flyer programme also successfully drove further passenger growth on its domestic and European scheduled routes.

A serious setback was suffered on 8 January 1989 when one of British Midland's newly-delivered, latest-specification Boeing 737-400s crashed into the M1 embankment when attempting to make an emergency landing at East Midlands Airport. The aircraft had diverted from its route from Heathrow to Belfast when a fan blade had broken in the left engine. The pilots had mistakenly shut down the right engine and the left engine had failed completely on the final approach. Of the people on board, forty-seven died and seventy-four sustained serious injuries. Michael Bishop was complimented on the manner in which this disaster was handled in the media. His increasing prominence in British civil aviation was recognised by the award of a knighthood two years later in 1991.

British Midland continued to grow, with annual passenger numbers in 2005 exceeding ten million. The airline re-branded as BMI and switched its airliner supplier to Airbus, accumulating a fleet of A320s, together with three wide-body A330s, used for long-haul services. Sir Michael Bishop and BMI then received a welcome boost in 2008 when the European Commission decided to grant legal recognition to "Secondary Slot Trading" by European airlines. This practice comprised the buying and selling of take-off and landing slots at congested airports. The effect was to raise significantly the value of BMI's Heathrow slots holding. Commencing in 1999, Lufthansa progressively increased its shareholding in BMI and it completed its take-over of the airline in June 2009, after purchasing Sir Michael's remaining shareholding. Sir Michael, who is now Baron Glendonbrook, retired from aviation with a substantial fortune.

BMI was now significantly loss-making, and the situation was so bad that, in March 2011, it decided to exit its previously much-cherished Heathrow to Glasgow route, claiming losses of £1m per month as a result of increased airport charges. On 22 December 2011, Lufthansa announced that it had agreed to sell BMI to IAG for £172.5m. Virgin Atlantic sought to make a counter-bid claiming that the acquisition would increase British Airway's share of slots at Heathrow to over fifty percent. The sale to IAG was completed on 30 March 2012, conditional upon the transfer of fourteen slots at Heathrow, which were later passed to Virgin Atlantic.

In 2002, BMI had set up a low-cost operation, Bmibaby, using the early series Boeing 737 aircraft, which had been displaced from its scheduled operations as Airbus aircraft were introduced. British Airways had no interest in continuing this operation. A buyer could not be found and so Bmibaby was closed down in September 2012. BMI's separate regional subsidiary was sold by IAG in June 2012 and continued to operate as Flybmi until it filed for administration on 16 February 2019. British Midland was now another Independent British airline which had been hoovered up by British Airways and its last remnants had also made their final farewells.

Dan-Air became renowned during the 1950s and 1960s for its ability to source and make productive use of second-hand aircraft. It had operated the ex-BEA Ambassadors successfully, and since 1966, Dan-Air had commenced purchasing most of the available de Havilland Comet airframes, forty-nine in total. It had then been able to maintain an operational fleet of over twenty Comets for both scheduled and inclusive tour services. Some eight million passengers were transported on Dan-Air's Comets during their service period with the airline until 1980.

A Dan-Air Boeing 727-200 at Luton in February 1981 with a VC10 of RAF Transport Command parked behind. Air Team Images

The Short 360, pictured at Munich in September 1990, was a successful British-built small airliner, operating here on regional services for Air Europe. Air Team Images

However, the airline's mix 'n match fleet strategy was not favoured by all at a time when its main competitor, Britannia Airways the in-house airline of Thomson Travel, was building up a fleet of fuel-efficient Boeing 737-200s. Matters came to a head in the mid-1970s. Two senior Dan-Air executives, Errol Cossey and Martin O'Reagan, failed to persuade Fred Newman, Dan-Air's Managing Director and majority shareholder, to implement actions progressively to replace its existing fleet with new jet aircraft. Newman had elected, instead, to follow the previous practice, in this case by purchasing second-hand trijet Boeing 727s from Japan Airlines.

Cossey and O'Reagan left Dan-Air in the late 1970s and approached Harry Goodman, the Chief Executive of ILG, who then accepted their proposal to set up an in-house airline to service ILG's Intasun Travel business. Intasun was second only to Thomson Travel in the United Kingdom market and currently chartered most of its inclusive tour flights from Dan-Air. However, the combination of higher oil prices following the Oil Crisis, compounded by the thirsty Dan-Air Comets, was driving up charter rates. On 25 April 1980, Dan-Air suffered a serious blow when one of its 727s crashed during a flight from Manchester. The Fight Crew had wrongly executed a holding pattern and the aircraft had hit high ground, near North Tenerife airport. All one hundred and forty-six people on board were killed.

Air Europe commenced operations in May 1979, initially with three new, one hundred and thirty seater Boeing 737-200s. During the following ten years, Air Europe expanded and, by 1989, it was operating thirty-one modern jet aircraft and was carrying nearly six million passengers a year, primarily from Gatwick, where it had become the largest resident operator.

By the early 1990s, both Dan-Air and Air Europe were facing mounting difficulties. Having failed to agree to a merger with BCal, Air Europe sought to increase pressure on Dan-Air by stating that Intasun would not be chartering any of its aircraft for the 1990 summer season, also that it was proposing to cancel its maintenance contract with Dan-Air Engineering at Lasham.

Dan-Air responded to the threats from Air Europe by appointing "Company Doctor" David James to carry out an assessment of the business. A re-financing was arranged, which enabled Dan-Air to continue operations in the meantime.

Meanwhile, Air Europe, undercapitalised and utilising an unsound financial structure with most of its assets being leased, ceased operations in March 1991 after its parent company, ILG, entered administration. There were four thousand job losses at Air Europe and many of its passengers were stranded at airports across Europe. In a similar fashion to BIA, other factors in the collapse included the downturn in leisure travel due to recessionary conditions in the UK and the effects of the First Gulf War.

Dan-Air lost £35m in 1991. David James prepared a five-year business plan, but sufficient funds could not be raised for its implementation. Following unsuccessful talks with Virgin Atlantic, a rescue was arranged with British Airways in early 1992, which acquired Dan-Air for a nominal £1, together with taking on £50m of its financial commitments. British Airways also acquired the twelve Boeing 737s that Dan-Air had belatedly purchased, including a number of short-haul routes operated from Gatwick. Around five hundred of Dan-Air's two thousand five hundred employees joined British Airways. Dan-Air had become yet another British civil aviation memory.

Invicta International Airlines Hugh Kennard sold his first airline, Air Kruise, to British Air Services in 1953, where he served as Joint Managing Director until the BUA take-over in the early 1960s. He then established Air Ferry in July 1962, later selling the airline to BUA. Invicta was registered in late 1964 by Hugh Kennard with the backing of the Minster Asset Group. Operating from Manston, Invicta carried out mostly inclusive tour flights with a small fleet of Vikings and DC-4s, supplemented in 1968 with some ex-British Eagle Viscounts.

Minster Assets later merged Invicta with its other airline, British Midland, but Kennard considered that the arrangements were not working satisfactorily.

In early 1969, Kennard purchased back the DC-4s and relaunched Invicta, also acquiring a number of ex-Trans-Canada Airlines Vanguards for inclusive tour and charter work. By early January 1973, Invicta needed to be rescued, and the European Ferries Group took a seventy-six percent stake. This ownership started badly when, on 10 April 1973, an Invicta Vanguard flying from Bristol to Basle crashed in the Jura mountain area. One hundred and eight of the one hundred and forty-five people on board died; a later Court of Enquiry determined that heavy snow storms were largely responsible.

Pisa April 1975. Package holidays in the 1970s. Invicta International's sole Boeing 720 collects passengers returning from a Thomson Holidays cruise. The Author

Invicta nevertheless remained in business and added a sole Boeing 720 to its fleet for the 1975 summer season, flying mostly Thomson Travel Group charters. By the commencement of 1976, Kennard was once again the airline's sole owner, leading the business for a further five years before selling out and returning to his first love, with a classic car restoration business in Canterbury. Invicta did not survive long without Kennard's direction and became insolvent in April 1982. Kennard died in 1995 without achieving the same fame as other contemporary aviation entrepreneurs, but leaving behind a significant contribution to British military and civil aviation after a colourful life.

Flybe was originally known as **Jersey European Airways**, which had been launched in 1979. Within a few years, the airline was acquired by the steel industrialist Jack Walker, who funded significant expansion. Walker sold his steel business to British Steel in 1989 and he then also became the owner of Blackburn Rovers Football Club, which achieved considerable success in the mid-1990s. The airline adopted the name, British European, in 2000 which had been vacant since the 1974 creation of British Airways. However, despite having the use of a name with a great history, the times were rapidly changing due to the increasing online purchasing of airline tickets. Accordingly, a further name change to Flybe was made two years later.

Pictured at Southampton, in June 2006, Flybe was once the world's largest operator of the de Havilland Canada Dash-8. Air Team Images

Pictured at Glasgow in April 2024, the Brazilian Embraer ERJ190 is an ideal aircraft for operations from airports with short runways, such as London City Airport. Air Team Images.

Flybe was an early operator of BAE 146s and later of Brazilian-produced Embraer ERJ regional jetliners, together with its fleet of Dash-8s. In March 2007, Flybe acquired BA Connect from British Airways, which included BA's regional services, excluding those operated from London City Airport. Flybe was actually paid to take on this operation and BA also acquired a fifteen percent shareholding in Flybe in order to provide further funding.

Flybe floated on the London Stock Exchange in December 2010 and, in May 2013, it raised further finance by selling its Gatwick slots to EasyJet for £20m. In February 2019, Flybe was sold to Connect Airways, a consortium including Virgin Atlantic and Stobart Aviation and, by early 2020, the airline was operating more than a third of all United Kingdom domestic flights. However, the Covid-19 pandemic then struck and Flybe filed for administration on 5 March 2020. The airline was briefly resurrected in 2022 but entered into administration for the final time on 28 January 2023.

Pictured at Glasgow in November 1988 is a Loganair Britten-Norman N-2 Islander. Over 750 Islanders remain in current use and it is the only complete British-built airliner still in production. Air Team Images

Pictured at Southampton in June 2024, the ATR 72 is a very successful aircraft operated by many regional airlines, such as Loganair. Air Team Images

Loganair is a Scottish airline, originating in the early 1960s, and which has subsequently been through a multitude of different ownerships and associations. It took over a number of former Flybe routes and has since leased some additional slots at Heathrow from British Airways. Together with routes previously operated by the defunct Flybmi, Loganair now serves over forty destinations in the United Kingdom, the Republic of Ireland and continental Europe.

Loganair's fleet comprises over thirty aircraft, primarily Embraer Regional jets and also including the ATR 42/72 twin turboprop Regional airliners. The ATRs are produced at Toulouse by the very successful joint venture between Airbus and the Italian Leonardo S.p.A.

Laker Airways had steadily increased its business during the late 1970s. In addition to its New York route, Skytrain had extended its services to Los Angeles, Miami and Tampa. Laker introduced fully bookable "Super Economy" Skytrain fares, which were approximately half those of its competitors and significantly lower than their Super APEX fares. Laker now had a fleet of eleven DC-10s together with three Airbus A300s, Laker Airways being the first British operator of this aircraft.

A Laker Airways Airbus A300 operating a Skytrain service from Gatwick in February 1982, in the final hours before the banks and suppliers closed down the airline. Air Team Images.

Freddie Laker, who had now become one of British Prime Minister Margaret Thatcher's "Golden Boys", alongside the inventor Sir Clive Sinclair, was knighted in 1978 for his services to the aviation industry. However, the established transatlantic airlines were continuing their retaliatory actions towards Skytrain with Pan Am dropping its lowest Economy Class rates by up to two thirds. British Airways, TWA and other competitors on the routes followed suit. Also, passengers were increasingly choosing to fly on the four-engine Jumbos offered by these competitors in preference to Laker's DC-10 trijets. The DC-10's high-profile accidents were still in the minds of the Public.

At a late stage, Laker introduced a Skytrain premium "Regency" service but the various adverse trends were having a cumulative effect. Skytrain's passenger loads and cash flow had fallen by half between October 1981 and February 1982. Laker Airways was thinly capitalised, with Laker personally owning ninety percent of the small amount of share capital through an off-shore holding company and with his first wife holding the remaining equity. The airline had very few owned assets, and it had incurred huge aircraft and aero-engine leasing obligations.

It could be argued that, had there been significant external shareholders with their equity investments being at serious risk, then warning bells might have been sounded earlier. Some kind of shareholder-led rescue operation might have then been possible. As it was, Laker Airways was now at the mercy of the banks, together with McDonnell Douglas and the engine supplier, General Electric, as its major creditors.

It has been alleged that some of the other European operators of the DC-10 indicated they would cease to do future business with the two American companies if they acted to rescue Laker Airways. In any event, in the early morning of 2 February 1982, Laker Airways collapsed with debts of £270m (£1.2bn today). Laker's previous "Golden Rule" of cash always changing hands in his direction had been sadly left far behind. The collapse was one of Britain's major corporate failures. A shattered and exhausted Freddie Laker retreated to his Grand Bahamas water-front house, resolving to take legal action against those who he considered had conspired to put his company out of business by predatory pricing.

Legal actions were commenced against the IATA airlines which Laker believed were involved in the conspiracy. A $50m out-of-court settlement was subsequently agreed and British

Airways agreed to contribute a further $35m. In his typical style, Sir Freddie insisted on all airline staff being paid outstanding wages. Also, he demanded that all transatlantic passengers who had travelled, post the Laker Airways collapse, should be issued with a £30 voucher as an admission of the alleged conspiracy to hold fares artificially low and to inflate them once Laker Airways had ceased business. In a separate out-of-court settlement, British Airways paid Sir Freddie £8m personally.

Laker then bought a property in the exclusive Palm Beach city of Boca Raton, splitting his time between there and his retained Grand Bahamas residence. However, the irrepressible Freddie Laker was not yet finished with aviation. He befriended the businessman Tiny Rowland, the CEO of Lonrho, a large conglomerate with a variety of business interests, including the ownership of the Princess Hotels, Casino and Country Club in Freeport. Laker became a consultant to the company and to the Grand Bahamas Tourist Promotion Board. He also established Princess Vacations International based in Miami in order to bring tourists to the Grand Bahamas on flight-inclusive gambling packages.

Sir Freddie then decided that he could cut out the involvement of third-party airlines in these packages by re-entering the airline business, which he did with Laker Airways (Bahamas). This new venture commenced in May 1992, with Boeing 727 services from Freeport to various destinations on the American East Coast. In 1996, a more ambitious and separate Laker venture, Laker Airways Inc., which was reminiscent of Skytrain, leased two DC-10s to link Fort Lauderdale with Gatwick and later Orlando with Manchester and Prestwick. However, this operation ceased two years later. Laker Airways (Bahamas) continued until flights ended in 2005, by which time relations with Lonrho had deteriorated and the company was then wound up.

On 9 February 2006, following complications during surgery to implant a pacemaker, Freddie Laker died in a small Florida hospital close to Boca Raton. He was aged eighty-three and his fourth wife, former air hostess Jacqueline Harvey, who he had married in 1985, was by his bedside together with his surviving children. The "not very bright" boy from Kent, who had left school at sixteen, had travelled a very long way in life. His much-delayed final retirement had sadly been very short and the last phases of Laker's career had not been the success for which his many admirers might have wished. However, beyond doubt, was that Laker had lived and died as an undisputed hero of British civil aviation.

A Rolls-Royce RB211-535 powered Boeing 757, at Kos in October 1988, one of a fleet of eleven operated by Monarch Airlines. This aircraft served with the airline for more than twenty years. The Author

Monarch Airlines had replaced its faithful Britannias, as planned, during the mid-1970s with Boeing 720s. By 1981 it was operating a mixed fleet of eleven aircraft, including also Boeing 737-200s and One-Elevens. In 1981 Monarch placed an order for a small fleet of the RB211-535 powered Boeing 757 200 series.

By the early 2000s, the airline's historic dependence on and involvement in the package holiday market, through Cosmos Holidays, had come under increasing pressure from the low-cost operators. Holidaymakers were booking cheap flights and were then making their own accommodation arrangements.

Monarch attempted to adopt a low-cost model and to change from being a predominantly charter airline to a "no frills" scheduled leisure carrier, but, in the financial year 2009, it made a loss of £32.3m. The controlling Mantegazza family injected £45m in order to keep Cosmos and Monarch afloat but a further large loss was made in 2012. At this point, the family decided to exit the business and Monarch downsized its operations, carrying 5.7 million passengers in 2015, a nearly twenty percent reduction on the previous year. In the following years, Monarch struggled on, with increasing difficulties, but it was becoming clear that it had lost any USP (unique selling point).

The renewal of Monarch's essential ATOL licence was due on 30 September 2017. The CAA granted a twenty-four-hour extension, but insufficient supporting finance was available. In the early morning of 2 October 2017, all Monarch flights ceased, and the airline entered administration. 110,000 passengers were stranded abroad and 300,000 future bookings were cancelled. Thirty-eight aircraft carried out what was the United Kingdom's largest-ever post-war repatriation. Monarch had failed because of a confused and variable strategy and it had become a clear casualty of the movement towards low-cost air travel.

Thomas Cook Airlines was created following a consolidation of the United Kingdom Inclusive Tours market in March 2007, when My Travel Group (previously known as Airtours) and Thomas Cook AG had agreed to merge to form Thomas Cook Group plc. Both companies operated in-house airlines, and they were combined, under the name Thomas Cook Airways, to carry just over eight million passengers in 2009 on a fleet of Airbus A321s and A330s.

In the following decade, the Thomas Cook Group experienced increasing financial difficulties. From midnight on 23 September 2019, airports in the United Kingdom began to impound Thomas Cook Airlines' aircraft, upon their arrival, for default in payment of airport charges. By 2 am, the CAA had announced that the Thomas Cook Group had entered administration. The CAA then initiated an even larger repatriation exercise than that required for the Monarch failure in order to return the 150,000 stranded British holidaymakers, using forty aircraft. Thomas Cook would later re-emerge as a travel company but not as an airline operator. Easyjet acquired the Thomas Cook Airlines slots at Gatwick and Bristol, with Jet2.com doing likewise at Birmingham, Stansted and Manchester.

XL Airways was originally launched as Sabre Airways in late 1994 and subsequently grew to become an airline servicing fifty destinations with a fleet of around thirty-five, mostly Boeing aircraft. It ceased operations in September 2008 when its parent company filed for administration, citing volatile fuel prices, the economic downturn and the inability to obtain further funding. 90,000 passengers were stranded, more than two-thirds of whom had booked package holidays and so were covered by the ATOL scheme. The remaining passengers had to arrange their own return flights but were mostly offered spare seats on the aircraft chartered by the CAA. This failure was a further reminder to travellers of the risks of booking flights and accommodation separately, to which the ATOL scheme did not apply, instead of choosing ATOL-protected package holidays.

Britannia Airways was to be the only survivor of the 1960s British Independent airlines. With financial backing from the Canadian Thomson organisation, Britannia had grown steadily and strongly, much assisted by Thomson's acquisition of the Lunn Poly travel agency in 1972, which it used to build up a large United Kingdom travel business. Meanwhile, Britannia resisted pressures from the United Kingdom civil aircraft manufacturing industry, in the late 1960s, to replace its Britannias with the One-Eleven. Instead, it chose the Boeing 737-200 and, by 1984, it was operating twenty-nine of this type, having become Britain's largest independent charter airline.

Pictured at Corfu in May 2004, Britannia Airways operated a fleet of Boeing 767s, commencing from the mid-1980s, for more than twenty years. Air Team Images

By the early 1990s, Britannia was also flying the higher-capacity narrow-body Boeing 757s and it then expanded into long-haul routes, becoming the first European airline to operate the new wide-body Boeing 767. In 2000, the Thomson Travel

Group, including Britannia Airways, now known as Thomson Airways, was acquired by Germany's TUI Group.

In March 2007, the merger of TUI AG's travel division with First Choice Holidays was announced. First Choice had developed its own in-house airline, Air 2000, which operated about forty aircraft, predominantly Boeings. These aircraft were incorporated into Thomson Airways. The combined airline is now known as TUI Airways and it carries large numbers of United Kingdom package holiday passengers annually on an all-Boeing fleet of sixty-seven aircraft, including the latest 737s and Dreamliners.

Terrorism

On 12 October 1967, there was news that a BEA Comet 4B had disintegrated above the Turkish coast, killing the fifty-nine passengers and seven crew members on board. Subsequent investigations proved that an explosive device had been detonated within the aircraft's cabin, causing a rupture of the controls. The Comet had broken up during the ensuing dive.

This early incident was followed, on 9 September 1970, by the seizure of a BOAC VC10, flying from Bahrain to Beirut, by hijackers from the Popular Front for the Liberation of Palestine. The VC10 was forced to land at "Dawson's Field" twenty miles north of Amman, Jordan. Here, it joined two other hijacked aircraft and all three were blown up on the ground. The passengers and crew hostages were subsequently released.

On 3 March 1974, another British Airways VC10 was hijacked, this time on the way from Beirut to London and the aircraft was forced to divert to Schiphol, Amsterdam. All ninety-two passengers and ten crew were released, but the hijackers then doused the aircraft with fuel and it was totally destroyed in the ensuing fire. These incidents were of major concern to British civil aviation and to world-wide aviation generally, which had also been affected by other acts of terrorism. However the aviation community and international law were as yet unclear on how to deal with this new menace.

The risks of terrorism were further highlighted in June 1985 when Sikh extremists bombed an Air India aircraft flying from Montreal to London with the loss of all three hundred and twenty-nine people on board.

On 21 December 1988, a very high-profile and horrifying incident occurred when a Boeing 747 Jumbo operating Pan Am flight 103 and bound for New York was destroyed by a bomb when flying over the Scottish town of Lockerbie. All two hundred and fifty-nine people on board were killed, together with eleven people on the ground. It was not until 2003 that the late Libyan leader, Muammar Gadaffi, belatedly accepted responsibility for this atrocity. A Libyan Intelligence Officer was put forward for trial and was jailed for life. Libya paid some compensation to the victims' families.

Early on the morning of the 11 September 2001, initial media reports stated that a light aircraft had collided with one of the Twin Towers of the World Trade Centre in New York. The situation was rapidly clarified with the horrifying news of a series of terrorist attacks involving four passenger aircraft which had been hijacked over mainland America. The attacks had been instructed by Osama bin Laden, the leader of the Al-Qaeda terrorist group, and had been implemented by members of the group, some of whom had been attending flight training courses in the USA.

Two Boeing 767s operated by American Airlines and United Airlines, respectively, had been hijacked en route from Boston to Los Angeles. The American Airlines aircraft had been deliberately flown into the North Tower at 08.46, followed, at 09.03, by the United Airlines aircraft hitting the South Tower. Both buildings were set on fire and subsequently collapsed, causing extensive dust clouds, which were later responsible for a number of related deaths. At 09.37, an American Airlines Boeing 757 en route from Washington Dulles airport to Los Angeles was flown into the west wall of the Pentagon in Washington, housing the US Defence Department. The fourth aircraft, a United Airlines Boeing 757, en route from New York, Newark airport to San Francisco, had been forced to change course towards Washington, possibly to attack either the United States Capitol or the White House. By this stage, the courageous passengers had been alerted to the other attacks. They confronted the hijackers but, at 10.03, the 757 was flown into a field near Shanksville, Pennsylvania, sadly causing the deaths of all on board. There was no damage to property or death to persons on the ground.

Two thousand, nine hundred and seventy-seven people were killed in the "nine eleven" attacks. Civil aviation in the USA was suspended for ten days, and there were longer-term implications for worldwide aviation. A particular change was the requirement for all airliners, with seating for in excess of sixty passengers, to be equipped with armoured and locked Flight Deck doors. In 2002, the European Commission introduced

Common Rules and Basic Standards on aviation security, including today's requirements for the screening of passengers, cabin and hold baggage, cargo, mail and airport supplies. Also strict procedures were introduced for airport security, checks and searches and for staff recruitment and training. Similar rules and standards have been adopted worldwide.

A further aviation tragedy, which was associated with but not directly terrorism-related, occurred on 24 March 2015 concerning a Germanwings Airbus A320 flying from Barcelona to Dusseldorf. The aircraft had reached its cruise altitude of 38,000 ft when the co-pilot, Andreas Lubitz, took advantage of the Captain's temporary absence from the Flight Deck to lock the cabin door and initiate a controlled descent to below 6,000 ft. In accordance with the prevention of terrorism requirements, the door was armoured and, despite valiant attempts with an axe, the Captain was unable to regain access. Lubitz then deliberately flew the aircraft into the Alps and all one hundred and forty-four people on board were killed.

It was later ascertained that Lubitz had hidden the results of a psychological assessment declaring him unfit for work because of suicidal tendencies. The EU Aviation Safety Agency subsequently ruled for two authorised personnel to be present on Flight Decks at all times, a rule which was later dropped. Lufthansa, the owner of Germanwings, paid €75,000 compensation to the family of every victim.

Whilst today's passengers often find airport security procedures to be irksome and time-consuming, there is a general appreciation that there are very good reasons for them. As previously mentioned, most airports now discourage visitors other than passengers or persons delivering or collecting them to or from flights, and plane spotters are generally no longer able to access airport terraces. These security procedures appear to be working well, and there have been no recent significant events of terrorism involving aircraft. However, everyone involved in aviation continues to remain vigilant.

The final British-built airliners

The Aircraft and Shipbuilding Industries Act 1977 created British Aerospace, a new statutory corporation. The Act effected the nationalisation of BAC, Hawker Siddeley Aviation, Hawker Siddeley Dynamics and Scottish Aviation. British Aerospace was later re-registered as a public limited company, and it was privatised by the Conservative Government in the mid-1980s.

It could be argued that British civil aircraft manufacturing would have been better served had such nationalisation taken place much earlier. The 1960s One-Eleven and the Trident second generation jet projects had been partially overlapping and competing. A single company might have combined these projects and then might possibly have developed a viable successor aircraft, such as the Three-Eleven, which had been mooted towards the end of the 1960s but which had never materialised.

In 1973, Government launch aid was still available for some civil projects and Hawker Siddeley had been successful in obtaining 50% support for its 146 Regional jet, a short-haul airliner seating up to one hundred passengers. Launch aid conditions, however, now involved the Government receiving a share of revenues from each aircraft sold. Sales of two hundred and fifty 146s would be required in order to reach break-even.

The 146 was a high-wing, cantilever monoplane with a T-tail and powered by four American-produced Avco Lycoming turbofan engines mounted on pylons beneath the wings. British Aerospace decided to continue with the 146 project and designated the new aircraft as the "Whisperjet", reflecting the aircraft's quietness. The 146 also had excellent short take-off and landing capabilities, making it suitable for operation from city-location airports.

British Aerospace's 1986 airliner offering. Two 146s flying with a 125 corporate jet and a Jetstream (centre), originally a Handley Page project. Air Team Images.

Dan-Air, contrary to its usual policy of buying only second-hand aircraft, was to be the first 146 operator, in May 1983, and the RAF introduced the aircraft into service in 1986 as a VIP transport. British Airways also used the type to launch the first jet services from London City Airport in 1987. The aircraft also sold well in both the USA and Australia. In 1993, it was superseded by the upgraded Avro RJ series and this successful project ended in 2001 with a total of three hundred and ninety-four aircraft having been produced.

Pictured at the Isle of Man in January 1997, this British Airways ATP is displaying one of the more than thirty Utopia tail fin designs. These designs occasioned strong objections from Lady Thatcher and from many others. Air Team Images.

The Iranian Revolution in 1979 resulted in the overthrow of the Pahlavi dynasty and replaced the Shah of Iran, Mohammed Reza Pahlavi, with the religious cleric Ayatollah Ruhollah

Khomeini. A drop in Iranian oil production followed, which occasioned another oil crisis in 1979, with oil prices doubling over the following twelve months. In response and also with mounting environmental concerns about aircraft noise, British Aerospace believed that there was a market for a short-range, low-noise, fuel -efficient turboprop airliner. Its ATP (Advanced TurboProp), with a passenger capacity of sixty to seventy, was a larger development of the successful Avro 748, but with the Rolls-Royce Darts replaced by more powerful Pratt & Whitney PW 126 turboprops, driving six-bladed propellers.

The ATP first flew in August 1986 with British Aerospace targeting to sell three hundred and fifty aircraft. However, Fokker had already moved to upgrade its Friendship, in the form of the Fokker 50, which first flew at the end of 1985. There was also strong competition from the already successful similar concept Canadian Bombardier Dash 8 and from the ATR 42/72 Regional turboprops which, today, are still rolling off the final assembly line at Toulouse, with around 2,000 units now having been sold.

British Aerospace achieved some initial ATP sales, with British Midland commencing operations with the type in 1988 and with British Airways also later operating the aircraft. British Aerospace strongly targeted the US market, but Air Wisconsin was the only purchaser. In mid-1997, British Aerospace announced the termination of ATP production after the sale of only sixty-five aircraft.

Sir Anthony Milward's 1971 retirement prediction that British Airways would not buy another British-produced aircraft was not entirely correct. The airline had, in fact, purchased both the

146 and the ATP but these were to be the last British-built airliners available for the airline to acquire. In 1992, British Aerospace wrote down the value of its civil aircraft manufacturing business by £1bn. Following the 1999, British Aerospace merger with Marconi Electronic Systems, the name BAE Systems was adopted which more correctly reflected its ongoing and current role as a technology-led defence, aerospace and security solutions provider.

In November 2001, BAE Systems announced the closure of the remainder of its civil aircraft manufacturing business with 1,669 job losses and a further £400m write-off. The Financial Times commented that a line had finally been drawn under a business that had once threatened the viability of the entire British Aerospace Group.

Scottish Aviation and, later British Aerospace, had made a success of Handley Page's Jetstream, but production had ceased in 1993 after sales of three hundred and eighty-six aircraft. The HS 125 business jet had also been a very successful aircraft, but British Aerospace had sold its Business Jets Division to the American Raytheon in 1993. Short Brothers Limited discontinued production of its successful 330/360 commuter aircraft in 1991.

As a result, the only civil passenger aircraft still being produced in the United Kingdom today is the Britten-Norman BN-2 Islander, a utility aircraft and small regional airliner. The Islander remains in very small-scale production, now back at its original home in the Isle of Wight and with 1,280 aircraft having been built since 1965.

Lord King and the Aviation Virgin

The American "Lend Lease" programme during the Second World War had been critical in achieving the Allies' ultimate success. At the same time, it had also assisted a number of enterprising individuals to make their careers and, in some cases, war-time fortunes.

John Leonard King, born in Brentford, Middlesex, in August 1917, was the second of four children of his postman father and seamstress mother. King left school at the age of twelve for factory work, later becoming a car salesman. The young entrepreneur then set up a taxi business and later acquired a Ford Cars sub-agency, which he named Whitehouse Motors. At the outset of the Second World War and recognising that there would, therefore, be minimal scope and fuel available for wartime private motoring, King diversified into general engineering. Using sophisticated American machine tools which were supplied under the Lend-Lease programme, King's company took on extensive and profitable war-time Ministry of Defence manufacturing contracts, primarily for aircraft parts.

Having duly prospered during the Second World War, King then moved to Canada but soon returned to England with the bold project of building a factory on wasteland at Ferrybridge, Yorkshire. The resulting Pollard Ball and Roller Bearing Company grew into the third-largest ball-bearing business in the United Kingdom, also spanning several continents.

In 1968, the Government's IRC enforced a merger of the three largest British Bearing manufacturers, as a result of which Pollard was sold for £10m (£200m today). King received £3m (£60m) personally and then became Chairman of Dennis

Specialist Vehicles and, in 1972, also of the engineering giant Babcock International plc. He was knighted in the 1979 New Year's Honours and he soon came to the attention of the newly-elected British Prime Minister, Margaret Thatcher, who described King as being her "favourite businessman". In early 1981, King was appointed as Chairman of British Airways, which was then substantially loss-making. King's brief was to restore profitability and then to privatise the airline.

Sir Richard Branson is a controversial figure for many, but beyond question are his entrepreneurship and his business achievements. From a middle-class background, Branson had attended the prestigious, independent Stowe School, where it had been discovered that he was severely dyslexic and with no head for numbers. Leaving Stowe in 1967, with a single A Level in Ancient History, Branson recalls, in his autobiography, that the Headmaster's parting words were, "I predict that you will either go to prison or become a millionaire". Both of these outcomes would later come to pass!

Branson's entrepreneurial instincts were already evident at school through the "Student" magazine, which he had first conceived and published before he left Stowe. This enterprise led to a mail-order business for pop records under the name "Virgin". This name was adopted because Branson and his staff freely admitted that they were complete virgins in business. By late 1983, Virgin Music had grown to be the leading independent record label with a turnover of nearly £100m (£400m today). Along the way, Branson had spent a night in Dover prison for breaching the Customs and Excise Act 1952 by operating a scheme to avoid purchase tax on records. Virgin was subsequently heavily fined for these breaches.

Branson's mother had worked as a Stewardess on Avro Lancastrians in the immediate post-war years but, other than his ballooning exploits, there seems to be nothing else in Branson's background to indicate any particular interest in aviation. In early February 1984, an American lawyer, Randolph Fields, approached Branson with a proposal to establish an airline, initially to service the Gatwick to New York (Newark) route. The route was now available following the collapse of Laker's Skytrain. The idea fired Branson's imagination, and he arranged to meet with Freddie Laker, who provided some initial guidance on the venture, including the suggestion that Virgin should offer an Upper (Business) Class in addition to Economy Class. Laker freely admitted that Skytrain's total reliance on Economy Class passengers had been a mistake and that the subsequent introduction of Skytrain's Regency Class was too late.

Fields had already recruited some ex-Laker senior staff, who were now based in a rented Gatwick warehouse and were in the process of obtaining the necessary CAA approvals. There was also the task of procuring suitable aircraft and trained staff for the proposed new airline. Following intensive negotiations with Boeing, the newly-named Virgin Atlantic Airways took a one-year lease of a Boeing 747 Jumbo and experienced Flight Crew were recruited via Industry contacts. The Cabin Crew were kitted out in the highly distinctive red Virgin uniforms.

On 18 June 1984, the rented Jumbo, the Maiden Voyager, arrived from Seattle for final CAA licence testing. The following day, with Branson and a hundred Virgin staff on board, the Jumbo took off from Gatwick. Shortly after take-off, there was a loud bang and the Jumbo lurched to the left, with flames and smoke pouring from an engine. The aircraft had suffered a bird strike. The damaged engine, which was uninsured pending the grant of the CAA licence, subsequently needed to be written off!

29 February 1984. Richard Branson celebrates the projected launch of Virgin Atlantic Airways later that year. Lord King was no admirer of the entrepreneur, who he termed as being "the grinning pullover".
Mirrorpix

This freak accident almost ended the venture in its infancy, but the Virgin Group had just enough resources to enable a replacement engine to be acquired and fitted. The CAA licence was duly obtained, and Virgin Atlantic now commenced operations on the Gatwick to Newark route. The new airline was on its way to eventually replacing British Caledonian as the "Second Force" British international airline.

Virgin Atlantic's early marketing strategy was excellent and included two ploys, also suggested by Sir Freddie, in order to attract Upper-Class passengers. One was the issue of a free Economy Class ticket for every Upper-Class ticket sold, which appealed particularly to middle-ranking executives wishing to take partners along. The second incentive was a complimentary limousine service to and from the airport. Given the opportunity, executives would increasingly fly Virgin Atlantic Upper-Class, which was perceived as being equivalent in quality to most other airlines' First Class. The in-flight entertainment was good and flying on Virgin was perceived as being a more fun experience than on the established carriers.

Back at British Airways, in the early 1980s, the new Chairman had not taken long in introducing some radical changes, and, within two years, King had replaced half of the British Airways Board with his own appointees. In 1983, Colin Marshall was hired as the airline's new Chief Executive. Marshall had left school at sixteen for a career at sea, initially as a trainee Purser, but he had then lived and worked in the United States, rising to the position of President and Chief Executive of the Avis car rental company. 15,000 employees were removed from the British

Airways payroll and actions were initiated to upgrade the aircraft fleet.

Late 1980s at newly-opened Heathrow Terminal 4. BA Tristars painted in the red tail Negus livery, together with Boeing 747s and 757s displaying the replacement Landor scheme. British Airways Museum.

Mid-1980s. Sir Colin Marshall (left) and Lord King celebrating their bargain-basement purchase of the Concorde fleet. British Airways Museum.

The now Lord King of Wartnaby (having been granted a life peerage in July 1983) then drove through a deal with the Government to ensure that the loss-making Concorde operations became profitable. Lord Heseltine, the responsible minister, claimed he was effectively forced to sell the Concorde fleet to British Airways for £16.5m (£70m today) plus the first years' operating profits. Heseltine, acknowledging that the planes were sold for "next to nothing", commented:

"If you have both hands tied behind your back and no cards and a very skilful negotiator on the other side of the table – I defy you to do any better".

British Airways' ageing fleets of the faithful One-Elevens and Tridents were progressively being replaced by the predicted non-British produced aircraft in the form of growing numbers of Boeing 737s. The Boeing 747 Jumbo fleet was increased and updated by the introduction of the Rolls-Royce RB211-524 powered 400 series aircraft.

British Airways had already announced its intention, at the end of 1979, to purchase the twin-engine Boeing 757, previously the 7X7 concept project. The 757s would replace its Trident 3 aircraft, and they were to be powered by the latest technology, fuel-efficient Rolls-Royce RB211-535 engines. The first of an initial order for nineteen 757s entered service in early 1983. This important order enabled Rolls-Royce to establish a much stronger marketing position in the USA. A major breakthrough in America was achieved in May 1988 with an American Airlines order for fifty RB211-535 powered 757s, with an option for the supply of a further fifty aircraft.

In preparation for the planned Stock market flotation, the legal status of British Airways was changed, in 1984, from that of a Crown Corporation to a public limited company. Lord King had demonstrated that he was a determined and, at times, ruthless businessman who was solely focused on achieving the tasks set for him by Margaret Thatcher's Government.

His Lordship would form a very quick view of people. He would fix them with his piercing blue eyes and then evaluate them against two criteria. First, if they had the required skills and so were potentially of value and second, whether or not he liked them. He also had a human side and, by all accounts, King was dedicated to his first wife, Lorna, who he had met during his early days as a car salesman. He was deeply affected by her death from cancer in 1969. Very much a supporter of the British Establishment, King had then married Isabel Cynthia Monckton, the daughter of the 8th Viscount Galway.

Lord King's weekly schedule would commence early on Monday morning by being chauffeur-driven to London in his British Racing Green Bentley Mulsanne Turbo from his country estate, Friars Well, Wartnaby, Leicestershire. During weekends at Wartnaby, he played the part of the country squire, supporting local activities, including being Master of Foxhounds for the Belvoir and Badsworth hunts. During the week, King resided at an Eaton Square, Belgravia flat, mostly conducting daily business matters from Babcock International's King Street offices. Parked in the King Street office basement, alongside the Bentley, was King's privately owned, navy blue, London taxi, which was used for local commuting.

One individual who had passed both of Lord King's evaluation criteria was the rotund and amiable Edward G "Ted" Lunn, the Babcock International plc Company Secretary and the Author's then immediate boss. Ted had started his career post-war as a wages clerk at BEA, and he had aspired to his current position through ability, study and hard work. In addition to his Company Secretarial skills and being also an elegant Minutes writer, Ted was a brilliant mimic with a seemingly inexhaustible fund of jokes. He would often use his comedic talents to diffuse tensions as Babcock navigated the difficult transition from heavy engineering into becoming the widely-based defence and engineering services group that it is today.

Lord King's second-floor office overlooked St James's Square. The Secretariat's offices were at the other end of the floor with less attractive views across King Street towards the Head Office of Hawker Siddeley, which was situated almost directly opposite. At least once a month, the aroma of Havana cigars would be scented as, much to the annoyance of the building's rudimentary air conditioning system, Lord King strode along the floor from his office, heading towards the Secretariat. He was always immaculately tailored, usually in three-piece suits, with his matching tie and pocket handkerchief, together with his trademark gold pocket watch and chain.

These visits were ostensibly for business updates but from the ensuing peals of laughter usually emerging from Ted's office, we concluded that the main purpose was probably for his Lordship to hear Ted's latest jokes. He would then most likely store them away for his future use in entertaining audiences on suitable occasions.

Dirty Tricks

By the end of 1988, Lord King had enjoyed a stellar seven years at British Airways, including its successful 1987 flotation and the subsequent absorption of BCal. The remaining blot on the horizon was Virgin Atlantic Airways, led by its flamboyant founder, Richard Branson. Branson and Lord King were certainly not to have any "meeting of minds" as had been the case in 1904 for the previous "unlikely pair". Both men were successful entrepreneurs, but the similarities ended there.

Lord King, from his modest beginnings and with limited formal education, had risen to great heights in his much cherished British Establishment. Branson, from his upper middle class and public school background, had then adopted what Lord King probably considered to be a Bohemian lifestyle with his casual dress and manner. The scene was set for a major future confrontation, but worldwide civil aviation was first disrupted by the First Gulf War.

Large numbers of foreign workers had fled from Iraq to Jordan. Branson knew the American-born Queen Noor of Jordan through his earlier ballooning activities and he volunteered a Virgin Atlantic aircraft to fly quantities of blankets and medical supplies to Amman. This relief mission was successfully accomplished and, on 23 October 1990, another Virgin Atlantic humanitarian flight took place, this time to Baghdad to rescue Western hostages held by Saddam Hussain. On board the flight was the former British Prime Minister, Sir Edward Heath, who successfully requested the release of the hostages. Lord King was indignant at this apparent upstaging of

British Airways, complaining that the Virgin Atlantic flights were little more than a publicity stunt for the airline.

In mid-January 1991, an intense six-week bombing campaign commenced to end the First Gulf War and to evict Iraq from Kuwait. On 24 February 1991, the land operation "Desert Storm" commenced with coalition forces, led by US General "Storming Norman" Schwartzkopf, Jr, entering Kuwait and expelling the Iraqi troops. The First Gulf War had ended, but it had occasioned a large escalation in aviation fuel prices, with passengers being disinclined to fly, particularly to distant international destinations, unless it was absolutely necessary.

In common with a number of other UK Independent airlines, Virgin Atlantic found itself increasingly financially stretched in the early 1990s. Virgin Atlantic's fleet, now comprising four Jumbos, was still operating primarily from Gatwick to New York, but with other US destinations having been added. Branson then had a stroke of good fortune. The Government agreed to transfer to Virgin Atlantic the four flights which had been previously operated by BCal each week to Tokyo.

The CAA then followed up with two key decisions, in 1991, which were favourable to Virgin Atlantic. The first was to enable Virgin to initiate a daily Tokyo frequency by transferring to Virgin Atlantic the two unused landing slots held by British Airways at Narita Airport, Tokyo. Lord King complained that this transfer was a "confiscation of his company's property". The second CAA key decision was its recommendation to the Department of Transport for the abolition of the previously-mentioned London Air Traffic Distribution Rules which were confining Virgin Atlantic to operations from Gatwick only. The

Secretary of State then confirmed that Virgin Atlantic could commence operations from Heathrow in July 1991.

Lord King raged that these two changes were hugely disadvantageous to British Airways. At the airline's AGM later that month he retaliated by announcing that the company would be ceasing its donations to the Conservative Party.

Relations, at the operating level, between British Airways and Virgin Atlantic had also become uneasy, since the 1988 BCal acquisition. Previously, BCal had serviced Virgin Atlantic's 747s but, post-merger, the responsibility had passed to British Airways and the hourly labour rates had been significantly increased. There had also been a dispute concerning a Virgin Atlantic aircraft which had been rendered out of service due to defective work by British Airways. British Airways had then refused to loan one of its spare aircraft as a replacement. As a result, Virgin Atlantic had incurred significant additional leasing costs and so it had transferred its servicing work to Aer Lingus in Ireland.

In October 1991 Sir Freddie Laker, still quietly mentoring Branson from behind the scenes, called from Florida to remind him that it was ten years since the commencement of the anti-competitive activities which had put Skytrain out of business. To prevent the same happening to Virgin Atlantic, Laker advised Branson to "cry foul", before it was too late.

On 11 December 1991, Branson wrote to the British Airways directors, including the now Sir Colin Marshall, who had been knighted following the airline's successful flotation. Attached to his letter was an eight-page annex setting out details of six types of "dirty tricks" that Virgin Atlantic alleged were being engaged in by British Airways. These "tricks" included numerous reported incidents of so-called "switch selling", where British Airways employees would call Virgin passengers at home and try to persuade them to switch their flights from Virgin Atlantic to British Airways. British Airways staff had also been seen intercepting Virgin passengers at New York's John F Kennedy airport and then offering them "incentives" to switch.

No substantive reply was received to Branson's letter other than in the form of an article published in early 1992 by British Airways' Public Relations Director, David Burnside, in "BA News". The article was titled "Branson Dirty Tricks Claim Unfounded". It was also alleged around this time that Burnside had instructed Brian Basham, a leading Public Relations Consultant, to prepare a report for British Airways on the Virgin Group and also on Richard Branson personally. Branson was advised that the contents of the "BA News" article were effectively calling him a liar and so were tantamount to libel.

Separately, Lord King had sent a standard response letter to viewers who had contacted him about a recent Thames TV programme entitled, "Violating Virgin?" which programme had been broadcast on 27 February 1992. This letter stated that: "The allegations by Mr Richard Branson that British Airways is engaged in a "dirty tricks" campaign against Virgin Atlantic are totally without foundation".

Branson was advised that this statement comprised a repeat of the libel in the "BA News" article. To Sir Freddie's delight, Branson now embarked upon the dangerous course of suing both British Airways and Lord King personally. In March 1992, after much agonising, Branson decided to sell Virgin Music to

Thorn EMI for £510m, with Thorn also taking on Virgin's debts, capped at £50m. Branson now had the funds both to keep Virgin Atlantic afloat and to pursue vigorously, his libel cases against British Airways and Lord King.

Branson also seized the opportunity presented by a weak market for new passenger aircraft to negotiate the purchase of ten new 747-400s from Boeing to serve the airline's rapidly developing route network. An order was also placed for eighteen new aircraft from Airbus. In each case the manufacturers agreed to include, in the package, the installation of individual seat-back videos also in Economy Class, thereby enabling Virgin Atlantic further to enhance its in-flight entertainment.

Pictured at New York JFK in August 2019, the Rolls-Royce Trent 500 powered Airbus A340, along with the airline's fleet of Boeing 747-400s, were the mainstays of the Virgin Atlantic fleet for nearly twenty years. Both aircraft were replaced, post-Covid-19. Air Team Images

In bringing the libel proceedings, which commenced on 20 March 1992, Branson was able to hire the formidable George Carman QC, the most feared and celebrated barrister of the time. Despite Carman's appointment, neither British Airways nor Lord King withdrew from the proceedings, nor did they seek to apologise. On the contrary, they brought counter-claims for damages for alleged libels in the contents of Branson's 11 December 1991 letter. However, as the litigation progressed, disillusioned British Airways staff presented further evidence, most of which was adverse to the airline's defence. On 7 December 1992, British Airways paid £495,000 into the Court and dropped its counter-claims in an attempt to settle the litigation.

Branson was advised that a settlement was the safest course, and payments of £500,000 to Branson personally and of £110,000 to Virgin Atlantic were then negotiated by the lawyers, together with an amount of £3m as a contribution towards the claimant's legal fees. In finalising the settlement, on 11 January 1993, Counsel for British Airways and Lord King stated that:

"British Airways and Lord King accept that the allegations against Richard Branson and Virgin Atlantic are wholly untrue."

Counsel then proceeded to offer unreserved apologies; however, no members of British Airway's senior management or its directors attended Court. Counsel's statement further commented that the incidents involving British Airways employees were "regrettable" but emphasised that the airline's directors were not party to any concerted campaign against Richard Branson and Virgin Atlantic. Branson now considered that he had been sufficiently vindicated in the matter. Apart from the lawyers, he was the only "winner" from the "Dirty Tricks" affair, and he was now able to focus his attention on the future development and expansion of Virgin Atlantic.

Branson was knighted in 2000 for "services to entrepreneurship", but the way ahead for Virgin Atlantic would not be easy. When interviewed by The Sunday Mirror in January 2000, Sir Richard acknowledged these ongoing difficulties with the words:

"If you want to be a millionaire, start with a billion dollars and start a new airline."

The Virgin Group today remains the majority owner of Virgin Atlantic Airways with America's Delta Airways being the minority shareholder. Branson had considered this tie-up with Delta to be essential following losses of £233m incurred between 2010 and 2013. The airline was then badly hit by the 2020 Covid-19 pandemic and, on 4 August 2020, Virgin Atlantic filed for Chapter 15 bankruptcy protection in New York. Large numbers of staff were laid off, and it was necessary to retire the faithful Boeing 747-400s, which had given such sterling service since the mid-1990s.

A £1.2bn refinancing package was arranged and, today, Virgin Atlantic Airways continues in business, returning to small profitability in the financial year to 31 December 2024. The airline is in the process of increasing its mixed fleet of Airbus and Boeing aircraft to comprise forty five aircraft with an average age of less than seven years. Just under six million passengers are carried annually, currently to thirty-two destinations, with an average load factor of around eighty percent.

Lord King was severely wounded by the "Dirty Tricks" affair, and he left British Airways later in 1993, ahead of his scheduled retirement date and with the somewhat meaningless title of "Chairman Emeritus". He died at his Leicestershire estate in 2005 at age eighty-seven. The much-admired Sir Colin Marshall, later Lord Marshall of Knightsbridge, succeeded Lord King as Chairman and served the airline in that role until 2004.

Low-cost air travel

Freddie Laker is still identified by many as being the founder of low-cost air travel. This assessment may well be correct in the case of long-haul destinations, but for short and medium-haul routes, the accolade must go to Texas-based South West Airlines. After several years of legal fights, South West eventually commenced operations in June 1971. Its successful launch was mostly attributable to local attorney Herb Kelleher, who became Chairman of the Board in 1978 and who subsequently led South West as CEO and President until 2001. South West's plan was to connect the "Texas Triangle" (a region of Texas containing the State's five largest cities and including the majority of its population – twenty-one million people in 2020) with a low-cost air service, eliminating unnecessary activities and using a single aircraft type, the Boeing 737.

South West's simple proposition was to "Keep planes flying because this is where they make money and keep fares low enough to keep people travelling". South West flew "point to point" often to secondary airports, thereby achieving further operating cost reductions. It later also operated the "Hub-and-Spoke" system used by other operators but on a "rolling hub" basis so that traffic was equalised throughout the day, so far as practicable, again to achieve cost efficiencies. In 1979, US President Jimmy Carter sponsored the Airline Deregulation Act, which enabled South West to commence services to adjacent States, then expanding into both East and Southeast USA during the 1990s.

South West Airlines has been consistently named by Fortune magazine as one of the most admired companies in America. Today, it is America's third-largest airline, serving airports in forty-two states and also numerous destinations in Central America. It operates a fleet of over eight hundred Boeing 737 aircraft and employs nearly 75.000 people.

Representatives of both Easyjet and Ryanair visited South West at the early stages of their development. Also, it is known that Richard Branson shared a number of long lunches with Herb Kelleher, who remained Chairman of South West until May 2008. Kelleher was then given the title of Chairman Emeritus but perhaps more meaningfully so than Lord King's 1993 appointment at British Airways. Despite his hard smoking and drinking lifestyle, Kelleher lived until age eighty-nine, dying in January 2019.

Stelios Haji-Ioannou was born on 14 February 1967 into a wealthy Greek-Cypriot ship-owning family. After graduating from the London School of Economics in 1987, he then obtained a Master's Degree in Shipping, Trade and Finance from the Bayes Business School of the University of London. In 1992, Stelios borrowed £30m from his father, which he used to set up Stelmar Shipping. The venture was successful, and shares in the oil tanker operator were later floated on the New York Stock Exchange.

In the course of establishing Stelmar, Stelios spent a considerable time shuttling by air between London and Athens. He also met Richard Branson a number of times during this period. These experiences resolved Stelios to start an airline. He introduced the subject during dinner with his father at the family's summer house, south of Athens, in the early summer of 1995. His shrewd plan was, initially, to set up a marketing organisation in order to build an airline brand and then to commence operations with two wet-leased ACMI (Aircraft, Crew, Maintenance and Insurance) Boeing 737s from GB Airways, a British Airways franchisee. Stelios's father listened, approved and wrote a cheque for the required £5m start-up funds, but stipulating that the airline should be based elsewhere than in Greece.

Stelios had decided on the name Easyjet simply because the word "easy" kept coming to mind. He then chose the United Kingdom as a base because it was the largest possible European market in an English-speaking country. Near to capacity Heathrow was rapidly eliminated and so was Gatwick, which was also becoming full. The choice was then between Stansted and Luton. The latter was chosen on price considerations. Stelios moved from his elegant Curzon Street, Mayfair offices to a considerably less salubrious small pre-fabricated, albeit initially rent-free, building at Luton airport, which became the headquarters of the United Kingdom's newest airline.

A small design agency created the brand, and for a corporate colour, Stelios chose the shade of orange known as Pantone 021C, which has been used ever since. A visit was made to the offices of the CAA and the required Operating Licenses were subsequently obtained. Stelios then proceeded to sign the lease for the two 737s. Another early decision was to cut out travel agents as middlemen and to sell flights direct to customers initially by phone and now, of course, over the Internet, with all payments to be made by credit card.

The new airline was also grappling with other start-up issues, including the choice of Cabin Crew uniforms. A solution unexpectedly emerged when the office manager noticed someone wearing a Benetton orange polo shirt. An urgent visit to the nearest Benetton shop verified that the said polo shirt and a matching sweatshirt almost exactly matched the Easyjet Pantone. The shop's entire stock of polo and sweatshirts was duly acquired, and Benetton was then contacted in Italy to provide one hundred and fifty orange polo shirts and one hundred and fifty orange sweatshirts.

Benetton Head Office was unable to supply in the required timescale so a second purchasing mission was despatched from Luton, heading for every Benetton shop in the surrounding area. By the end of the day, all of their available stocks of orange polo and sweatshirts had been acquired. With the Cabin Crews now suitably kitted out and with everything else in place, the first Easyjet flights commenced between Luton and Glasgow in mid-November 1995.

Ryanair had been established some ten years earlier, in Waterford, Southern Ireland, as a small conventional regional airline. In 1988, a brilliant and determined, twenty-seven year old Trinity College, Dublin educated, financial expert joined the small carrier as its Chief Financial Officer. Michael O'Leary immediately commenced the process of converting Ryanair to a low-cost airline, and he made visits to South West Airlines in order to study its operations in detail. O'Leary was appointed Chief Executive Officer of Ryanair in 1994 and today still leads the total operation as Group CEO of Ryanair.

Well known for speaking his mind, O'Leary responded to Easyjet's 1995 entry into the market by stating that it was not, in fact, the first low-cost airline to fly from London to Scotland. He claimed that Ryanair had already started flying from London to Glasgow in the previous month. However, the relevant Ryanair flights were actually between Stansted and Prestwick, Ayr, an airport which is some thirty-one miles south of Glasgow. Ryanair has subsequently continued its policy of using secondary airports across Europe, albeit with very low fares partially facilitated by low and, in some cases, no airport handling charges. This style of operation remains a continuing fundamental difference between the two competing airlines.

In 1992, the European Commission deregulated the airline industry in Europe, giving carriers from one EU country the right to operate services between other EU states. This change provided a major opportunity for low-cost airlines to expand their operations widely into Europe. The subsequent phenomenal growth of both Easyjet and Ryanair is well documented and is fully evident to today's air travellers from simple observations at most British airports.

Ryanair floated on the Dublin and American NASDAC Stock Exchanges in 1997 and O'Leary then applied part of the proceeds to place a $2bn order for forty-five new Boeing 737-800 series aircraft. In late 2001, undaunted by the possible longer-term adverse effects on worldwide aviation of the nine-eleven terrorist attacks on America, O'Leary then ordered a further one hundred and fifty-five 737s from Boeing at heavily discounted prices. Ryanair's growth was further facilitated by its 2003 acquisition of the ailing Buzz from KLM and as routes potential in Europe grew with more member states progressively joining the European Union.

In subsequent years, O'Leary has repeatedly courted both Airbus and Boeing for the supply of new replacement aircraft. In November 2018, Ryanair ordered one hundred and thirty-five of the latest Boeing 737 MAX aircraft. At the height of the Covid-19 pandemic, in November 2020, O'Leary is said to have re-negotiated this order, seizing the opportunity to purchase an additional seventy-five aircraft at substantial discounts from the list price. Ryanair has remained loyal to Boeing but clearly has always extracted the best possible terms.

Ryanair currently operates nearly six hundred 737s, comprising the largest airline fleet in Europe and the sixth largest in the world. O'Leary is the owner of just under four percent of Ryanair and he has become one of Ireland's wealthiest business people.

Back at Easyjet, Stelios obtained an Aircraft Operator's Certificate, in 1996, in order to enable the airline to commence the flying of its own aircraft. In March 1998, Easyjet acquired the Swiss airline TEA, Basel and established a significant operating base which it still maintains today at Geneva airport. In November 2000, Easyjet floated on the London Stock Exchange and purchased the low-cost carrier Go Fly, in May 1998, thereby doubling its fleet of Boeing 737s. The airline was now well established, and Stelios began to cease his day-to-day involvement whilst maintaining a substantial family shareholding.

In 2002, Easyjet decided to commence the replacement of its Boeings by announcing an order for one hundred and twenty Airbus A319s, with an option for another one hundred and twenty aircraft. Its Airbus fleet was expanded further in 2007 with the purchase of GB Airways, which added nine A320s and six A321s. Easyjet later negotiated with Airbus for the exchange of some of its A319s for higher capacity A320s.

Today, Easyjet operates around three hundred and forty A320 family aircraft and it has outstanding orders with Airbus to continue the replacement of its entire fleet with the latest fuel-efficient A320neos (new engine option). Easyjet is currently the second largest budget airline in Europe behind Ryanair. More recently, it has aggressively entered the package holiday market through Easyjet Holidays, aiming for twenty-five percent or more of its passengers to travel on these package holidays in future years.

An Airbus A320, one of Easyjet's fleet of over three hundred A320 family aircraft, at Milan in December 2024. A Boeing 737 MAX of Ryanair is landing behind. Air Team Images

In 2010, Stelios, who was knighted in 2007 for services to entrepreneurship, left the Easyjet Board and then gave an interview to the Management Today magazine in which he complained that, despite the huge expansion of its services, Easyjet had "created no shareholder value for ten years". He was concerned about the airline's expansion policies, particularly the extent of its new aircraft purchases.

In April 2020, during the early stages of the Covid-19 epidemic, Stelios publicly called for the removal of the Easyjet CEO and Chairman following their failure to terminate an outstanding order with Airbus for one hundred and seven A320 series aircraft.

The world's demand for new A320s has continued to increase, and production is now completely booked through

2030. The cancellation of Easyjet's order would have lost the airline its place in the A320 queue – so cancellation would almost certainly have been the wrong course of action.

In early 1980, a small airline, Express Air Services, was providing daily freight flights to the Channel Islands using a sole Handley Page Herald aircraft; one of the few remaining examples of this 1960s aircraft still flying. After securing Post Office contracts in the early 1980s, the airline adopted the name Channel Express and progressively increased its fleet of Heralds. In the following two decades, the airline continued to expand from its base at Bournemouth International Airport, with a mixed fleet rising to over thirty aircraft.

In 2002, Channel Express established the low-cost brand Jet2.com and the new leisure airline operated its first service to Amsterdam from its base at Leeds Bradford Airport on 12 February 2003. The airline carried just over 600,000 passengers, in 2003, and further European sun and city destinations were added with flights being provided also from Manchester Airport from the following year. Interest in package holidays had declined from the late 1980s as holidaymakers had taken advantage of the cheap flights now available and the ability to book accommodation direct. Jet2.com had seen and had now taken the opportunity of re-inventing a variety of good value and secure package holiday options.

Pictured at Mallorca in October 2024 is a Boeing 737-8, one of a number supplied new to Jet2.com. Air Team Images

By 2013, Jet2.com had grown very significantly, carrying 5.5 million passengers during the course of that year. Expansion continued so that, in 2016, 6.7 million passengers were carried. This was the year that the airline had received its first new Boeing 737-8, from an order for thirty of these aircraft which had been placed during 2015. Jet2.com had previously only operated second-hand aircraft. Three years later, Jet2.com carried over 14 million passengers using a fleet of over one hundred owned and leased aircraft. In September 2021, Jet2.com placed an order for thirty-six Airbus A321neos with an option for a further twenty-four aircraft. Two years later, the airline celebrated its twentieth birthday by announcing that Jet2.com Holidays had surpassed TUI as the United Kingdom's largest air tour operator and that Jet2.com had been ranked in a Which? Survey, as being the best airline for short-haul flights.

In the year to March 2024, nearly 18 million passengers were carried by Jet2.com, of which nearly seventy percent were travelling with Jet2.com Holidays. In 2025, Jet2.com has expanded further by operating flights from thirteen UK airports to seventy European destinations. These are commendable achievements for an airline starting from such modest beginnings. The Jet2.com story clearly has some way to run.

Third and fourth generation jets/aero-engines.

By the mid-1990s, it had become clear that new generations of jet airliners and aero engines would be required to provide services into the twenty-first century. Britain would no longer be a participant in the production of such complete civil aircraft, and what little remained of the Industry was now in the process of final run down.

The Dutch aircraft manufacturer, Fokker, would not be involved either. Fokker had achieved considerable post-Second World War success, particularly with its Friendship regional airliner, which had sold over eight hundred units by 1986. Fokker had then sold two hundred and forty F28 Fellowships, a Rolls-Royce Spey engined commuter jet, seating up to eighty-five passengers. The Friendship's successor, the Fokker 50, powered by two Pratt & Whitney Canada PW127B turboprops, had been less successful, with sales of two hundred and thirteen aircraft up to 1997. Fokker had also developed the F28 into the Fokker 100, but costs were spiralling out of control and it had become necessary for the Dutch Government to underwrite a bailout.

The Fokker 100 was powered by the new Rolls-Royce Tay, developed from the Spey but featuring a scaled-down fan from the RB211-535, thereby generating a higher bypass ratio. Had the Tay been available earlier, it might have been used to extend the life of the One-Eleven. The Fokker 100 and its smaller version, the Fokker 70, achieved over two hundred and eighty sales but these volumes were insufficient to stave off the bankruptcy which occurred on 15 March 1996. As a consequence another great aircraft manufacturer once an important Rolls-Royce customer, had disappeared.

The remaining major participants in worldwide civil aircraft manufacturing were now just the Boeing Corporation, which incorporated McDonnell Douglas following a 1997 merger, together with the Airbus. consortium

Boeing. From the mid-1980s, Boeing had commenced the replacement of its successful 727 trijet by the 757 twinjet, and Boeing had sold 1050 units up to the end of 757 production in 2004. The wide-body 767, of which freighter versions are still being manufactured today, has sold over 1300 aircraft to date. Boeing had also continued to modernise the 747 Jumbo, particularly with the 747-400 launched in 1984.

Pictured at Heathrow in March 2004, this British Airways Boeing 777-200 displays another of the unpopular Utopia tail fin designs which were dropped during the mid-2000s. Air Team Images

Otherwise, Boeing stuck closely to its 1970s concepts of various "tubes" powered by twin, pylon-mounted, massive turbofans. Boeing's policy was much aided by the further modification of ETOPS by the FAA in 1988 to allow an 180-minute diversion period. Its capable twin-engine 777, the first Boeing aircraft to use "fly by wire" controls, had entered service with United Airlines in 1995 and was rated to 180 ETOPS. This change opened up further significant sales potential for the aircraft.

Today's 777s have replaced the Jumbo as the workhorse of the sky for long-haul route purposes. They are able to carry up to three hundred and seventy passengers to worldwide destinations, with the 777-300 ER version having a range of up to 8,500 nautical miles. As of June 2024, more than 1700 Boeing 777s had been delivered. Boeing is currently developing the new 777X, powered by the General Electric GE9X turbofan producing a massive 134,000 lbf, but the programme and consequent deliveries to airlines are well behind schedule.

By 1997, the highly successful Boeing 737 short to medium-range, narrow body, twin-jet had already been in service for nearly thirty years, with a number of upgrades having been made during that period. In that year, the Next Generation (NG) Boeing 737- 600/900 series was launched with uprated CFM56 high-bypass turbofans produced by CFM International, a company formed in 1974 and jointly owned by General Electric and France's SAFRAN (formerly SNECMA). The NG 737s are capable of seating between one hundred and eight and two hundred and fifteen passengers.

The fourth generation 737 MAX, powered exclusively by the "modestly-named" CFM LEAP (Leading Edge Aviation Propulsion) turbofans, entered service in May 2017. In late 2018 and in early 2019, two 737 MAX aircraft crashed occasioning the deaths of three hundred and forty-six passengers and crew. 737 MAX aircraft were grounded, and subsequent investigations found inadequacies in the software architecture of control systems and faults in the FAA's certification procedures.

The aircraft returned to service in November 2020, but a further incident occurred in January 2024 when a doorway closure blew out on an Alaska Airlines flight, causing an uncontrolled decompression of the aircraft. There were no fatalities and subsequent investigations revealed the cause as being unrelated to the previous incidents. The incident was deemed to be due to a Boeing maintenance failure to install door plug bolts after repair work, thereby occasioning further concerns about safety procedures at Boeing.

The 737 MAX incidents are estimated to have cost Boeing in excess of $20bn in fines, compensation and legal fees. At the end of 2024, 737 MAX aircraft deliveries were around 1600 units. Despite lost orders for around 1200 aircraft attributable to loss of customer confidence following the 2018/19 incidents, there are still outstanding orders for a further 4,700 aircraft. Around 19,000 Boeing 737s of all types have been delivered or ordered since its introduction in 1967.

A TUI Boeing 787 Dreamliner departing from a wet Manchester in December 2023, heading for sunnier climes. More Dreamliners and various Jet2.com aircraft, providing package holiday flights, are parked behind. Air Team Images

In contrast to the 737 MAX, the Boeing 787 Dreamliner was a completely new aircraft, first flying at the end of December

2009 and entering airline service two years later. The 787 was the first airliner with an airframe made primarily of composite materials and it is able to carry up to three hundred passengers over distances of up to 8,500 nautical miles. Over 1900 Dreamliners have been ordered, of which over 1,100 have been delivered. The Rolls-Royce Trent 1000 is an engine option for the Dreamliner chosen initially by many operators, including British Airways and Virgin Atlantic, which airlines respectively operate thirty-eight and seventeen Rolls-Royce-powered aircraft.

The 737 MAX issue and other quality concerns have placed the Boeing Corporation in operational and financial difficulties. The Corporation has also been hit by strikes by its 30,000 employee members of the International Association of Machinists and Aerospace Workers Union. Boeing incurred a financial loss of over $11bn in 2024 and both its CEO and Chairman stepped down during the year. Until six years ago, Boeing broadly shared the civil aviation market with Airbus, but the split is now around 60:40 in favour of Airbus.

Boeing's troubles might also have opened the door for competition from China for the supply of short/medium haul airliners. China's narrow-body Comac C919, powered by CFM International LEAP engines, is a potential future competitor to both the 737 MAX and the A320 family. China Eastern Airlines commenced services with C919s in May 2023. There are significant current outstanding orders for the aircraft, predominantly from Chinese domestic carriers, and certification for operations in other world markets is now being pursued.

Airbus. The continued development of the A320 has enabled Airbus to offer several variants with passenger capacities of between one hundred and seven and two hundred and thirty seats. In January 2016, Airbus introduced the A320neo, which has sold extremely well. Total sales of the A320 family have now matched those of the 737 with an incredible 11,500 plus units being delivered, with a further 7,000 units on order.

An Airbus A330-200 at RAF Cosford in June 2024, one of fourteen operated for the RAF by the Air Tanker consortium. This aircraft bears the Global Britain livery and is used as a VIP transport. Air Team Images

Despite taking the lead in the early 1970s, with the launch of its twin-engine A300, Airbus was still not entirely convinced with Boeing's 1970s predictions that twin wing-mounted turbofan configuration aircraft were the only way forward. Accordingly,

Airbus hedged its bets for large, longer-haul aircraft in the early 1990s by launching both the wide-body four-engine A340 and the A300s successor, the twin-engine A330. However, the tide was turning, and the A340 managed sales of only three hundred and eighty units, quite low by modern-day standards, with production ending in 2011. Both British Airways and Virgin Atlantic successfully operated A340s until their withdrawal from service in 2020.

The A330 still remains in production with orders for nearly 1,800 aircraft, of which just over 1.600 have been delivered. The Rolls-Royce Trent 700 turbofan was an engine option for this aircraft and the Trent 7000 is the exclusive engine choice for the more recent A330neo. Virgin Atlantic currently operates a fleet of eighteen A330s.

Airbus's replacement for the A340 was the A350, a completely new design constructed largely of carbon-fibre-reinforced polymers. The fuselage can accommodate up to four hundred passengers in a nine-abreast cross-section. The A350 is exclusively powered by the Rolls-Royce XWB engines and it entered service with Qatar Airways in January 2015. Over 600 aircraft of more than 1300 on order are now operational. Sales of the A350 have benefitted from delays in the development programme for the new Boeing 777X, despite Boeing claiming that its new aircraft has ten percent better efficiencies.

Pictured at Heathrow in January 2022, this Rolls-Royce XWB 97 powered Airbus A350-1000 of Virgin Atlantic is a state-of-the-art airliner. Rumoured list prices are in excess of $300 million! Air Team Images

British Airways and Virgin Atlantic both operate A350s, with current fleets of eighteen and twelve aircraft, respectively and remain fierce competitors. On 8 November 2021, there was a historic moment for British civil aviation when two A350-1000 aircraft, operating British Airways flight BA001 and Virgin Atlantic flight VS3 respectively, took off simultaneously for New York on Heathrow runways 27L and 27R. Nearly thirty years had passed by since the days of the "Dirty Tricks" affair.

Post Covid-19 some airlines early-retired the huge Airbus A380. Shown here, at Heathrow in December 2024, is one of British Airways' fleet of twelve aircraft which are still employed on high passenger volume routes. Air Team Images

In October 2007, the incredible four-engine Airbus A380, the world's largest and only full-length, double-deck airliner capable of carrying over five hundred passengers, entered service with Singapore Airlines. A rationale for the launch of the A380 was the Hub-and-Spoke system under which airlines would use their A380s to ferry large numbers of passengers to their strategically located hubs for onward flights to end destinations.

In practice, however, the increasing range capabilities of aircraft and continuing improvements in airport facilities world -wide has partially diminished the importance of hubs by increasing point-to-point flights, without the need to change aircraft. When A380 production terminated in 2021, Airbus allowed Emirates to cancel its remaining unfulfilled orders in favour of replacement orders for A330s and A350s. Emirates still operates over one hundred A380s, ferrying passengers to its Dubai hub and has stated that it intends to operate a progressively reducing fleet of A380s until 2035.

Between 2018 and 2020 Airbus extended its operations further by taking control of Bombardier's regional jet business, also including de Havilland Canada, which had previously been purchased by Bombardier from Boeing. The Bombardier business is now known as the Airbus Canada Limited Partnership and the Bombardier C Series five-abreast narrow body airliner has been adopted by Airbus to become the A220. Production of the wings and central fuselage section of the A220 is carried out at the Belfast facility of Spirit Aerosystems. Airbus has recently announced its intention to acquire this part of the Spirit Aerosystems business, but there are doubts as to the future of the remaining Belfast operations. Over 900 A220s, powered by the Pratt & Whitney PW 1500G geared turbofan engine, have been ordered, of which around 400 have been delivered, with Air France being the largest European operator. The Dash-8 programme and the de Havilland Canada brand were sold by Airbus to new Canadian owners in 2019 and Dash-8 production is currently suspended.

Airbus today remains an extremely successful producer of civil aircraft, with an order backlog of over eight thousand aircraft which it is struggling to reduce, despite having geared up its facilities to increase its annual output to over eight hundred aircraft.

The impressive front fan of the massively powerful Rolls-Royce XWB-84 engine. Rolls-Royce Museum. The Author

Aero-engines. Rolls-Royce has made a dramatic operational and financial post-2020 Covid-19 pandemic recovery in recent years The critical Engine Flying Hours numbers are now at pre-Covid levels and are forecast to continue increasing in future years. The Rolls-Royce XWB-84s, powering the A350-900 aircraft, are each rated at 84,000 lbf, with the even more impressive XWB-97, which powers the A350-1000, each producing a staggering 97,000 lbf. These are tremendous power outputs when compared with the struggles of Stanley

Hooker's team in the early 1970s to obtain the contracted 40,600 lbf from the predecessor RB211!

The advances in aero-engine technology over the past fifty years are a little short of incredible, but the production of high-performance aero-engines remains a very complex and high-risk business. In the autumn of 2024, both British Airways and Virgin Atlantic criticised the performance of the Rolls-Royce Trent 1000 engines installed in their Dreamliner fleets, claiming that maintenance downtime was three times more than had been indicated. This situation, together with the non-availability of replacement parts, had led to the partial grounding of their respective Dreamliner fleets and the cancellation of routes and services previously scheduled for 2025.

British Airways' dissatisfaction with the Trent 1000 was demonstrated, in May 2025, when its parent, IAG, placed a big order for new large-sized, long-haul aircraft, including thirty-two Boeing 787 Dreamliners. IAG specified the General Electric GEnx-1B engine instead of the Trent 1000 for its new Dreamliners.

Rolls-Royce, which is expecting a nearly ten percent increase in the number of its engines in service during the remainder of this decade, is now investing £55m in its Maintenance, Repair and Overhaul capacity, particularly at its Dahlewitz, Germany facility, with the objective of improving its after-market support for Trent engines. These improvements include the introduction of Durability Enhancement packages, which are targeted to more than double the "time on-wing" of Trent 7000 and 1000 engines.

Improvements in the performance of the Airbus A330neo are already evident and IAG has recognised this success by including twenty-one A330neos, with options for a further thirteen aircraft, in its May 2025 order.

Rolls-Royce has also experienced issues with the reliability of its XWB engines. In November 2023, the Chairman of UAE's Emirates Airline stated that Emirates, an operator of XWB-84 powered A350-900s, would not be placing orders for the XWB-97 powered Airbus A350-1000 until Rolls-Royce has provided satisfactory guarantees concerning the durability and maintenance costs of the aircraft's engines. Rolls-Royce claims it has a potential solution to prolong the operational life of the XWB-97 by installing gadolinium zirconate-coated turbine blades. Emirates, however, has yet to make a commitment to order the A350-1000 and appears to be keeping faith with its delayed order for Boeing 777X aircraft.

Rolls-Royce is not alone in experiencing engine performance and maintenance issues. Pratt & Whitney is currently dealing with corrosion and cracks in turbine and compressor disks in its GTR (Geared Turbofan) engines powering some of the latest Airbus 320 family aircraft. The problems arise from contamination of the powder metal used to make these critical items. A large number of aircraft are consequently grounded due to engine issues and the delivery of new A321neos to the rapidly growing low-cost airline, Wizz Air, has fallen seriously behind schedule because of delays in engine supply.

A further sharp reminder of the need to remain ever vigilant in the high-pressure environment of civil aviation in the Modern

Era arose in early September 2024 when a Cathay Pacific A350-1000 experienced an in-flight engine fire in one of its XWB-97s soon after take-off from Hong Kong on a flight to Zurich. The fire was promptly detected and extinguished, but Cathay Pacific immediately grounded its A350-1000 fleet pending checks, which found defective fuel lines on the engines of fifteen aircraft. The European Union's Safety Agency (EASA) then followed up with a requirement for one-time, special fleet inspections.

The International Airlines Group (IAG)

By the early 2000s, British Airways had retained its position as the UK's primary transatlantic carrier with Virgin Atlantic now established as the United Kingdom's designated second carrier on these routes. On the other side of the Atlantic there had been all change. Juan Trippe, the founder of Pan Am, passed away in April 1981 after seeing his creation suffer years of declining profitability, commencing in the 1970s and worsening during the 1974 Oil Crisis. Pan Am had sold its transatlantic routes to United Airlines in the late 1980s, but bankruptcy could not be avoided. The airline finally ceased operations in December 1991, with Delta Airlines acquiring most of its remaining assets. TWA, the other American "Chosen Instrument", where Howard Hughes had long ceased his involvement, dying in 1976 after an eccentric and reclusive lifestyle in his declining years, had suffered similar financial problems. In 1991, TWA sold its transatlantic routes to American Airlines. Ten years later, America purchased the remaining TWA assets and operations, and another famous civil aviation name had disappeared.

Former Civil Service and British Airways in-house lawyer Robert Ayling succeeded Sir Colin Marshall as Chief Executive of the airline in 1995. The slogan: "The World's Favourite Airline" was adopted, and Ayling commissioned a new "World Images" livery, code-named "Utopia", which introduced tail-fin art intended to represent communities in countries served by the British Airways route network. Some of the designs were attractive, but many observers were not impressed by the overall concept. Former Prime Minister Margaret Thatcher showed her displeasure at a Conservative Party conference by famously covering the tail of a model 747 with tissue paper and declaring: "We fly the British flag, not these awful things". The tail-fin art was progressively removed and was replaced by the current stylised Union Flag scheme known as "Chatham Dockyard". This design is derived from a Union Flag flown by Lord Nelson, whose fleet was based at Chatham Royal Dockyard.

Robert Ayling departed as Chief Executive shortly afterwards in March 2000 but, whilst previously in office, he had recognised the threat of the emerging low-cost carriers. However, Ayling did not consider that British Airways could or should follow suit, deciding that the best way to respond was for British Airways to set up its own low-cost subsidiary, Go Fly.

Ayling had met Stelios Haji-Ioannau at an airline conference in New York in 1996, and later meetings took place with the possibility of British Airways making an investment in Easyjet. Nothing materialised from this exercise other than the subsequent announcement by British Airways of the creation of Go Fly, its own low-cost airline. An upset Stelios described Go

Fly as being a "photocopy of the Easyjet business plan", an allegation dismissed by Ayling. Shortly afterwards, a telephone call was received by Stelios from a long-established British civil aviation entrepreneur, now based in Florida. Sir Freddie Laker urged Stelios to "sue the bastards".

Following a subsequent meeting with Sir Freddie in London, Stelios decided to follow his advice and to commence legal actions, also making complaints to the European Commission that British Airways was unfairly cross-subsidising its subsidiary. Meanwhile, Go Fly with the former British Airways New York General Manager, Barbara Cassani, as its Chief Executive, commenced operations on 22 May 1998 with a flight to Rome, followed the next day by a flight to Milan. On board the second flight was a group of ten individuals attired in orange Panatone 021C boiler suits. Stelios and nine of his Easyjet colleagues had booked seats on the flight as a publicity stunt and in a creative effort to upstage the event.

A Go Fly Boeing 737-300 which later served with Easyjet after the airline was purchased from its Management in 2003. Air Team Images

Robert Ayling's replacement was the seasoned, no-nonsense Australian airline executive Rod Eddington. Eddington rapidly reviewed British Airways' operations and questioned, not unreasonably, if it was sensible for British Airways to pour cash into a low-cost airline, which in some areas was competing with and undermining its full-service operations. It clearly did not make sense, given the evolving market situation at that time.

In 2001, British Airways agreed to a Cassani-led Management buy-out of Go Fly and the airline was subsequently sold to EasyJet two years later at a substantially higher price. Eddington steered British Airways through the aftermath of the dreadful nine eleven attacks, reversing most of the policies of his predecessor, including the difficult decision to end the operational life of Concorde.

Eddington retired in 2005 and was replaced by the Aer Lingus Chief Executive, the very capable and combative Willie Walsh. In 2008 British Airways received a major boost with the opening of its new home at Heathrow Terminal 5, capable of handling over seventy million passengers a year. In July 2010 the European Commission and the US Department of Transportation approved a plan for British Airways to merge with Iberia, the Spanish flag carrier, together with entering into a coordination agreement with American Airlines on transatlantic routes. These arrangements commenced in October 2010, and IAG was created to act as the new publicly-quoted holding company.

In April 2013, IAG completed the acquisition of Vueling, the Barcelona-based Spanish low-cost airline. Today, IAG also includes the long-haul operator, Level, providing services out of Barcelona to North and South America. Qatar Airways is closely associated with IAG and currently holds a twenty-five percent shareholding.

One battle which Michael O'Leary did not win was for the ownership of the Irish flag carrier, Aer Lingus. In October 2006, the Irish Government floated the company on the Dublin and London Stock Exchanges. Ryanair acquired a sixteen percent holding, and O'Leary immediately launched a take-over bid claiming that this was a "unique opportunity to form an Irish airline". The bid was rejected, but Ryanair further increased its shareholding. In June 2007, the European Commission announced it would block a bid from Ryanair on the grounds that the combined airlines would control eighty percent of European flights from Dublin, thereby reducing consumer choice and potentially increasing fares. Ryanair made two subsequent take-over attempts, but the European Commission was unmoved.

In January 2015, IAG announced that the Irish Government had agreed to accept its €1.4bn offer for Aer Lingus. Ryanair was now effectively forced to accept in respect of its then nearly thirty percent shareholding. The transaction was duly completed with Aer Lingus joining IAG in September 2015.

By 2023, IAG was the world's third-largest airline group in terms of annual revenue, carrying a total of over 115 million passengers, with an average load factor of eighty-five percent on a fleet of nearly six hundred aircraft. Within IAG, British Airways operates a fleet of over two hundred and fifty aircraft, including its A350s and A380s together with a large number of Airbus A320 family aircraft for short to medium-haul routes. Fifty-nine Boeing 777s together with its thirty-seven Boeing 787s are operated on long-haul services. European services from London City airport are provided by British Airways primarily using a fleet of Embraer Regional jets.

To survive in such a highly competitive market, British Airways has adopted a low-cost model for its short and medium-haul services. The "world's favourite airline" slogan was dropped in 2001 when Lufthansa overtook British Airways in terms of passenger numbers. In relation to people, IAG has moved a long way from BEA's archaic 1960s employment practices, with women occupying more than a third of senior leadership roles and with an ambition to increase this allocation further to forty percent through more inclusive recruitment.

IAG operates around one hundred and forty A320 family aircraft, but in October 2022, it ordered fifty Boeing 737 MAX aircraft, together with options for a further one hundred aircraft. IAG states that the new aircraft will be introduced progressively to replace less efficient aircraft across its various member airlines' short to medium-haul fleets. However, IAG also remains an Airbus customer, confirming an order for an additional thirty-seven A320neo aircraft at the time of the announcement of its order for the 737 MAX.

In the 2025 AirlineRatings.com survey, Iberia and British Airways were placed fourteenth and fifteenth, respectively, in the "Hybrid" category, a category which comprises those airlines offering both "Full Service and "low-cost" flights. Delta, United and American Airlines were rated more highly in fourth, fifth and sixth places respectively.

In the Full Service only category, as a further indication of the rapidly changing power base of world civil aviation, Qatar Airways, Cathay Pacific, Singapore Airlines, Emirates and Etihad were all within the top ten positions, with Virgin Atlantic in thirteenth place. Within the low-cost category, Easyjet and Ryanair occupied fifth and seventh places, respectively with IAG's Vueling trailing behind in twentieth place. These ratings indicate that there is clearly work to be done in order to improve current customer perspectives of the IAG constituent airlines.

Open Skies and Markets

The previously-mentioned Airline Deregulation Act 1979 in the USA had taken the sector out of the political sphere in favour of a liberalised economic approach. The associated American International Air Transportation Act of 1979 facilitated an increasing number of liberal Bilateral Air Services Agreements between the USA and a large number of countries. In Europe, there was increasing realisation that airlines should no longer be used as instruments of national policy. A major breakthrough was achieved in 1992 when the Netherlands signed an "Open Skies" Agreement with the USA providing for free market competition with no restrictions on international route rights or on the number of designated airlines or on capacity frequencies and types of aircraft. Ticket pricing should, in the future, be determined only by market forces.

Following the creation of the Single European Market, in 1993, the European Commission removed all barriers to a free aviation market in Europe, thereby creating the second-largest aviation area in the world behind the USA. The European Commission also allowed cross-border majority airline ownership together with the right for companies from any member state to set up and operate an airline in another member state. As previously mentioned, these changes provided the low-cost carriers with practically unlimited freedom to choose routes, capacities, schedules and fares, with commercial considerations being the primary driving force. This situation was hugely different from the restrictive environment which had served to stifle the growth of civil aviation in the

United Kingdom and in Europe in the post-war period and prior to the commencement of the Modern Era.

The low-cost carriers established bases across Europe, with Easyjet today having twenty-nine such bases, including Easyjet Europe, which is based in Vienna with an Austrian Air Operator Certificate. This arrangement has enabled Easyjet to secure flying rights, post-Brexit, for its network of services within and between EU Member States.

Significant changes for the State-owned airlines across Europe commenced in the early 2000s when Belgium's SABENA, the national carrier since 1923, filed for bankruptcy in November 2001 in the wake of the nine-eleven attacks. - followed SABENA into bankruptcy in April 2002. In May 2004, Air France-KLM was created by way of the merger of the French and Dutch airlines. More recently, in October 2023, Air France-KLM agreed to make an investment in Scandinavian Airlines (SAS) in order to enable the struggling airline to exit bankruptcy proceedings in the USA. Air France-KLM is also rumoured to be eyeing the acquisition of an interest in the Portuguese national carrier, TAP.

Lufthansa is the owner of SABENA's successor, Brussels Airlines and also of Swiss International Airlines which assumed the operations of Swissair. Lufthansa acquired Austrian Airlines in 2009, and it holds a large minority stake in Italy's flag carrier, ITA Airways. ITA is the successor to the defunct Alitalia, and Lufthansa has the option to acquire the remainder of the shares by 2029.

The days of Western Governments operating and supporting airlines as symbols of national prestige are clearly long gone. Michael O'Leary, some years ago, made the following forecast about civil aviation in Europe:

"I think it is inevitable that in the next five or six years, Europe consolidates around four large carriers, each with about a 20% share, IAG, Lufthansa, Air France-KLM and Ryanair. Everybody else either disappears, merges, gets taken over, or partners with one or other of those big four".

O'Leary, once again, is in the process of being proved substantially correct with his predictions whilst apparently conceding that Easyjet will continue to operate alongside the big four. Also, O'Leary was probably not expecting the entry into the market of the Hungarian, FTSE 250 quoted, Wizz Air. Starting operations in November 2017, the new airline, based at Luton, took over the landing slots vacated by the demise of Monarch Airlines. The Wizz Air group of airlines has grown significantly across Europe and currently operates two hundred and fifteen Airbus A320 family aircraft, serving two hundred destinations and, in 2024, carrying 62 million passengers. Despite this strong competition, Ryanair continues relentlessly to drive forwards with the simple proposition that it will always offer its passengers the lowest fares.

The hugely significant US-EU Open Skies Agreement came into operation on 30 March 2008. It granted authorisation to every US carrier and to every EU carrier to fly between every city in the EU and every city in the US. There are no restrictions on the number of flights, aircraft, and routes, and fares are to be set according to market demand. The restrictive Bermuda 11 Agreement was discontinued at this point, and London Heathrow was opened to full competition. The Open Skies

Agreement encourages cooperative agreements, including code-sharing, where two or more airlines sell and market the same flight under their own branding and flight numbers.

In addition, to ensure maximum competitiveness in these now completely open markets, international airlines have increasingly grouped into alliances, the two largest being the Star Alliance and Skyteam. IAG is a member of the third and smaller One World alliance, of which the largest members are American Airlines, Cathay Pacific, Japan Airlines, Qantas and Qatar Airways. These alliances facilitate full coordination of the major airline functions on routes, including scheduling, pricing, revenue management, marketing and sales.

In 1974, the Governments of Bahrain, Oman, Qatar and the United Arab Emirates (UAE) took control of Gulf Air, an airline which had previously been operated for them by BOAC. Gulf Air became the flag carrier for the four Middle Eastern nations, using Bahrain as a hub airport and also focussing operations on Abu Dhabi rather than on the rapidly developing nearby Dubai. This situation did not meet the aspirations of the UAE's Prime Minister and the ruler of Dubai, Mohammed bin Rashid Al Maktoum, to turn Dubai into a world-class metropolis. Accordingly, in 1985, Dubai-based Emirates was founded by Ahmed bin Saeed Al Maktoum, its present chairman, and it commenced services in July 1987.

The subsequent growth of Emirates has been nothing short of phenomenal, and it is now the world's fourth-largest airline by scheduled revenue passenger kilometres flown. Emirates has the world's largest Airbus A380 fleet, with over one hundred aircraft, and it is also the world's largest operator of the Boeing

777, with a fleet of over one hundred and thirty of this type. In addition, Emirates operates a large fleet of 787 Dreamliners, together with a fleet of sixty-five Airbus A350-900s in service and on order. In July 2003 a second national airline for the UAE, Etihad, was established in Abu Dhabi. Etihad currently operates a fleet of eighty-nine aircraft sourced from both Airbus and Boeing, including a small fleet of A380s which it has progressively reintroduced into service post the Covid-19 pandemic.

Qatar Airways was established by the Government of Qatar in late 1993, with operations commencing from Doha in January of the following year. In a similar fashion to Emirates, the subsequent expansion of Qatar Airways has been astonishing with a large fleet including the latest types from both Airbus and Boeing. Qatar withdrew from Gulf Air in 2002, and Gulf Air is now a comparatively small airline wholly owned by the Government of Bahrain. It operates thirty-one A320s on short-medium haul routes and ten Boeing 787s on longer-haul routes.

Emirates, Etihad and Qatar Airways(now collectively known as the "ME-3"), have achieved amazing growth, largely attributable to the exercise of Sixth Freedom rights, gained by way of Bilateral Air Services Agreements, under which passengers are carried from one country through the home country of the airline and then onwards to a third country. Using these rights, the Gulf States have taken full advantage of their key geographic locations to ferry passengers from throughout the world to large hub airports, particularly at Dubai and Doha. Here they are de-planed in order to join connecting flights to their ultimate destinations. Emirates Airlines operates a daily

A380 service from Gatwick to Dubai International Airport, which is the world's busiest airport by international passenger traffic, handling over 90 million passengers annually. Terminal 3, the base of Emirates, is the largest airport terminal in the world.

In April 2024, it was announced that Dubai's second, Al Maktoum, Airport is to be expanded. The current airport will be closed in due course, with all operations being transferred to the Al Maktoum airport, which will, appropriately, be re-named "Dubai World Central". This expanded airport will have the capacity to handle 260 million passengers annually. Meanwhile, Qatar's huge and fabulously appointed Doha Hamad Airport, together with Singapore's Changi Airport, are currently considered to be the best in the world.

Collectively, the ME-3 now has a combined wide-body aircraft capacity which is greater than that of the entire US wide-body fleet. This vast expansion of the ME-3 has not been welcomed by all airline industry participants. In particular, the "US-3", comprising American, Delta and United Airlines, has requested re-negotiation of the Open Skies Agreements, arguing that they have conferred disproportionate benefits on the ME-3 by opening up the US market whilst providing virtually no benefits in return. They further argue that the ME-3 has been provided with large subsidies from their relevant Governments in order to facilitate the massive expansion of their aircraft fleets.

The response of the ME-3 has been to deny that subsidies have been provided and that any re-negotiation would defeat the fundamental principle of Open Skies. It has also countered that, instead of complaining, the correct response for the US-3 was to modernise their fleets and to compete on service and in-flight entertainment. This unhappy situation remains unresolved.

There can be little doubt, however, that the power base of modern civil aviation now lies in the Middle East, although the existing carriers in the region will soon be facing competition from Riyad Air, a new Saudi Arabia-based carrier which has been established to help to increase tourism to Saudi Arabia. Riyad Air has ordered a fleet of over one hundred and thirty new aircraft, but delays in the delivery of these aircraft, particularly from Boeing, have deferred the commencement of operations. Riyah Air has also announced future alliances with Air France - KLM and with Delta/Virgin Atlantic.

Strong competition is also provided by Turkish Airlines. In the early 1980s, the Turkish Government recognised its national airline as being its gateway to the world. At the time, Turkish Airlines operated a fleet of thirty aircraft and carried three million passengers a year. As of June 2024, the airline from its Istanbul hub was serving three hundred and forty-nine destinations and providing more non-stop services than any other airline. Its fleet, now amounting to over four hundred modern aircraft, will soon include seventy, Rolls-Royce powered, Airbus A350s.

If alive today, the founders of British civil aviation would be amazed to know that Britain's former colony, Singapore, a very successful independent city-state since 1965, now operates one of the world's top airlines with a fleet of one hundred and sixty state-of-the-art aircraft. Singapore Airlines' ultra-long-range A350-900s can transport its passengers non-stop from Los Angeles to Singapore, covering the 8,700-mile journey in less than eighteen hours. The A350 is certified to ETOPS 370, enabling it to fly for more than six hours on just one of its Rolls-Royce Trent XWB-84s.

Finally, it is important not to overlook India and China, the world's most populous nations. Per-capita air travel in India is currently little more than a quarter of that of China, which itself is far below the level of air travel prevailing in the Western economies. Both of these countries hold the potential for a huge further growth in the volume of worldwide air travel.

The Protection of the Environment

During the Formative Years and well into the mid-twentieth century, civil aviation activity was at such a relatively low level that the question of its damage to the environment was not a material consideration for most Government or Industry leaders. Certainly, in early 1962, environmental considerations could hardly have been front of mind when the British and French Governments signed up for a hugely expensive project in order to produce a noisy and thirsty supersonic airliner to transport small numbers of privileged passengers across the world. Only in the mid-1970s, when the US EPA began to make unfavourable rulings against Concorde, initially about aircraft noise, did the protection of the environment become of greater significance.

The huge subsequent increase in air travel and the consequent environmental impact has now made effective protection of the environment an existential issue for civil aviation. It is estimated that flying is responsible for around 2.5% of global greenhouse gas emissions and for 8% of United Kingdom emissions. Although the per passenger/kilometre carbon dioxide created from flying has more than halved since 1990, the significant increase in flights over the past thirty years means that carbon dioxide emissions have more than doubled to over one billion tonnes annually.

Carbon dioxide production is not the only issue because the contrails (water vapour from aircraft exhausts) emitted from aircraft flying at high altitudes are reputed to have a significant effect on increasing global warming. Whilst air travel is certainly responsible for increasing carbon dioxide emissions, the environmental damage caused by the generation of the electricity required to power the world's increasing need for air conditioning is even greater. However, the combined effects of both of these activities are increasingly detrimental to the environment.

The aim of the airline industry and that of many Governments is stated to be to achieve net zero emissions by 2050. A Royal Society Report in February 2023 concluded that net zero could be achieved only by reducing the amount of air travel, together with increasing carbon offset projects. A possible alternative was to replace fossil aviation fuel with a low or zero-carbon energy source and the Report considered four possible fuel options to address aviation Industry emissions: hydrogen, ammonia, synthetic fuels and biofuels.

The Report concluded that there was currently no single net zero alternative to jet fuel. Accordingly aircraft and aero-engine manufacturers are focussed on addressing environmental issues through the production of ever more efficient and quieter aircraft powered by engines which use Sustainable Aviation Fuel (SAF). SAF is certified jet fuel which blends conventional fossil fuel with biomass from a range of renewable materials, such as cooking oils, fats, plant oils and municipal, agricultural and forestry waste. Depending upon the blend and the type of biomass used, there is the potential to lower CO_2 emissions significantly. A further benefit is that the burning of biofuels does not emit sulphur dioxide.

Airbus is targeting that, by 2030, all of its aircraft will be capable of flying on one hundred percent SAF. However Airbus commented in March 2025 that its next single-isle jet would be "evolutionary rather than revolutionary" and that the development of a radical hydrogen-powered regional aircraft had been delayed. Airbus also advised that the aviation industry's goal of reaching net zero by 2050 was feasible but acknowledged that the cost of SAF, which is currently nearly three times that of kerosene jet fuel, together with the limited availability of suitable renewables, are still issues to be resolved.

To enhance the United Kingdom's production of renewable energy, with the objective of completely removing its dependence on fossil fuels, Rolls-Royce has been chosen by the Government to implement a Small Modular Reactors (SMRs) programme. SMRs can be built on smaller sites, closer to where the electricity is needed, at a much lower cost and in a shorter timescale. Britain's existing nuclear reactors are nearing the end of their operational lives, with only one new large nuclear plant under construction, which is well behind schedule. SMRs are based on existing technology, and, in the case of Rolls-Royce, the reactors are derived from the company's extensive involvement in producing power plants for Britain's nuclear submarines.

If Rolls-Royce is successful in its nuclear efforts, then the additional revenue stream from a SMRs programme could assist the company in remaining a strong competitor in world aerospace.

All of the British airlines are working to reduce their environmental impact, and they all have large outstanding orders for more efficient aircraft. British Airways has committed to using ten percent of SAF for its operations by 2030 and is seeking to replace more than a third of its fleet over the next five years with more fuel-efficient aircraft. The Boeing 737 MAX aircraft, which are now in service with and on order by Ryanair, are able to carry four percent more passengers whilst consuming sixteen percent less fuel and cutting noise levels by fifty percent. As mentioned earlier, both Easyjet and Jet2.com are also in the process of further modernising their fleets, and Easyjet has committed to achieving a carbon intensity reduction target of thirty-five percent by 2035.

In 1971, American manufacturers decided to discontinue their efforts to produce a larger supersonic aircraft competitor to Concorde. After Concorde operations ceased in 2003 there have been no subsequent supersonic passenger flights. However, the American Boom Technology company is proposing the "Boom Overture", a supersonic airliner capable of travelling at Mach 1.7 over distances of up to 4,900 miles, Test flights are currently taking place with the aircraft, which is built primarily from composite materials, being powered by four turbofan engines. Boom Technology claims a large potential market but admits that fuel efficiency will be lower than subsonic alternatives. Other companies are also active in this area, some working on aerodynamic designs intended to reduce the volume of sonic booms and thereby make supersonic travel over land a legal possibility.

It remains to be seen if these projects will come to commercial fruition and how they could be reconciled with the ongoing drive to reduce the impact of civil aviation on the environment. The availability of good-quality video conferencing and facilities such as DocuSign make it appropriate to question the need for supersonic travel also the current extent of business travel. For instance, the Author's expensive twenty-four-hour Concorde round trip to New York in June 1989 would certainly not have been necessary with the availability of today's technology.

Governments continue to seek to balance the protection of the environment against the freedom of the individual to travel and to choose their mode of transport. In June 2023, the French Government formally introduced a ban on domestic short-haul flights where there is a rail alternative of under two and a half hours. Spain is reported to be planning to introduce a similar ban. The French Government will review the effectiveness of these measures after three years.

In the United Kingdom, Air Passenger Duty (APD) was introduced in 1994 by the then Chancellor, Kenneth Clarke, who also claimed the associated environmental benefits of discouraging internal flights. However, the Government then later proceeded effectively to contradict itself by halving APD for UK Domestic flights from April 2023. However, despite this apparent change in Government policy there has been no emergence of an airline providing a comprehensive network of

United Kingdom domestic air services, similar to that previously operated by Flybe. Loganair and some other small carriers have taken over a number of Flybe's former routes, but there has been no overall successor to Flybe.

The 2024 Autumn Budget announced a thirteen per cent APD increase on all commercial flights from 2026, with swingeing increases for corporate jets. Michael O'Leary reacted on behalf of Ryanair, describing this as "an idiotic decision" which would serve only to make air travel much more expensive for families and to render the United Kingdom a less competitive destination. O'Leary further stated that Ryanair would cut flights to and from United Kingdom airports by ten per cent, which could lead to as many as five million fewer passengers being carried from those airports. Ryanair has reacted to similar trends across Europe, to impose taxes on aviation and increase airport charges, by reducing the number of its European services. Easyjet has also reduced its UK domestic flights programme for 2025.

The Airports Act 1986 was passed as part of Prime Minister Margaret Thatcher's privatisation agenda. As a result, all major British airports today are now in private ownership. The Government has no direct control over London's Spanish-owned Heathrow or over French majority-owned Gatwick airports, both of which are heavily congested at times. This poor state of affairs can be attested by the many passengers who have either frustratingly sat in aircraft queuing for take-off or who have been delayed aboard aircraft held in holding patterns, awaiting a landing slot.

The Labour Government, elected in the autumn of 2024, appears to be supportive of both the long-mooted third runway at Heathrow and of the proposed conversion of Gatwick's backup northern runway into much much-needed fully-fledged second runway. However, beyond the exercise of taxation and planning controls, the British Government, in reality, has very limited direct influence or leverage in order to initiate and implement the capital projects needed to bring about the necessary long-term changes. It is estimated that a third runway at Heathrow will cost £20-25bn. This amount will need to be privately funded, which will be no easy task.

Epilogue

Air travel is no longer the privilege of just the better off. It is vastly more available in the Modern Era and it has opened up huge, exciting and safe travel opportunities for the many.

Britain's post-war loss of Empire led to a much more visible and cosmopolitan society the development of which has been greatly assisted by the growth of civil aviation. The United Kingdom still retains a significant presence in aerospace and in airlines. Government figures in 2022 showed that aerospace activities were a major contributor to the Economy. The British Aero Industry exported seventy percent of its output, it directly employed 108,000 highly skilled people and it created 5,200 apprenticeships.

The wings and other components for the highly successful range of Airbus airliners are still produced in the United Kingdom. The Trent family of engines, developed from the 1970s Rolls-Royce RB211, has enabled Britain to remain a major supplier of gas turbine engines for large-sized, long-haul civil aircraft, with nearly 2,000 of the latest Trent XWB engines being in service or on order.

Rolls-Royce also has a significant Defence business and a successful "Pearl" range of business jet engines, including the engines powering corporate America's favourite transport and play thing, the Gulfstream Executive jet. Rolls-Royce still employs around 21,000 people in the United Kingdom and it spends £800m each year on research and development.

However, passengers travelling short or medium-haul are unlikely to see Rolls-Royce badges displayed on the engine pods of the A320 family and the Boeing 737 jets operated by most airlines on these routes. Rolls-Royce does not currently produce an engine for this sector of the market, having sold its shares in International Aero Engines to Pratt & Whitney in 2012. International Aero Engines produced the V2500 engine which was an early competitor to the extremely successful CFM International 56/LEAP engines. CFM International currently dominates the short/medium-haul market and well over 30,000 engines have been produced, of which 1400 engines were delivered in 2024 alone. Higher output targets are scheduled for future years.

Because Rolls-Royce does not currently participate in the engines market for short and medium-haul aircraft, it has only a twelve percent share of the overall commercial passenger jet market. In 2018, Rolls-Royce signed an Agreement with Airbus to develop a range of advanced, geared UltraFan engines. The UltraFan claims significant fuel consumption improvements over current engines. Some of these improvements are derived from the use of huge titanium-tipped carbon composite fan blades. Ironically, it was the failure of the carbon fibre "Hyfil" fan, during RB211 testing in 1970, which precipitated the company's Receivership early in the following year. Hopefully history will not be repeated.

Rolls-Royce has recently announced the production of a smaller, 30,000 lbf, UltraFan demonstrator for testing alongside its original more powerful demonstrator. There are rumours that the company has approached the British Government for funding support towards the estimated £3bn of developing the UltraFan to power the next generation of narrow-body aircraft for short/medium-haul routes. Rolls-Royce claims that this is a "once in a generation opportunity" which could create and sustain 40,000 skilled jobs in the United Kingdom and provide £100bn or more of benefits to the Economy.

The British Government still supports aerospace projects generally through the Industry Aerospace Technology Institute Programme, including making grants of £685m to Airbus and to Rolls-Royce over the period 2022-25, with a further £975m earmarked for grants in the following five years. No decision has yet been made on whether or not to offer specific support to the UltraFan.

The twenty-first century BAE Systems is a widely-based defence, aerospace and security solutions company, with an annual turnover of around £25bn and employing over 90,000 people worldwide. BAE Systems retains an interest in aviation through its collaborations with Airbus and Leonardo on the Eurofighter Typhoon. It also works with Lockheed Martin on the latest Γ35 stealth fighter, now in service with the United Kingdom's Joint Strike Force.

Pictured in the mid-1990s is an ex- British Airways Tristar followed by two VC10s, all three aircraft then operating as RAF air tankers. Current and future RAF aircraft are now purpose-designed and are competitively sourced. Air Team Images

Aircraft sourcing for the RAF is no longer a political matter and the RAF is much freer to tender competitively, worldwide, for the equipment that it really needs.

At the end of the Second World War the British Government had almost complete de facto control over the British Aero Industry and also over British civil aviation. Its role today is more appropriately confined to promoting safe and efficient air services through the CAA, although it retains the power to tax aviation. The new rates of APD are estimated to generate £110m in revenue in 2025/26. The Industry body, Airlines UK, concurs with Ryanair's Michael O Leary that this tax constitutes unhelpful Government "meddling" in the sector, serving only to make the

United Kingdom a less competitive aviation base and destination.

British airlines are now much fewer in number than in the immediate post-war years, but Easyjet and Ryanair (Irish registered but a public company operating predominantly from the United Kingdom) operate on a vastly larger scale than their predecessors and provide extensive services to and within Europe. Jet2.com has largely taken up the mantle of those 1960s/1970s entrepreneurial British inclusive tour operators and their associated Independent airlines with the slogan "Package holidays you can trust". British Airways and Virgin Atlantic continue to provide a significant British civil aviation presence in the wider international markets.

The founding personalities of British civil aviation, if alive now, would probably be saddened, puzzled and disappointed to discover that all of the great British aircraft manufacturing names have disappeared. However, as practical and pragmatic people, they would be pleased to see that Britain still retains a sizeable and specialised aerospace industry.

What is absolutely certain is that those courageous and talented entrepreneurs would be amazed at the massive scale of worldwide civil aviation in the Modern Era. They would be surprised at the many changes in the key airline players but proud that the surviving British airlines are well-established and are still battling hard in order to keep the Union Jack flying across the world.

For those readers who have enjoyed these stories of British civil aviation and are now wishing to learn more and to explore aspects of the subject in further detail, there are many specialist publications. Also, the United Kingdom is well served by a number of excellent aviation museums, including the Rolls-Royce Heritage Museums at Derby and Bristol and the British Airways Speedbird Heritage collection at the airline's Heathrow headquarters. There are also the RAF museums at Cosford and Hendon, together with the Imperial War Museum at Duxford, the Brooklands museum at Weybridge and Aerospace, Bristol at Filton. Smaller aviation museums, just to mention two, are the Avro museum at the former Hawker Siddeley assembly and test facility at Woodford, near Stockport and the de Havilland museum at London Colney. The British Caledonian website is also worth a visit in order to learn more about a long-disappeared Independent airline

A number of the British airliners and other aircraft referred to in this book can be viewed at many of the museum locations, together with numerous other static exhibits. Any one of the above museums is most definitely worth a visit for an entertaining and interesting day out.

Annex 1 – Barnes Wallis and Neville Shute Norway

Barnes Neville Wallis was born in Ripley, Derbyshire, in 1887, and he spent the majority of his career working for Vickers-Armstrongs, initially on the R100 airship project. Following Vickers' acquisition of Supermarine in 1928, Wallis was despatched to the Southampton facility to "improve the efficiencies" of the Supermarine design department. Supermarine's Chief Engineer, the legendary RJ Mitchell, was away on holiday, and the inoffensive but naïve Wallis made the disastrous mistake of occupying his office. Upon his return, an enraged Mitchell banished Wallis to a remote part of the factory from where he later scuttled back to Vickers-Armstrongs at Weybridge, never to return again to Southampton in Mitchell's time. It is disappointing that the relationship between these two great British aeronautical engineers started so poorly, with Mitchell's early death in 1937 preventing any further engagement.

Barnes Wallis was later responsible for the successful Vickers-Armstrongs Wellington bomber from which the Viking airliner was developed. Wallis also designed the "bouncing bomb" of "the Dam Busters" fame, and he is brilliantly portrayed by Michael Redgrave in the still regularly shown 1955 epic war film of that name, telling the story of Operation Chastise. On the night of 16/17 May 1943, nineteen Avro Lancaster bombers, led by one of the RAF's youngest Wing Commanders, the already highly-decorated and fearless twenty-four year old Guy Gibson, successfully attacked three dams in the Ruhr valley. The Lancasters dropped Wallis's "bouncing bombs", and the attack occasioned catastrophic flooding, disrupting German arms production.

Gibson was awarded the Victoria Cross for his leadership and courage during the mission. After his Lancaster had delivered its bomb, Gibson then sought to draw fire from other attacking bombers by flying escorting them during their bombing runs. Nevertheless, eight of the Lancasters and fifty-three of their young crew members did not return.

Wallis, initially elated with the success of his bombs, was distraught when the extent of the losses was revealed to him. Until retirement in 1971, Barnes Wallis worked on many projects, including Concorde and the European consortium-produced Panavia Tornado multi-role combat aircraft. In later life, and much chastened by his wartime experiences, Wallis's guiding principle was to test all designs thoroughly so as to minimise risks to aircraft crews.

Neville Shute Norway. Aeronautical engineer, the founder of Airspeed Limited and, later, a world-renown author.

Neville Shute, Norway, born in 1899, worked alongside Barnes Wallis in the 1920s at Vickers-Armstrongs on the R100 airship project. Following the cancellation of the project, Shute Norway bravely formed the Airspeed Company where Sir Alan Cobham was also an initial shareholder. Writing under his pen name of Neville Shute, Shute Norway would later become a hugely successful novelist. His delightful and touching novel "No Highway", published in 1948 but still a good read today, tells the story of the Reindeer aircraft, which was discovered to be suffering from metal fatigue. Shute Norway had considerable technical knowledge of this topic and it is probable that the 1948 and 1949 Atlantic Ocean Avro Tudor incidents were attributable to this cause. However, in his Author's Note, Shute states that the Reindeer is "not based on any particular commercial aircraft" and, at the time of publication, there had only been one Tudor crash.

No Highway had nevertheless exposed the emerging risk of metal fatigue as new airliners began to fly faster and higher. The book was described by Flight magazine as "one of the few novels to reveal a new engineering truth": the concept of metal fatigue. The novel was the basis for the 1951 film "No Highway in the Sky" with James Stewart playing Mr Honey, the heroic aviation boffin.

Shute carried out valuable Second World War work on secret weapons development but then left Britain in the early 1950s, having concluded that the British tax system was too penal. He continued his highly successful writing career in Australia, where he completed the remainder of his twenty-three books, including "On the Beach" and "A Town like Alice" which was later voted seventeenth in the Readers List of the Modern Library's 100 Best Novels of the 20th Century. Unlike Wallis, who had lived into his early nineties, Shute's life was cut short, dying at age sixty in Australia following a stroke on 12 January 1960. He was still proudly holding his British citizenship.

Annex 2 – The Munich Air Crash

On 6 February 1958, less than a year after the Football League had lifted its ban on football clubs travelling by air, a BEA Airspeed Ambassador was returning seventeen members of the Manchester United football team, together with a number of support staff and journalists, from a European Cup match in Belgrade. A direct flight from Belgrade to Manchester was beyond the Ambassador's range and so the aircraft, piloted by two experienced captains, both former RAF Flight Lieutenants, had stopped to refuel at Munich.

The aircraft's first two take-off attempts from Munich had been abandoned because of a boost surging on the port engine. In deteriorating weather conditions, the pilots fatefully decided to make a third run. Both engines performed satisfactorily, but a build-up of slush on the runway slowed the aircraft. It failed to gain altitude and ploughed through a fence at the end of the runway, then hitting some buildings, one housing a parked fuel truck which ignited. Of the forty-four people on board, twenty died at the scene and three more in hospital.

Although the casualties were much lower than those involved in the Llandow Tudor accident earlier in the decade, the Munich incident drew huge national attention. The Manchester United Manager, Matt Busby, suffered serious injuries and eight of the famous "Busby Babes" were among the dead, including the team captain, Roger Byrne. England International, Duncan Edwards, survived the crash but died from his injuries a fortnight later. One of the survivors was Bobby Charlton, who was later to become one of England's highest-capped players and a member of the 1966 FIFA World Cup-winning England team.

Whilst, even in those early post-Second World War years, the risks of flying were small in comparison with most other modes of transport, the Munich crash was a sad and high-profile reminder of what could happen when things went wrong. The accident also opened up new legal territory with significant personal injury claims being made, including a claim by Manchester United, seeking £250,000 for the lost potential transfer fee values of its deceased players.

Annex 3 – Operation Black Buck

The 1982 Falklands War included some notable British aviation aspects. On 2 April 1982, the Argentine Junta, under the leadership of General Leopoldo Galtieri, mounted amphibious landings on the Falkland Islands, which were British Dependent Territories. The garrison, comprising a small number of British marines, together with the Governor were removed from the Islands and flown to Argentina, from where they were repatriated to the UK.

On 6 April 1982, the resolute British Prime Minister, Margaret Thatcher, convened a War Cabinet, which authorised the assembly of a task force, eventually comprising one hundred and twenty-seven ships. The first part of the task force set sail in early April, led by two aircraft carriers, HMS Hermes and HMS Invincible, carrying forty-two Harrier "jump jets". The Harriers would play a key role in the conflict despite being outnumbered, three to one, by the Argentinean jets now in the process of establishing a base at Port Stanley airfield in the Falklands. The ocean liners, SS Canberra and Queen Elizabeth 2, were requisitioned and were quickly adapted to carry the Third Commando and the Fifth Infantry Brigade down to the Falklands.

Despite the early 1960s removal of their original raison d'etre, a small number of Vulcan V Bombers were still flying. There was about to be a final dramatic event in their operational lives. The RAF had a base on the far distant British overseas territory of Ascension Island, located in the South Atlantic. By 30 April 1982, a group of elderly RAF jets had been assembled at the base. The purpose was to carry out a series of five Operation Black Buck attacks. Three were targeted on the Port Stanley airfield, and the other two were directed to the destruction of Argentinian mainland radar installations.

The missions involved round trips of 8000 nautical miles (9,200 miles), taking over sixteen hours. The force for the first mission comprised two Vulcans, supported by no less than eleven Victor aerial refuelling tankers. Some very rapid modification work on the Vulcans had been required, including obtaining components from a variety of sources to render their in-flight re-fuelling systems operational. Also, Dual Delco Carousel navigation systems had been removed from some of the RAF's stored, ex-BOAC, Super VC10s and had been installed in the Vulcans.

The sound, at take-off in the late evening of 30 April 1982, of the over fifty Rolls-Royce engines powering the first mission aircraft must have been quite magnificent. Disappointingly for its crew, the lead Vulcan was forced to return early with technical problems, but the reserve aircraft, XM607, battled on to the Falklands and successfully achieved hits on the runway and surrounding area.

After numerous in-flight re-fuellings on both the outward and inward legs, the Vulcan and all of the supporting Victors safely returned to base.

This mission and the subsequent Black Buck attacks were brilliant logistical achievements by the RAF. They were morale-raising for the Nation and they demonstrated the vulnerability of the Port Stanley airfield, thereby contributing to the successful recovery of the Falkland Islands from Argentina on 14 June 1982. The conflict lasted seventy-four days. Six hundred and forty-nine Argentine military personnel, together with two hundred and fifty-five British servicemen and three Falkland Islanders, had been killed. It is unlikely that Britain will ever again attempt a military exercise of this type and scale.

The Vulcans left RAF service soon afterwards, but at the very end of their operational lives, they had at last proved their worth. The V Bombers were a fascinating and expensive part of British aviation history, but their era was now drawing to an end. The first of the V Bombers, the Valiants, had already left service, as early as 1964, following the discovery of cracks in their wing spars. The Victors continued on as air tankers, serving with distinction in the First Gulf War, before the V Bombers saga finally ended when the Victor tankers were withdrawn from RAF service and replaced by VC10s in 1993.

Bibliography

The following is a list of the principal publications consulted:

British Independent Airlines 1946-76 – The Aviation Hobby Shop, December 2000. ISBN 0907178820

Losing my virginity – Richard Branson, 1998. ISBN 1852276843

Wings across the world (The History of British Airways) – Harald Penrose 1980 ISBN 0304306975

The challenge of BEA – Garry May 1971. ISBN 72340447 X

No Frills – Simon Calder, 2002. ISBN 185227932 X

A Market for Aircraft (Hobart Paper 57) IEA/Keith Hartley, 1994. SBN 25556055-X

Empire of the Clouds – James Hamilton-Patterson, 2010. ISBN 979057124795-0

No Highway - Nevil Shute, 1948. ISBN 9780099530091

Air Bridge – Hammond Innes, 1951. Fontana Books

Dowding of Fighter Command – Vincent Orange, 2008. ISBN-13:9781906502140.

Acknowledgements

All photographs in this publication, which are indicated as having been sourced from Air Team Images, have been authorised for use in this publication only and should not be reproduced, stored or transmitted in any form or by any means without the permission of Air Team Images Limited.

All rights are reserved in images which are indicated as having been provided by the Author and such images should not be reproduced, stored or transmitted in any form or by any means without the permission of the Author.

All rights are reserved to the relevant copyright owners of all other images in this publication, where such images are not in the Public Domain and copyright may still be applicable to such images. Images which have been provided by way of Creative Commons (CC) Licences are attributed to the original creator where known.

Index